AF505967

French Politics, Society and Culture Series

General Editor: **Robert Elgie**, Paddy Moriarty Professor of Government and International Studies, Dublin City University

France has always fascinated outside observers. Now, the country is undergoing a period of profound transformation. France is faced with a rapidly changing international and European environment and it is having to rethink some of its most basic social, political and economic orthodoxies. As elsewhere, there is pressure to conform. And yet, while France is responding in ways that are no doubt familiar to people in other European countries, it is also managing to maintain elements of its long-standing distinctiveness. Overall, it remains a place that is not exactly *comme les autres*.

This new series examines all aspects of French politics, society and culture. In so doing it focuses on the changing nature of the French system as well as the established patterns of political, social and cultural life. Contributors to the series are encouraged to present new and innovative arguments so that the informed reader can learn and understand more about one of the most beguiling and compelling of all European countries.

Titles include:

Jean K. Chalaby
THE DE GAULLE PRESIDENCY AND THE MEDIA
Statism and Public Communications

Pepper D. Culpepper, Peter A. Hall and Bruno Palier (*editors*)
CHANGING FRANCE
The Politics that Markets Make

David Drake
FRENCH INTELLECTUALS AND POLITICS FROM THE DREYFUS AFFAIR
TO THE OCCUPATION

David Drake
INTELLECTUALS AND POLITICS IN POST-WAR FRANCE

Graeme Hayes
ENVIRONMENTAL PROTEST AND THE STATE IN FRANCE

David J. Howarth
THE FRENCH ROAD TO EUROPEAN MONETARY UNION

Andrew Knapp
PARTIES AND THE PARTY SYSTEM IN FRANCE
A Disconnected Democracy?

Michael S. Lewis-Beck (*editor*)
THE FRENCH VOTER
Before and After the 2002 Elections

John Loughlin
SUBNATIONAL GOVERNMENT
The French Experience

Mairi Maclean, Charles Harvey and Jon Press
BUSINESS ELITES AND CORPORATE GOVERNANCE IN FRANCE AND THE UK

Mairi Maclean and Joseph Szarka (*editors*)
FRANCE ON THE WORLD STAGE
Nation State Strategies in the Global Era

Susan Milner and Nick Parsons (*editors*)
REINVENTING FRANCE
State and Society in the Twenty-First Century

Gino G. Raymond
THE FRENCH COMMUNIST PARTY DURING THE FIFTH REPUBLIC
A Crisis of Leadership and Ideology

Sarah Waters
SOCIAL MOVEMENTS IN FRANCE
Towards a New Citizenship

Reuben Y. Wong
THE EUROPEANIZATION OF FRENCH FOREIGN POLICY
France and the EU in East Asia

French Politics, Society and Culture
Series Standing Order ISBN 0-333-80440-6 hardcover
Series Standing Order ISBN 0-333-80441-4 paperback
(*outside North America only*)

You can receive future titles in this series as they are published by placing a standing order. Please contact your bookseller or, in case of difficulty, write to us at the address below with your name and address, the title of the series and the ISBN quoted above.

Customer Services Department, Macmillan Distribution Ltd, Houndmills, Basingstoke, Hampshire RG21 6XS, England

---

France on the World Stage

Nation State Strategies in the Global Era

Edited by

Mairi Maclean

Professor of International Business
Bristol Business School
University of the West of England

and

Joseph Szarka

Reader in European Studies
Department of European Studies
University of Bath

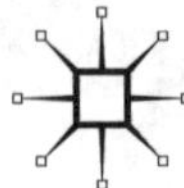

First published 2008 by
PALGRAVE MACMILLAN
Houndmills, Basingstoke, Hampshire RG21 6XS and
175 Fifth Avenue, New York, N.Y. 10010
Companies and representatives throughout the world

PALGRAVE MACMILLAN is the global academic imprint of the Palgrave Macmillan division of St. Martin's Press, LLC and of Palgrave Macmillan Ltd. Macmillan® is a registered trademark in the United States, United Kingdom and other countries. Palgrave is a registered trademark in the European Union and other countries.

ISBN-13: 978–0–230–52126–1   hardback
ISBN-10: 0–230–52126–6   hardback

This book is printed on paper suitable for recycling and made from fully managed and sustained forest sources. Logging, pulping and manufacturing processes are expected to conform to the environmental regulations of the country of origin.

A catalogue record for this book is available from the British Library.

Library of Congress Cataloging-in-Publication Data

France on the world stage : nation-state strategies in the global era
  / edited by Mairi Maclean and Joseph Szarka.
       p. cm. — (French politics, society and culture)
    Includes bibliographical references and index.
    ISBN 0–230–52126–6 (alk. paper)
  1. France—Foreign relations—21st century.   2. Globalization—
  France.   3. France—Politics and government—21st century.   I.
  Maclean, Mairi, 1959–   II. Szarka, Joseph.
  DC430.F73 2008
  327.44—dc22   2008011124

10   9   8   7   6   5   4   3   2   1
17   16   15   14   13   12   11   10   09   08

Printed and bound in Great Britain by
CPI Antony Rowe, Chippenham and Eastbourne

Contents

List of Tables and Figures

Tables

Figures

Acknowledgements

Many people have helped, directly and indirectly, with the compilation of this volume, the origins of which lie in a conference entitled 'France on the World Stage' held at the University of the West of England, Bristol, on 8 July 2005, organised jointly with the University of Bath, under the aegis of the South West Wales and West of England Regional Centre for Contemporary French Studies. We are grateful to the French policy sub-group of the Political Studies Association and the Association for the Study of Modern and Contemporary France for kindly sponsoring the event. Our thanks go to our guest speakers from France and the USA, Professor Guillaume Parmentier of the Centre Français sur les Etats-Unis at the Institut Français des Relations Internationales in Paris, Professor Bernard Barraqué of the Ecole Nationale des Ponts et Chaussées in Paris, and Professor Herman Lebovics of the State University of New York (Stony Brook), USA; their presence was a privilege. We wish to thank all those who contributed to the conference, and all who attended, many of whom travelled from other countries in order to participate. Lorraine Kirby, Pat Diango and Pam Talbot helped in many ways with organisation, and Jeremy Fogg with technical matters. We also wish to thank Robert Elgie for his sound advice as series editor, and Alison Howson, Gemma d'Arcy Hughes and Amy Lankester-Owen of Palgrave for their kind assistance in the production of this volume.

Mairi Maclean and Joseph Szarka

Notes on Contributors

Laurent Binet is a graduate of Sciences-Po and the Celsa-Sorbonne. He currently teaches in the Department of French at the University of Bristol, having been a lecturer at the University of Bath and a PR consultant in Paris. His research focuses on French politics and Eurosceptic discourses in France since 1992.

Tony Chafer is Professor of Contemporary French Area Studies and Director of the Centre for European and International Studies Research at the University of Portsmouth. He has published widely on Franco-African relations and his book *The End of Empire in French West Africa: France's Successful Decolonization?* was published in 2002. He is currently working on a British Academy research project entitled 'Towards a new policy partnership? France and Britain in Africa since Saint-Malo'.

David J. Howarth is Senior Lecturer at the University of Edinburgh. He is the author of *The European Central Bank* (Palgrave Macmillan, 2003, 2005, first and second editions) (with Peter Loedel); *Contemporary France: Politics and Society* (2003) (with Georgios Varouxakis); and *The French Road to European Monetary Union* (Palgrave Macmillan, 2001).

Raymond Kuhn is Professor of Politics at Queen Mary, University of London. He has written widely on French media policy and political communication, including a single authored study *The Media in France* (1995). He is currently writing a book on the French media in the digital age to be published by Palgrave Macmillan.

Mairi Maclean is Professor of International Business at Bristol Business School, University of the West of England. She was previously Reader in European Business at Royal Holloway, University of London. Her recent books include *Business Elites and Corporate Governance in France and the UK* (Palgrave Macmillan, 2006), written with Charles Harvey and Jon Press, and funded by the Leverhulme Trust and Reed Charity; *Economic Management and French Business from de Gaulle to Chirac* (Palgrave Macmillan, 2002); and *Michel Tournier: Exploring Human Relations* (2003). Her current research interests include corporate governance, business elites, business history and business transformation. She is author of numerous articles in the fields of international business and political economy.

Guillaume Parmentier is the Director of the Centre for America and Transatlantic Relations (CART), which he created in January 2007, and a non-resident professor of International Relations at the University of Paris II. He has published widely on France and international relations. His last (edited) book, entitled *Les Etats-Unis aujourd'hui, choc et changement*, was published in 2004.

Gino Raymond is Professor of Modern French Studies at the University of Bristol. He has taught in both France and Britain and published widely on the varied manifestations of French political culture. His recent books include *The French Communist Party under the Fifth Republic* (Palgrave Macmillan, 2005) and *Redefining the French Republic* (edited with Alistair Cole, 2006).

Albrecht Sonntag is Professor at the Ecole Supérieure des Sciences Commerciales d'Angers (ESSCA), where he holds the chair in European integration and manages the school's international programmes. He graduated from Stuttgart University and holds a doctorate in sociology from the Université de Nantes. His recent research has focused on European identity and collective memory, the legitimacy of European institutions, and Franco-German relations. He has published extensively in French, English and German in both academic journals and publications for a wider public. He is the author of a forthcoming book on international football as a source of collective identities in the age of globalisation.

Nicholas Startin is Senior Lecturer in French and European Studies at the University of the West of England in Bristol. His main area of research is contemporary French politics and in particular the impact of Euroscepticism and globalisation on the domestic political agenda in France; he also conducts comparative research on the far-right in contemporary Europe with a particular focus on the French Front National, having published in both these areas.

Joseph Szarka is Reader in European Studies in the Department of European Studies, University of Bath, England. His research interests are in politics and policy studies, specialising in environmental, economic and energy policy-making. He has published widely in international journals and his books include *The Shaping of Environmental Policy in France* (2002) and *Wind Power in Europe: Politics, Business and Society* (Palgrave Macmillan, 2007).

Jean-Marc Trouille is Senior Lecturer in European Business Management at Bradford University School of Management, where he holds a Jean Monnet Chair in EU Economic Integration. His research interests lie in the field of European economic integration with particular reference to industrial policy, and to Franco-German economic and industrial cooperation.

Henrik Uterwedde is Deputy Director of the Deutsch-Französisches Institut, a think-tank specialising in modern France and Franco-German relations. He teaches at the universities of Stuttgart and Osnabrück. Current research fields include the state, economy and society in modern France, economic policy and models of capitalism in France, Germany and Europe.

Reuben Wong is Assistant Professor at the National University of Singapore (NUS). He teaches International Relations in the Political Science Department, and is a Council Member of the Singapore Institute for International Affairs. He was First Secretary in the Singapore Embassy in Paris (1995–98). He obtained an MPhil in European Politics from Oxford University, and a PhD in International Relations from the LSE on an NUS Graduate Scholarship. He is the author of *The Europeanization of French Foreign Policy: France and the EU in East Asia* (Palgrave Macmillan, 2006).

List of Abbreviations

AC!	Agir ensemble contre le chômage
ADEME	Agence de l'environnement et de la maîtrise de l'énergie
ADSL	Asymmetric digital subscriber line (broadband)
AFEP	Association française des entreprises privés
AII	Agence de l'innovation industrielle
AKP	Adalet ve Kalkinma Partisi
AMF	Autorité des marchés financiers
ANP	Advanced Nuclear Power
AOL	America OnLine
ARF	ASEAN Regional Forum
ASEAN	Association of Southeast Asian Nations
ASEM	Asia-Europe Meeting
ASMCF	Association for the Study of Modern and Contemporary France
ATTAC	Association pour la taxation des transactions financières et pour l'aide aux citoyens
BEPG	Broad Economic Policy Guidelines
BNP	Banque nationale de Paris
CAC	Cotation assistée en continu
CAP	Common Agricultural Policy
CEO	Chief executive officer
CERI	Centre d'études et de recherches internationales
CFA	Communauté française d'Afrique
CFSP	Common Foreign and Security Policy
CGP	Commissariat général du plan
CIA	Central Intelligence Agency
CMF	Conseil des marchés financiers
CNPF	Conseil National du Patronat Français
COB	Commission des opérations de bourse
COP	Conference of the Parties
CPNT	Chasse, pêche, nature, traditions
DATAR	Délégation à l'aménagement du territoire et à l'action régionale
DFI	Deutsch-Französisches Institut
DGCID	Direction générale de la coopération internationale et du développement

EADS	European Aeronautics, Defence and Space Company
EC	European Community
ECB	European Central Bank
Ecofin	Economic and Financial Affairs Council
ECOWAS	Economic Organisation of West African States
EdF	Electricité de France
EDP	Excessive deficit procedure
EEA	European Environment Agency
EG	Economic governance
EIDHR	European Initiative for Democracy and Human Rights
EMS	European Monetary System
EMU	Economic and Monetary Union
EP	European Parliament
ERM	Exchange Rate Mechanism
ESDP	European Security and Defence Policy
ETS	Emissions Trading Scheme
EU	European Union
FDI	Foreign direct investment
FIFA	Fédération internationale de football association
FN	Front National
G7	Group of seven most industrialised nations (USA, Japan, Germany, UK, France, Italy and Canada)
GAC	General Affairs Council of the EU
GATT	General Agreement on Tariffs and Trade
GDP	Gross domestic product
GHG	Greenhouse gas
ICCPR	International Covenant on Civil and Political Rights
IEA	International Energy Agency
IFRI	Institut français des relations internationales
IMF	International Monetary Fund
INSEE	Institut national de la statistique et des études économiques
IRIS	Institut des relations internationales et stratégiques
ISAF	International Security Assistance Force
ITER	International Thermonuclear Experimental Reactor
LCI	La chaîne info
LCR	Ligue communiste révolutionnaire
LO	Lutte ouvrière
MATE	Ministère de l'aménagement du territoire et de l'environnement

MC	Military Committee (of NATO)
MEDD	Ministère de l'écologie et du développement durable
MEDEF	Mouvement des entreprises de France
MPF	Mouvement pour la France
MRC	Mouvement républicain et citoyen
MtCO$_2$	Million tonnes of carbon dioxide
MW	Megawatt
NAP	National Allocation Plan (under EU ETS)
NATO	North Atlantic Treaty Organisation
NEPAD	New Partnership for Africa's Development
NGO	Non-governmental organisation
NRE	Nouvelles Régulations Economiques
OECD	Organisation for Economic Co-operation and Development
ORTF	Office de radiodiffusion-télévision française
OSCE	Organisation for Security and Cooperation in Europe
PCF	Parti communiste français
PDG	Président directeur-général
PKO	Peacekeeping operations
PSA	Political Studies Association
RECAMP	Renforcement des capacités africaines de maintien de la paix
RES	Renewable energy sources
RPF	Rwanda Patriotic Front
RPF	Rassemblement pour la France
RPR	Rassemblement pour la République
SACEUR	Supreme Allied Commander Europe
SEC	Security and Exchange Commission
SECAM	Séquentiel couleur à mémoire
SEM	Single European Market
SGP	Stability and Growth Pact
SME	Small and medium-sized enterprise
SOSR	SOS Racisme
SOX	Sarbanes-Oxley Act
TCA	Trade and Cooperation Agreement
TGV	Train à grande vitesse
TWh	Terawatt hour
UDF	Union pour la démocratie française
UK	United Kingdom
UMP	Union pour un mouvement populaire
UN	United Nations

UNCHR	United Nations Commission on Human Rights
UNFCCC	United Nations Framework Convention on Climate Change
UNSC	United Nations Security Council
USA	United States of America
USSR	Union of Soviet Socialist Republics
VCR	Video cassette recorder
VDI	Verein deutscher Ingenieure
WTO	World Trade Organisation

1
Globalisation and the Nation State: Conceptual Lenses on French Ambitions in a Changing World Order

Mairi Maclean and Joseph Szarka

Introduction

The purpose of this book is to examine the ways in which France's relations with the international community have evolved in a period of accelerating globalisation. It considers the role of the nation state and its capacity for political initiative, examining French strategies to consolidate French influence on the world stage. It questions whether an intermediary country such as France can continue to 'punch above its weight' in a changing world order. Thus, the book considers France both as a passive and an active actor. In other words, as well as assessing the impact of globalisation on France, it addresses French strategies to avert unwelcome outcomes and to deepen global developments by reinforcing French influence and policy preferences around the world.

This volume grew out of a conference entitled 'France on the World Stage', organised jointly by the University of the West of England and the University of Bath. It was held at Frenchay, Bristol, under the aegis of the French policy sub-group of the Political Studies Association (PSA), the Association for the Study of Modern and Contemporary France (ASMCF), and the South West Wales and West of England Regional Centre for Contemporary French Studies, and took place on 8 July 2005.

The date is significant since on 7 July 2005, London was the target of a terrorist attack. Four Islamist suicide bombers detonated their home-made bombs in the morning rush-hour, causing carnage in the British capital. Trains approaching the underground stations of Aldgate, Russell Square and Edgware Road were attacked. The bombers had targeted the four corners of the city, North, South, East and West. In the event, the Northern line was spared by its temporary closure, one of the terrorists transferring to a London double-decker bus and blowing it up in Tavistock Square.

The relationship of the so-called '7/7' terrorist attack to the present volume is not just that it coincided with the conference, such that some of the participants, passing through London en route to Bristol, were caught up in the chaos that ensued. (One American professor – who had escaped 9/11, having owned an apartment blocks away from the World Trade Centre – staying overnight near Russell Square, heard the blasts, yet stalwartly made it to the conference the next day on the first train out of Paddington.) The wider relevance of these events lies in the fact that terrorism now spans the globe – just as politics, culture and the environment have also become global in a way which few would have predicted even twenty years ago. Attacks by the supranational terrorist organisation Al-Qaeda over the past ten years have affected no fewer than 26 countries around the world, in locations as far afield as New York, Washington, Bali, Nairobi, Sharm el-Sheikh and, of course, Madrid. Confronted with world-wide terrorist attacks – though often targeted at Western interests – the population looks for protection, action and resolution to the nation state in the first instance. Indeed, not just in security terms, but also in the geopolitical, economic and environmental domains, the nation state remains a central actor in international relations, confounding the predictions of observers who suggested that in the twenty-first century the nation state may have had its day (Beck, 2000; Guéhenno, 1995; Ohmae, 1995, 2005).

Against the background of these multiple dimensions of globalisation, this introductory chapter raises key questions and issues in current debates regarding the role of the nation state and its capacity for initiative in a changing world order. We review some of the most relevant components of the literature on globalisation and path dependencies, seeking to develop conceptual lenses through which to view the two-way interactions between international processes and nation state strategies. We then examine the enduring nature of French ambitions on the world stage, using those lenses to identify continuities and discontinuities in national strategies. In a final section, we provide an overview of this volume, setting out the main themes of the chapters and situating them in relation to our key issues.

Conceptual lenses

The globalisation debate raises major questions related to the will, purpose, opportunity and scope for action of the nation state. Faced by rapid evolution in the external environment, to what extent are nation states free to choose their strategies? Can congruence be deliberately and deliberatively attained between purpose and opportunity, or is the available scope for action irrevocably dictated by external necessity and internalised habits?

The literature on path dependency indicates that whilst adaptive capacity is not permanently moulded, it is significantly constrained by past decisions. The notion of path dependency stresses that choices entail consequences, enacted over the long term through a variety of chain reactions. Once made, decisions cannot be undone and the repertoire of future options is altered. As a concept, path dependency owes much to the work of North (1990: 6), who explained how 'informal constraints embodied in customs, traditions, and codes of conduct … not only connect the past with the present and the future, but provide us with a key to explaining the path of historical change'. North pointed to important lock-in effects occurring in national political and business systems, influenced by the timing of industrialisation (Fligstein and Freeland, 1995; Pedersen and Thomsen, 1997), as a result of which sub-optimal structures endure over long periods, even when a potentially superior alternative arises. In this way, historically derived perceptions persist, reflecting 'the complexities of deciphering a complex environment with the available mental constructs – ideas, theories, and ideologies' (North, 1990: 96). Systems become self-reinforcing (to a degree), as regulation fosters particular institutional structures which, in turn, strengthen existing patterns of regulation. This perspective indicates that actors involved in rule-making at the *international* level still remain substantially embedded in national cultures and environments, from which they extend their behaviours and strategies into the global domain (Djelic and Quack, 2003a). Change is not precluded, of course. For example, no predetermination acts to ensure that a 'particular economy – usually defined as being a national one – is fated to continue along its path' (Crouch, 2005: 3). Rather, path dependence tends to encourage incremental change within institutions and organisations (North, 1990) – unless, of course, a change, or even a revolution, is compelled by a crisis. Yet when change does occur, some elements of the 'new' may recast continuity in subtly altered ways.

The concept of path dependence not only helps explain the manner in which change occurs or fails to occur, but also draws attention to varying conceptualisations of the dependent variable 'change'. The conceptual lenses through which we view our object of study inevitably alter our perceptions. A commitment to identifying the effects of path dependence may diminish the capacity to recognise discontinuity in the object of study. Conversely, the vocation to implement change and enact a *rupture* (a break) which is regularly voiced by premiers across both sides of the Channel – currently Gordon Brown and Nicolas Sarkozy – may mask path continuities, deliberately or by omission. Thus, the ways in which the notion of path dependence is used – whether and how to stress continuity or discontinuity – constitutes a major alternative in terms of the conceptual lenses used to scrutinise the object of study.

Given the core themes of this volume, a concern with 'nation state strategies' over and against a preoccupation with 'globalisation processes' provides the other major alternative in terms of conceptual lenses. Depending on which set of lenses we don, our vision changes markedly. Globalisation may perhaps be the word which best encapsulates the changing landscape of the new millennium (Lyth and Trischler, 2004). It is often considered as the 'big idea' of our times (Held et al., 2000: 1). Although close to cliché, it may nevertheless capture the essence and lived experience of a 'new' epoch. For Beck (2000: 1), it involves an '*escape* from the categories of the national [sic] state'. While the nation state once determined the contours of society, in his view the 'world society' has emerged with globalisation. This 'global cosmopolitan society' (Giddens, 1999) undermines the integrity, role and action of the nation state, since 'a multiplicity of social circles, communication networks, market relations and lifestyles, none of them specific to any particular loyalty, now cut across the boundaries of the national state' (Beck, 2000: 4).

Yet the demise of the nation state has long been predicted. Daniel Bell (1987) considered it too small to solve the big problems, yet too big for the small problems. These sentiments were echoed by Kenichi Ohmae (1990, 1995), who recently claimed that a new world is assuming shape and form 'from the ashes of yesterday's nation-based economic world' (Ohmae, 2005: 1), in which success depends on action on the world stage. This 'hyperglobalist' perspective (Held et al., 2000: 3) regards economic globalisation as constituting a new era in human history in which the nation state is irrelevant, dysfunctional or counter-productive. According to Ohmae (1995: 5), traditional nation states have become 'unnatural, even impossible business units in a global economy', a view shared by Strange (1996: 4), who argued that 'the impersonal forces of world markets…are now more powerful than the states to whom ultimate political authority over society and economy is supposed to belong'. This observation was substantiated by Sklair (2002) who established that in 2001 four of the world's 10 biggest economic entities in terms of turnover were not countries but transnational corporations: behind the USA, Germany, the UK, Italy, Japan and France came US giants Ford Motor Company, General Motors, Wal-Mart and Exxon Mobil. Sklair ascertained that whilst fewer than 60 countries in 2001 had a gross domestic product (GDP) of $20 billion or more, as many as 245 companies were listed in the *Fortune* Global 500 as having greater annual revenues. With such unparalleled resources, transnational corporations can play fast and loose with their ties and obligations to local communities and environments (Beck, 2000).

Further, whilst the rapid pace of technology diffusion and industrial development has resolved the economic problems of at least some parts of the world, it has also created an unprecedented escalation in the levels of environmental hazards. Infamous disasters, which do not respect national boundaries – including the devastating nuclear accident at the Chernobyl power plant in the Ukraine in 1986, the Exxon Valdez oil spill off the coast of Alaska in 1987, and the explosion at the chemical plant in Bhopal in 1984 – have given rise to notions of a 'risk society' (Beck, 1992) or 'vulnerable society' (Theys, 1987), terms which are evocative of the new scale and enormity of the threats (Szarka, 2002: 157). Global climate disruption has emerged as the largest and most alarming of this new category of environmental threat, one which dwarfs the nation state and inevitably requires an internationally coordinated response.

However, more sceptical commentators question whether globalisation truly amounts to anything new (Held et al., 2000). Djelic and Quack (2003b: 302) suggest that globalisation is a 'contested and discontinued process' which shares 'quite a few similarities with earlier periods of internationalisation of economic activity'. According to Hirst and Thompson (1996), globalisation has acquired a chimerical quality, with the weight of evidence pointing not to a global integrated market but merely to heightened levels of internationalisation. Others, however, whom Held et al. (2000) define as 'transformationalists', view globalisation as a transforming force of unprecedented strength and reach, reshaping economies, societies, institutions and ultimately giving rise to a new world order dominated by the network society (Castells, 1996). Yet this does not mean that global homogeneity is a foregone conclusion. On the contrary, persistent divergence remains a possibility, even in the face of strong isomorphic pressures (DiMaggio and Powell, 1991), as long-standing cultural patterns reassert themselves, such that the processes of global convergence are challenged and disrupted by deep-rooted structural continuities expressed in national legal, institutional, political and intellectual practices.

French ambitions in a changing world order

Among the industrialised nations, France is perhaps the country to have experienced the greatest difficulty in coping with globalisation, or which has at any rate agonised most loudly over it.[1] Hostile reactions have led to the creation of an anti-globalisation movement which, through the activities of the Association pour la taxation des transactions financières et pour l'aide aux citoyens (ATTAC), has transformed itself into a movement promoting *altermondialisation* and seeking alternatives to neo-liberal economic globalisation.[2] Gordon and Meunier (2001: 8–11) listed four reasons why globalisation poses particular problems for France: it challenges a tradition of state-centred capitalism; threatens national culture and identity; calls into question the founding principles and values of the French Republic; and reduces France's international stature. This last-mentioned challenge highlights the French dilemma: despite recent expressions of hostility, stubborn resistance or simply disorientation, France has historically been a pioneer of internationalisation yet, having lost momentum in the recent period, struggles to recapture the initiative.

French history reveals a long tradition of leadership, and at times dominance, in military and economic power projection, in international diplomacy, in the dissemination of cultural practices and political ideas, and in the diffusion of 'universal' values. This legacy has produced a specific form of path dependency. In the late twentieth century, the Gaullist ambition to perpetuate national *grandeur* (greatness) produced a tension between a long-standing will to international leadership and the reality of diminishing national influence on the world stage. Internationalisation, and latterly globalisation, have exposed France's position as an 'intermediary' power some way behind the Cold War superpowers of yesteryear, the USA and the USSR, and the emerging powers of today's 'new world order', such as China. Thus, the spectre of national decline has, for some time now, haunted political debate in France.

One of its recent manifestations is a spate of publications on 'declinology'. Examples include *La France qui tombe* ('France in free-fall') by Nicolas Bavarez (2003); *La France est-elle encore une grande puissance?* ('Is France still a great power?') by Pascal Boniface (1998); *Adieu à la France qui s'en va* ('Farewell to France departing') by Jean-Marie

Rouart (2003); and *L'Arrogance française* ('French Arrogance') by Romain Gubert and Emmanuel Saint-Martin (2003). These titles pinpoint sites of national anxiety and insecurity, weaving a narrative of national economic vulnerability and fading international prestige, accompanied by loss of national identity and compensatory, overweening ambition.

Clearly, France has experienced great difficulty in coming to terms with a decline in status from its former pre-eminence as a leading military and colonial power, to being a nation of the second rank (Hoffmann, 1987; Kuisel, 1981). On the eve of the First World War, the French Empire spanned some 11,755,000 square kilometres, with a population of 41.1 million living outside France. It embraced a plethora of colonies across several continents: Asia (India, Indo-China, Kwangchou-Wan), Africa (Algeria, Tunisia, Congo, West Africa and the Sahara, Réunion, Madagascar, Mayotte Comoro Isles, and the Somalia Coast), Latin America (Guiana, Guadeloupe, Martinique, St Pierre et Miquelon) and the Pacific (Tahiti and islands, New Caledonia). Yet in 1940 this great imperial power was defeated in a matter of weeks by an invading German army, its alleged state-of-the-art fortifications, the Maginot Line, easily breached. In the recent period, France's cultural prestige also declined, as French eminence in literature and the arts diminished in *rayonnement* – in its radiance for the wider world (Rouart, 2003). France has found it hard to accept the diminished role offered to it by the post-war world. It is against this background of decline in international standing that General de Gaulle's obsession with *grandeur* and national prestige must be viewed (Maclean, 2002). Thus, the underlying question raised by the 'declinology' debate is the capacity of France as a nation to adapt to successive changes in the world order. In other words, what is the national capability to put aside out-dated and failing strategies, to develop new patterns of behaviour, and to forge a new role?

In practice, French political leaders have sought to find a compromise position that is more ambitious than simply acquiescing to externally imposed constraints, and more modest than the traditional search for *grandeur*. In the language of the Chirac presidency (1995–2007), this was described as an effort to *maîtriser la mondialisation*: although this expression has sometimes been misconstrued as a wish to roll back globalisation – surely an impossible task worthy of Canute – a more appropriate translation is to 'domesticate' or merely 'manage' globalisation. Indeed, part of the French approach has been communicative, seeking to make globalisation more comprehensible and more acceptable, as exemplified by former Prime Minister Jospin's call for 'globalisation with a human face' (Jospin, 2002: 10). But France has also developed substantive strategies to cope with and adapt to a changing world order. Key amongst these has been the preference to orchestrate a multipolar world order, a preference consistently followed in foreign policy-making under President Chirac (Boniface, 2007: 32). This involves setting behavioural 'rules' (Védrine, 2001: 14) – namely new forms of regulation – within international institutions, such as the United Nations (UN) and the World Trade Organisation (WTO). Such rule-making is conceived as the antidote to neo-liberal laissez-faire, and translates *la mondialisation maîtrisée* into practice. Within this multipolar order, the European Union (EU) – as the 'natural' extension and continuation of French ambitions – constitutes a leading pole and a major institutional venue for cross-border rule-making. France has thus made a major commitment to fuelling the motor of European integration. Yet these ambitions point to France representing a singular case in international relations.

A major impediment to French preferences for a multipolar order has been the USA acting as global hegemon. Wallerstein (1984) defined a hegemonic situation as one where 'power is so unbalanced that one power can largely impose its rules and wishes in the economic, political, military, diplomatic and even cultural arenas'. In the 1960s, American hegemony was already actively resisted by de Gaulle, who viewed US financial pre-eminence as tantamount to slavery (Maclean, 2002; Rueff, 1972). Since the end of the Cold War and the implosion of the USSR in the 1990s, the world is increasingly dominated by one superpower (Huntington, 1999), with the USA behaving more and more as if in a unipolar world (Patrick, 2001; Young, 2001) on issues as wide-ranging as world security and climate change, raising concomitant threats of financial imperialism and intellectual colonialism. By the 1990s, this unipolar world entailed a context where, for the French, globalisation was often synonymous with Americanisation, stirring the desire to preserve national difference and cultural diversity. Evidencing clear foreign policy continuity with the Gaullist period, Hubert Védrine, French Foreign Minister between 1997 and 2002, sternly declared that 'the very weight [of the Americans] carried them towards hegemonism, and the idea they have of their mission is unilateralism. And that is unacceptable'.[3] This tradition of outspoken criticism has given France a reputation as a difficult negotiating partner for the USA (Cogan, 2003).

Nowhere is French opposition to American projects more evident than in relation to the invasion of Iraq. When, following the attacks on the World Trade Centre of 11 September 2001, President George W. Bush called for coalition partners to join the USA in the so-called 'war on terror', France and Britain chose to follow different paths. Prime Minister Blair promised, apparently unconditionally, to stand 'shoulder to shoulder' with the Americans, first in Afghanistan, then more problematically in Iraq. Bush sought 'regime change', based on claims that Iraqi leader Saddam Hussein continued to stockpile weapons of mass destruction – although UN weapons inspectors could find none. In stark contrast, French political leaders were more circumspect. Védrine criticised the USA for acting 'unilaterally, without consulting others, taking decisions based on its own view of the world and its own interests … refusing any multilateral negotiation that could limit their decision-making, sovereignty and freedom of action'.[4] Following the passing of UN resolution 1441 in November 2002, unanimously agreed by the Security Council, which offered Iraq 'a final opportunity to comply with its disarmament obligations' (UN Security Council, 2002), Chirac declared himself willing in February 2003 to veto a second UN resolution, which would have sanctioned war against Iraq.

President Chirac galvanised international opposition against rushing into war, enlisting the support of Germany, other non-permanent members of the UN Security Council, and Russia. In the view of Gubert and Saint-Martin (2003: 11), the impression created by France in the spring of 2003 was that of 'a small country inflicting lessons of morality on the Empire' and constituted a prime example of French arrogance. In response, the USA and its immediate allies (foremost of which was the UK) decided that a second resolution was unnecessary, resolution 1441 being deemed to give all necessary authority to proceed with a war – which critics have since branded as illegal. Once France refused to join the coalition in the invasion of Iraq, the Bush administration dismissed France as 'old Europe' – as opposed to the 'new Europe' formed by East European countries – subsequently deciding to 'forgive Moscow, ignore Berlin and punish Paris' (Gubert and Saint-Martin, 2003: 10). French goods encountered a public boycott in the USA, with 'French fries' being renamed as 'freedom fries'! France was even castigated as part of what the American Fox News Channel termed the 'axis of weasels' (Panchadsaram, 2004), echoing the expression 'axis of evil' used by President Bush in his 2002 State of the Union address to describe Iraq, Iran and North Korea as sponsors of terrorism. This episode constituted a low point in the history of France-US relations. Yet it is marked by two ironies. One is that subsequent events proved France right regarding the non-existence of weapons of mass destruction in Iraq, and the likelihood that invasion would increase, rather than decrease, terrorist activities. The other, as pointed out by Boniface (2007: 71–2), is that France not only gained nothing from formulating the correct analysis, but has quietly been forced to side with the American-led 'war on terror'.

Frustrated ambitions related to reining in the US hegemon and the perverse outcomes of the failed Iraq adventure sharply illustrate the constraints impacting on France as nation state playing the role, in the Gaullist tradition, of an 'independent' actor on the world stage. Here, continuity is evidenced in the dogged pursuit of a variant of Gaullist foreign policy, yet discontinuity is displayed in the acceptance of the need to develop strategic alliances. The most evident manifestation of this incomplete struggle to moderate historical reflexes in favour of new learned behaviours, and so overcome *inherited* path dependency, lies in France's strategy towards Europe. As Jean Monnet (1976) expressed it, men may come and go, but the institutions they bequeath are more powerful, being able to shape and inform policy and events over long periods of time. In practice, designing Europe's institutional architecture is tantamount to *bequeathing* new elements of path dependency to future generations.

France learned to conceive of Europe as a means of extending French influence, recognising that French and European interests shared much common ground. Through playing a leading role in the European Community (EC), France discovered that it could transcend national limitations and enjoy an amplified role on the world stage, thus retaining more control over its own destiny than geopolitical and historical considerations alone would logically have permitted (Maclean and Howorth, 1992). As Hoffmann (1987: 49–50) noted, while the objectives of welfare, prosperity, security and independence were deemed by French political elites to be no longer achievable 'through national action and at the level of the nation', nevertheless these 'might still be reachable at the level of Europe'. President Mitterrand famously summed up France's European ambitions in his New Year's Eve address to the nation in 1988, 'France is our homeland, but Europe is our future' (Guyomarch et al., 1998: 1).

A key founding member of the Community, France was particularly active when the initial rules of the game were being shaped. Over the years, French influence in the EU has been arguably greater than that of any other member state. The lasting imprint of national French institutions and structures on the make-up and management of the EU is exemplified most clearly by the Common Agricultural Policy (CAP). A French invention designed to solve the problems of financing French farming, the CAP has survived in its essence, despite significant reforms, since it was conceived by de Gaulle in the 1960s. It is illustrated too by Economic and Monetary Union (EMU), a project driven by the French since the Giscard years (1974–81) as a solution to the problems of asymmetrical interdependence with Germany, brought to fruition with the advent of the euro in 1999 (Howarth, 2001; Maclean, 2002).

Today, however, the project of European integration has altered almost beyond recognition (Drake, 2005). With 10 new member states (mostly from Central and Eastern Europe) joining the EU in 2004 and a further two in 2007, its centre of gravity has shifted eastwards. Initial decisions on the enlargement of the EU were taken in the euphoric days which followed the Soviet Union's disintegration. As Jacques Delors, a Frenchman and former President of the European Commission, put it at the time: 'History is knocking at the door. Are we going to pretend that we cannot hear?' (Maclean and Howorth, 1992: 1). Yet, while enlargement provides Germany with a huge adjacent market, in economic terms the French have struggled to reap benefits. In political terms, the reweighting of votes which occurred in post-enlargement Europe has tended to favour small countries over larger ones to a greater extent than before; though old members may yet wield more influence than new arrivals.

However, the Franco-German relationship, seen for many years as the engine of the EU (Cole, 2001; Maclean and Trouille, 2001), declined during the 1990s. France found it difficult to come to terms with a reunited Germany, run by a younger generation of politicians from both East and West who were less willing to subordinate German preferences to French interests, and eager to develop relationships with new partners. The privileged status France previously enjoyed as co-leader of the EU with Germany is no longer guaranteed; hence the considerable efforts deployed in 2007 by newly elected President Sarkozy to revive the entente with Chancellor Merkel.

In the EU of 27 member states, and with further candidate countries (notably Turkey) keen to join, the 'European idea' is no longer as popular in France as it once was. The 2005 French referendum on the EU Constitutional Treaty sharply illustrated the divergences between elite and popular opinions. Although its drafting committee was chaired by Valéry Giscard d'Estaing, a former president of France, and despite support from the French political establishment, the Treaty was rejected by the French (and Dutch) electorates. The referendum's outcome revealed that the French ruling elite was spectacularly out of touch with grassroots anxieties regarding the negative impact of globalisation (perceived or real) on employment and living standards.

In 2007, the EU was in clear need of reform, with a 'simplified' version of the Constitutional Treaty having been prepared at the time of writing to streamline the functioning of European institutions. Yet behind the technical issues of institutional architecture lie substantive questions regarding the nature of the European project, the role of individual states, and the involvement of the electorate. What is the socio-economic purpose of the EU? Is it to facilitate and adapt to neo-liberal globalisation spearheaded by the USA, to simply resist that model, or to propose another? What is the political end-term of the EU – a federal state, a condominium or a continued form of political consortium? Does the EU have a military vocation, and does it lie within, beyond or separate to NATO? And how will future decisions on enlargement rebound on the formulation of a coherent vision of Europe's future? Is there, for example, an inherent contradiction between an 'economic Europe', based on free-market principles (allowing the entry not just of Turkey but perhaps other Mediterranean states, or ex-USSR states such as the Ukraine), and a 'political Europe', with common government premised on shared concepts of identity, citizenship and public space? Further, at the national level (whether in France or elsewhere), what are the specific responses of political elites to these questions? And to what extent are they prepared to listen to and respect the views and responses of their electorates? The findings of this volume will cast light on a number of these issues, but do not purport to settle debates that will remain open-ended for the foreseeable future.

Overview of the book

The chapters that follow will explore the theme of France as a nation with enduring aspirations to play a leading role on the European and international stage, examining its capacity for initiative in a world dominated by one superpower, and seeking to understand the causes and limits of national adaptation to a globalised order.

The first chapter concentrates on France's relationship with the USA which reached a nadir in 2002–03, as Guillaume Parmentier explains. While the dispute centred on the invasion of Iraq, it was symptomatic of deeper tensions between the two nations, embracing the international system as a whole, with contrasting, even dichotomous, messages sent by France and the USA to the world at large. Since the elections of May 2007, France has a new president, Nicolas Sarkozy, and a chance to improve relations with Washington after a period of friction.

French relations with two other important poles of the contemporary world order – Africa and Asia – then come under scrutiny. As Tony Chafer observes, French elites of different political hues have been united in regarding France's role in Africa as central to the nation's status as a world power. François Mitterrand firmly believed that France's future in the twenty-first century depended on retaining a 'special relationship' with former African colonies. Africa, especially when reduced to its French-speaking constituents, was considered a 'manageable' continent where the exercise of French influence would bolster national aspirations to world power status. France developed a Gaullist strategy to African countries based on bilateral relations, which has only been revised in recent years due to policy failures linked to collapsing regimes, leading to an incomplete transition to a multilateralist approach.

In contrast, Reuben Wong shows how French foreign policy in East Asia rapidly became 'Europeanised'. In examining foreign and security relations towards Japan, and policies over human rights in China in the period from 1985 to 2005, Wong documents substantial convergence between French and EU policies – to a degree which would have been unimaginable from a traditional, Gaullist foreign policy perspective. In large part, the explanation is that French resources were recognised as over-stretched and inadequate to meet national objectives in countries as distant, large and challenging as Japan and China; hence the EU came to serve as an indispensable intermediary.

Questioning the Gaullist heritage further, Albrecht Sonntag argues that the politics of prestige in which France has frequently engaged have left a burdensome legacy. France has proved unable to live up to self-imposed expectations of role and rank – imbued with notions of hierarchy, superiority and distinction – on the world stage. The call for the recovery of France's lost rank and status, he notes, is to be heard on every major party platform across the French political spectrum. Sonntag explains the persistence of the politics of prestige using a variant of the path dependency concept to show how culture, expressed through societal and institutional processes, can form 'prison walls' which limit adaptive capacity in relation to European construction and globalisation.

Because the theme of European integration is central to France's adaptation to a globalising world, three chapters in the volume explore EU perspectives. The analyses by Nick Startin and Laurent Binet focus on the causes and consequences of the failed 2005 referendum on the EU Constitutional Treaty. Startin uses a public opinion perspective, drawing extensively on poll data, to establish the motivations of voters, which is complemented by Binet's discourse analysis perspective dissecting the arguments put forward by politicians and other opinion leaders. Together these studies demonstrate that the rejection of the Constitutional Treaty was bound up with the Chirac administration, whose popularity had ebbed significantly after the 2002 electoral landslide, and with particular – and relatively new – causes of dissatisfaction with the EU itself. In the minds of many French voters, the EU provoked anxieties over enlargement and – most importantly – fears over globalisation. As Startin concludes, a failure to persuade the French that the EU can still serve as a force for good in the world will both damage the EU and put considerable strain on the future of the French Fifth Republic.

Further, French strategy towards Europe has been inherently ambiguous. Is the aim to build a fortress Europe, defended by protectionist barriers, or a federal bloc to rival the USA worldwide in economic and security terms? As regards monetary integration, Howarth responds that France uses Europe to 'to keep the world at bay'. His chapter shows that the technical issues related to the euro spilled over into broader policy aims related to European economic governance: both areas have served as transmission belts whereby successive French governments have sought to manage European and global constraints in order to satisfy national interests.

The focus then turns to French business and the economy against the backdrop of globalisation. Mairi Maclean considers the continuing internationalisation of French business made possible by extensive inward and outward foreign direct investment (FDI). She examines the extent to which the French national business system is now converging on the 'Anglo-American model', as international standards of corporate governance emerge. As Searjeant (2001: 31) observed, globalisation – like charity – 'should start at home', meaning that France's strength lies in recognising that globalisation works in the national interest, if as many domestic companies as possible can be helped into the driving seat.

Jean-Marc Trouille and Henrik Uterwedde examine the renaissance of 'industrial policy' – which sought to promote national champions, but which fell into obsolescence in the 1980s – in the new guise of a 'competitiveness policy', reflective of French concerns to consolidate global influence. They consider instances of Franco-German cooperation, a half-way house, perhaps, towards the creation of 'European champions'. They find that renewed French industrial policy contains innovative, forward-looking strategies which nevertheless rely on familiar – albeit recast – recipes.

In the environmental domain, Joseph Szarka considers the ways in which the French have engaged in international regime-building to develop climate protection policies, and reviews the rationale behind burden-sharing at the European level. This chapter elucidates the distinctive aspects of French national policy-making, whilst identifying how and why it is reaching its limits in the critical area of climate policy.

Here too the forces of path dependence co-exist, paradoxically and at times precariously, with concomitant factors for renewal.

In the communications and cultural domain, Raymond Kuhn explains how French television is ever more influenced by developments in the increasingly networked transnational media system. He argues that French television, now in the third age of its historical development (that of global digital media), may be regarded as both 'reaching out' – taking advantage of opportunities offered by globalisation to promote French cultural and economic interests abroad – whilst simultaneously 'pushing back', introducing regulatory measures designed to bolster and protect the national status of French television in response to external threats, real or perceived.

In the final chapter, Gino Raymond turns the spotlight on the specificities of the French Republic in the era of globalisation. He examines the riots which erupted during the autumn of 2005 in the deprived suburbs of Paris and other French conurbations, which constituted the worst outbreak of civil unrest for forty years, and scrutinises the implications for citizenship and democracy in contemporary France. Raymond predicts that, in conformance with the expectations of political elites and grassroots constituencies alike, action in the public space is likely to remain the favoured arena for the expression of political preferences, at a time when French society seeks, and is arguably desperately in need of, reconciliation with itself.

Summary remarks

To propose a conclusion at this stage would be inappropriate: the chapters which follow should be allowed to speak for themselves. However, some common lines of analysis and argument can be flagged.

Globalisation has unleashed isomorphic forces of unprecedented strength, reconfiguring economies, societies and institutions in new and unpredictable ways. Nevertheless as we review the outcomes of this research project focusing on 'France on the world stage', we have been struck repeatedly by the power of cultural reproduction and the reassertion of social patterns, albeit in new guises. In consequence, to toll the knell for the nation state at this stage seems premature. However, this is not to deny that the nation state is currently challenged in unprecedented ways. More pooling of national resources within the EU, more coalition-building and burden-sharing with international partners will clearly be needed to face collectively the challenges of security and defence, business and the environment.

Path dependency has often proved determinative, with indications across a range of domains – diplomatic, political, economic, environmental, cultural and societal – of France's difficulties in breaking away from familiar recipes and well-trodden paths. Yet incremental change has proved significant, with major innovations identified in each domain listed. Just as the shifting of the Earth's tectonic plates escapes our attention yet yields spectacular results, so incremental policy adjustments in evolving contexts have produced large-scale consequences. This volume cannot determine the extent to which the French populace has benefited or suffered from globalisation. But it does show that Gaullist foreign policy has been profoundly transformed in the context of a new world order. For France the stress no longer falls on the ideology of national independence, but on more pragmatic goals of multipolar diplomacy. Domestic politics and policy-making have been irrevocably shaped by the pressures of Europeanisation. French business and the economy have been extensively overhauled and modernised to compete successfully in global markets. Faced with global climate risk, environmental concerns have emerged from the domain of 'low politics', and precipitated an unprecedented round of international regime-building. Whilst the French often feel that their society and culture are under attack from globalisation – and particularly Americanisation – the realisation is dawning that transnational networked media (satellite and internet) offer new opportunities for the *rayonnement* (radiance) of French language and culture, and of French political values related to liberty, citizenship and the Republic. Global communications, exchanges and comparisons serve to test claims to a 'universal message', potentially diluting out-dated and inward-looking idiosyncrasies whilst strengthening and diffusing what is best in national models.

Notes

1. A statement of the anti-globalisation position can be found in Forrester (1996). See Bové and Dufour (2000) for a critique of globalisation as mere commodification. For a summary on the French debate on globalisation, see Kresl and Gallais (2002: 5–11).
2. For studies on ATTAC, see Ancelovici (2002) and Waters (2006).
3. Cited in Patrick (2001: 10).
4. See http://archives.cnn.com/2002/WORLD/europe/02/07france.bush, consulted 3 July 2007.

References

Ancelovici, M. (2002) 'Organising against globalisation: the case of ATTAC in France', *Politics and Society*, 30(3) (September): 427–63.

Bavarez, N. (2003) *La France qui tombe*, Paris: Perrin.

Beck, U. (1992) *Risk Society: Towards a New Modernity*, London: Sage.

Beck, U. (2000) *What is Globalization?* trans. P. Camiller, Cambridge: Polity Press.

Bell, D. (1987) 'The world and the United States in 2013', *Daedelus*, 116(3): 1–31.

Boniface, P. (1998) *La France est-elle encore une grande puissance?* Paris: Presses de Sciences-Po.

Boniface, P. (2007) *Lettre ouverte à notre futur(e) Président(e) de la République sur le rôle de la France dans le monde*, Paris: Armand Colin.

Bové, J. and F. Dufour (2000) *Le Monde n'est pas une marchandise*, Paris: La Découverte.

Castells, M. (1996) *The Rise of the Network Society*, Oxford: Blackwell.

Cogan, C. (2003) *French Negotiating Behavior: Dealing with La Grande Nation*, Washington, DC: United States Institute of Peace Press.

Cole, A. (2001) *Franco-German Relations*, Harlow: Pearson.

Crouch, C. (2005) *Capitalist Diversity and Change*, Oxford: Oxford University Press.

DiMaggio, P.J. and W.W. Powell (1991) 'The iron cage revisited: institutional isomorphism and collective rationality', in W.W. Powell and P.J. DiMaggio (eds), *The New Institutionalism in Organizational Analysis*, Chicago: University of Chicago Press.

Djelic, M.-L. and S. Quack (2003a) 'Introduction: governing globalization – bringing institutions back in', in M.-L. Djelic and S. Quack (eds), *Globalization and Institutions: Redefining the Rules of the Economic Game*, Cheltenham, UK and Northampton, MA, USA: Edward Elgar, pp. 1–14.

Djelic, M.-L. and S. Quack (2003b) 'Conclusion: globalization as a double process of institutional change and institution building', in M.L. Djelic and S. Quack (eds), *Globalization and Institutions: Redefining the Rules of the Economic Game*, Cheltenham, UK and Northampton, MA, USA: Edward Elgar, pp. 302–33.

Drake, H. (2005) *French Relations with the European Union*, London: Routledge.

Fligstein, N. and R. Freeland (1995) 'Theoretical and comparative perspectives on corporate organization', *Annual Review of Sociology*, 21: 21–43.

Forrester, V. (1996) *L'Horreur économique*, Paris: Fayard.

Giddens, A. (1999) *Runaway World: How Globalisation is Shaping our Lives*, London: Profile.

Gordon, P.H. and S. Meunier (2001) *The French Challenge? Adapting to Globalisation*, Washington, DC: Brookings Institution.

Gubert, R. and E. Saint-Martin (2003) *L'Arrogance française*, Paris: Balland.

Guéhenno, J.-M. (1995) *The End of the Nation State*, trans. V. Elliott, Minneapolis: University of Minnesota Press.

Guyomarch, A., H. Machin and E. Ritchie (1998) *France in the European Union*, Basingstoke: Macmillan.

Held, D., A. McGrew, D. Goldblatt and J. Perraton (2000) *Global Transformations: Politics, Economics and Culture*, Cambridge: Polity Press.

Hirst, P.K. and G. Thompson (1996) *Globalization in Question: the International Economy and the Possibilities of Governance*, Cambridge: Polity Press.

Hoffmann, S. (1987) 'France and Europe: the dichotomy of autonomy and cooperation', in J. Howorth and G. Ross (eds), *Contemporary France: a Review of Interdisciplinary Studies*, volume 1, London: Pinter. pp. 46–54.

Howarth, D. (2001) *The French Road to European Monetary Union*, Basingstoke: Palgrave Macmillan.

Huntington, S.P. (1999) 'The lonely superpower', *Foreign Affairs*, 78(2): 35–49.

Jospin, L. (2002) *My Vision of Europe and Globalisation*, Cambridge: Polity.

Kresl, P.K. and S. Gallais (2002) *France Encounters Globalisation*, Cheltenham, UK and Northampton, MA, USA: Edward Elgar.

Kuisel, R.F. (1981) *Capitalism and the State in Modern France: Renovation and Economic Management in the Twentieth Century*, Cambridge: Cambridge University Press.

Lyth, P. and H. Trischler (2004) *Wiring Prometheus: Globalisation, History and Technology*, Aarhus: Aarhus University Press.

Maclean, M. (2002) *Economic Management and French Business from de Gaulle to Chirac*, Basingstoke: Palgrave Macmillan.

Maclean, M. and J. Howorth (1992) 'Introduction: the "old continent" in turmoil, a new one in the making', in M. Maclean and J. Howorth (eds), *Europeans on Europe: Transnational Visions of a New Continent*, Basingstoke: Macmillan, pp. 1–17.

Maclean, M. and J.-M. Trouille (eds) (2001) *France, Germany and Britain: Partners in a Changing World*, Basingstoke: Palgrave Macmillan.

Monnet, J. (1976) *Mémoires*, Paris: Fayard.

North, D.C. (1990) *Institutions, Institutional Change and Economic Performance*, Cambridge: Cambridge University Press.

Ohmae, K. (1990) *The Borderless World: Power and Strategy in the Interlinked Economy*, London: Collins.

Ohmae, K. (1995) *The End of the Nation State: the Rise of Regional Economies*, London: HarperCollins.

Ohmae, K. (2005) *The Next Global Stage: Challenges and Opportunities in our Borderless World*, Upper Saddle River, New Jersey: Pearson/Wharton School Publishing.

Panchadsaram, S. (2004) 'France: a new member of the "axis of evil"?', http://www.etalkinghead.com/archives/france-a-new-member-of-the-axis-of-evil-2004-01-28.html, consulted 3 July 2007.

Patrick, S. (2001) 'Don't fence me in: a restless American seeks room to roam', *World Policy Journal*, 18(3): 2–14.

Pedersen, T. and S. Thomsen (1997) 'European patterns of corporate ownership: a twelve-country study', *Journal of International Business Studies*, 4: 759–78.

Rouart, J.-M. (2003) *Adieu à la France qui s'en va*, Paris: Grasset.

Rueff, J. (1972) *Combats pour l'ordre financier*, Paris: Plon.

Searjeant, G. (2001) 'Globalisation should start at home', *The Times*, 18 January, 31.

Sklair, L. (2002) *Globalisation: Capitalism and its Alternatives*, Oxford: Oxford University Press.

Strange, S. (1996) *The Retreat of the State: the Diffusion of Power in the World Economy*, Cambridge: Cambridge University Press.

Szarka, J. (2002) *The Shaping of Environmental Policy in France*, Oxford: Berghahn.

Theys, J. (1987) 'La société vulnérable', in J.-L. Fabiani and J. Theys (eds), *La Société vulnérable: évaluer et maîtriser les risques*, Paris: Presses de l'Ecole Normale Supérieure, pp. 3–35.

UN Security Council (2002) 'Security Council holds Iraq in "material breach" of disarmament obligations, offers final chance to comply, unanimously adopting resolution 1441 (2002)', New York: UN Press Release SC/7564, http://www.un.org/News/Press/docs/2002/SC7564.doc.htm, consulted 8 July 2007.

Védrine, H. (2001) *France in an Age of Globalization*, Washington: Brookings Institution.

Wallerstein, I. (1984) *The Politics of the World Economy: the States, the Movements and the Civilizations*, Cambridge: Cambridge University Press/Editions de la Maison des Sciences de l'Homme.

Waters, S. (2006) 'A l'Attac: globalisation and ideological renewal on the French left', *Modern and Contemporary France*, 14(2) (May): 141–56.

Young, H. (2001) 'We've lost that Allied feeling', *Washington Post*, 1 April.

2

French-American Relations after the Iraq War: How to Redefine the Relationship

Guillaume Parmentier

The years 2002–03 were a historical low point in the relationship between France and the United States of America (Friedman, 2003). After this nadir, the relationship could only improve. It would be mistaken, however, to be complacent since many of the root causes of the major disagreements over the last years have not yet been addressed. The dispute over the recourse to war in Iraq was only a symptom of deeper problems and divergences. The conflict was not just over Iraq, but over the international system. This means that relations will be harder to mend. The responses of France and the USA to terrorism likewise reveal how difficult it is to reconcile the positions of the two countries. When the Americans decided to launch a 'war' against terror – which in the French view could not be won – France wished to keep the target limited strictly to Al-Qaeda and its allies. Even though a sense of realism has led each partner to accept the need for the other's contribution, fundamental differences remain. To explore these differences, this chapter will start with an analysis of the underlying causes behind the tensions, particularly the distinct messages that each of the two nations has the pretension – indeed the audacity – to convey to the world. It will consider the evolution of Franco-American relations in the aftermath of the Iraq invasion and address the question of whether improved relations can be fostered by reform of the North Atlantic Treaty Organisation (NATO). Finally, the scope for a redefinition of the relationship through improved cooperation between the USA and the European Union (EU) will be discussed.

Two global visions

France is the only large European country never to have fought a war against the USA, and each is the other's longest-standing ally. Over the centuries, their relationship has always been essential, but it has encountered many ups and downs. Both countries have a global vision of the world as it is and, more important, as it should be. Each has the ambition of shaping the world according to its convictions, but these are not always perfectly compatible, giving rise to many tensions between the two nations.

The birth of both nations was founded on the ideas of the Enlightenment. Of course, France pre-existed the Enlightenment, but modern France recognises itself in its post-revolutionary image. Contemporary France sees itself as both an initiator and a result of the idea of liberty. Yet the USA is the first nation to be based on an idea – the idea of freedom – arising directly from concepts of the Enlightenment. Because France and the USA see themselves as the embodiment of these ideas, the messages they send to the world convey similar values, such as democracy, liberty, peace, tolerance and human rights.[1] However, given the distinct cultural contexts within which each nation has modelled these ideas, their expression has taken very different forms and the references in which each recognises itself are often at odds with those of the other. Whilst, for example, freedom is mainly associated with private enterprise in the USA, in France it is seen as a more individual issue, yet one which must be guaranteed by public authorities. Although these conceptions are not fundamentally exclusive, they are sufficiently distinctive to divide the leaderships of the two countries when problems arise on which their instinctive reactions differ.

Furthermore, the vision that the French have of themselves, as a result of their history, is that of a country resisting empires (which to many means the USA), whereas many Americans believe that their country acts for the common good and that its foreign policy is a gift to the world (or, in sociological parlance, an 'international public good').[2] Both nations consider their foreign policies to be a contribution to the world order. Yet in a global context where the USA enjoys overwhelming dominance in military power, economic might and cultural influence, these different visions easily lead to clashes. Both France and the USA tend to see their foreign policy in the mirror of the other country's positions. A tendency exists on each side to be obsessed by the other, while dismissing them as less important than they actually are. In France, commentators of an anti-American persuasion often portray the USA as all-powerful yet on the verge of collapse.[3] In the USA, the State Department has historically seen France as a spent force, while often tracing the difficulties of American foreign policy to French 'plots'.

The aftermath of the 2001–03 Iraq crisis

A legacy of negative feelings

France's reputation used to be good in the eyes of the American public, though poor among policy-making elites. Since the Iraq war, French standing in American opinion polls has sharply deteriorated. The French threat of a veto against the invasion of Iraq was perceived as a betrayal by many Americans who felt that at the very moment that the USA was hit, its closest allies were abandoning it. The fact that there was no link between Saddam Hussein and Al-Qaeda – a point later conceded by the administration – was lost on the American public. For a time, France's popularity was lower than Russia's.[4] In 2005, the American public had still not forgotten about the clash.[5] Subsequently France's image recovered in Washington circles, once its dire predictions over the Iraq operation were proved abundantly true (Ignatius, 2006). America's reputation in France declined regularly after President Bush rejected the Kyoto Protocol in March 2001 and the beginning of the so-called 'war on terror'.[6]

However, events after 11 September 2001 showed that the French felt strong solidarity with Americans in difficult times. The reaction of the French public and authorities was one of total identification with the Americans. On the following day, the newspaper *Le Monde* ran the title: 'We are all Americans' (Colombani, 2001). This headline accurately caught the mood of the public in France, in Europe and around the world. For the French, it expressed the feeling that, having experienced a number of terrorist attacks (albeit on a smaller scale), the atrocities of 9/11 would bring the USA closer to Europe in its assessment of the threats it was facing. The opposite proved true, however. The French had dealt with terror campaigns since the war in Algeria, in relation to Corsican and Basque terrorism, as well as attacks waged by Syrian-led Middle Eastern terrorists,[7] but they failed to understand fully the depth of America's reaction to the events of 9/11. Most Americans reacted as if the attacks had taken place mainly against their values: it was because they were Americans that they had been targeted. This feeling was exacerbated by the response of the Bush Administration and the President's statement that 'you are either with us or against us in the fight against terror' (CNN, 2001). No doubt the combination of surprise, the theatricality of the event and its repeated screening on television screens gave Americans the feeling that they were being singled out. In view of the difference in magnitude in human, economic and political losses, many Americans were shocked by the comparison with the kinds of terrorism that the

French and other Europeans had experienced. From the beginning therefore, the French (and European) reaction was at odds with that of the Americans.

As early as 12 September 2001, the UN Security Council under France's presidency passed resolution 1368 (United Nations, 2001), affirming that military action against the perpetrators of the attacks of 11 September constituted *legitimate* self-defence in the face of external aggression. Thus the perception of the attacks as an 'act of war' was the same on both sides of the Atlantic. This similarity of assessment and sense of solidarity did not, however, prevent the French from criticising the US response. In the French view, it was unnecessary and indeed inappropriate to respond immediately to one act of war by another. This would give Al-Qaeda excessive attention and importance, with the probable result that it would became the centre of Islamist anti-American opposition. The French considered therefore that staying firmly within UN rules was the key to any international response to the attacks. This was considered too soft and hence unacceptable by most Americans.

A transatlantic rift over foreign policy

The main cause of disagreement arose from each country's perception of foreign policy. This was linked not only to the specific question of Iraq, but to a fundamental difference in their approaches to war and the use of force. Whilst the French are certainly closer to the Americans than some other Europeans as regards their readiness to use force, they only favour its use within the limits of the UN Security Council. But the involvement of the UN does not seem as important to American leaders. After 9/11, many Americans believed that the international organisation was deeply flawed because it included countries whose behaviour was in obvious contradiction with many tenets of US and Western policy, whose respect for human rights was lacking, whose attitude to their neighbours was threatening and whose contribution to world order was negative. Why should such countries be considered a necessary part of the solution to international problems? But the perception of French and European leaders was different. They acknowledged that certain countries were delinquent in their attitude to international affairs and human rights, but argued that excluding them from the solution of international crises was a sure way to create a coalition of frustrated nations who would foment trouble and render solutions even more difficult. This clash of conceptions manifested itself clearly during discussions over the appropriate response to Saddam Hussein's regime.

The Iraq question changed the parameters of the transatlantic debate. In 2003, 84 per cent of Americans polled agreed with the statement that 'under some conditions, war is necessary to obtain justice', whilst only 39 per cent of French respondents agreed (German Marshall Fund of the USA, 2003). This may be due to a certain war weariness among the French: while the continental part of the USA has not been invaded since 1812,[8] France has had to fight recurrent aggressions. Above all, the differences lay in the fact that the USA portrayed the invasion of Iraq as closely linked to both the 'war' on terror and the 'war' against Al-Qaeda. While the French agreed on the necessity to fight international terrorism by destroying the Al-Qaeda network, they strongly objected to the syncretic American approach. They considered that the confusion between two entirely different types of 'war' could foster an undesirable unity among otherwise separate and competing groups and countries. Furthermore, a 'war on terror' was such a broad undertaking that it could only be lost. It is impossible to put an end to terror, which is a human feeling, and even to terrorism, which is a weapon that is easy to use and will be used by some, especially in an international system where power is distributed in a heavily unequal manner. The French position was reinforced when the US administration had to admit that there was no clear link between Saddam Hussein and Al-Qaeda. The French have come to consider that the Iraq war has increased the threat of terrorism by providing a base for Al-Qaeda in the Sunni part of Iraq and by increasing sympathy for the 'Muslim cause'. This gap in perceptions has led French public opinion – but not the French government – to consider the USA responsible for negative developments in international affairs during the recent period.[9] In this respect, French public opinion is in the European mainstream. But in the USA, the French reaction is often interpreted as a weaker ally's frustration over its incapacity to dictate the course of world affairs, resulting in natural resentment against the strongest power (Mandelbaum, 2005).

The divergences between France and the USA can be brought down to three major areas of disagreement: the importance of religion, attitudes towards the use of force and the view of the state (Mandelbaum, 2005: 141–86). Differences in the means to redress injustice and the use of violence in general have led to French criticisms regarding the use of capital punishment and the lack of gun control in the USA. Crucially, the role of the state is perceived in entirely different ways in the two nations. In terms of domestic policy, the French expect a more assertive state than do Americans.[10] Moreover, foreign policy is the ultimate justification for the power of the centralised French state. This is obviously a reason for the continued assertiveness of French foreign policy and for the widespread support the latter enjoys among French people. Indeed, France as a nation evolved as a means to protect the king's vassals from foreign encroachments (especially from the Holy Roman Empire, hence the touchiness about empires among the French). In contrast, the founding fathers of the USA were concerned that foreign policy would concentrate too much power in the hands of the President (Zoellick, 1999). However, since 9/11 at least, the USA expects a more assertive presence on the international scene, considering that the use of force is the best way to be respected. This attitude is strongly criticised by France. The French have become more 'European' in their increased reluctance to employ force, whereas they were less reticent in this respect until the end of the Cold War. They are more comfortable with foreign inter-vention when this is done wearing an international or European hat than when France goes it alone. This is now true even in former French Africa, as witnessed by the UN cover given to the operation in the Côte d'Ivoire. This reticence about the use of force has not, however, had a similar restraining effect on the conduct of French foreign policy nor on the public assertiveness of French leaders on international matters, including those where France's declarations can only have a symbolic effect. This style of diplomacy is expected of its leaders by the French population, as was clear during the 2003 crisis when President Chirac's opinion poll ratings increased enormously and when Foreign Minister Dominique de Villepin became a celebrity among his fellow-countrymen due to his televised exchanges with his American counterpart. These dif-ferent approaches to the role of the state in international affairs are also reflected in the views held by the French and the Americans towards institutions or agreements that may restrain their governments, such as the International Criminal Court or the 1997 Kyoto Protocol.

Yet it would be mistaken to couch this opposition in stark national terms. What made the 2003 configuration exceptional was precisely that 9/11 created a façade of unity among Americans, a factor that French leaders underestimated. Americans have since become increas-ingly divided on foreign policy. In 2004, 85 per cent of Republicans approved of President Bush's international policies, while 80 per cent of Democrats disapproved (German Marshall Fund of the USA, 2004). Moreover, the French have more difficulty agreeing with the views of the Republican Party on key international issues than with those of the Democratic Party (Mandelbaum, 2005: 151). By the late 2000s, the prevailing feeling in the USA was that the Iraq adventure was disastrous. The defeat of the Republicans in the November 2006 mid-term elections had its roots in the unpopularity of the administration's Iraq policy. The results can be interpreted as a desire for a change in American foreign policy (Luce, 2006). Although it is too early to tell whether the shift in power will heal the transatlantic rift, foreign policy differences between France and the USA may be somewhat smoothened out – at least in the rhetoric, now that the Bush administration is forced to deal with a Democratic House and Senate. The 'checks and balances' on which the American constitution is based will reassert themselves, after the recent dominance of partisan politics and the unusual party spirit of the Republican Party had temporarily undermined them.[11] In addition, the election of Nicolas Sarkozy as French President in May 2007 may lead to a significant change in Franco-American relations. It is revealing that, during the presidential campaign, taking a position for or against a policy pursued or advocated by the USA was equivalent to making a political statement. The relationship with the USA is as much a domestic as a foreign policy issue in France. It has a direct influence on domestic approval rates and can be used on both sides to generate political capital. When in September 2006, Nicolas Sarkozy (then Interior Minister) visited President Bush and used the occasion to criticise the manner in which President Chirac and Dominique de Villepin had handled the relationship with the USA during the run-up to war in 2003, the visit triggered a national debate about transatlantic relations and France's role in the world. The discussion drew in France's leading politicians. Laurent Fabius, former Prime Minister and then a candidate for the Socialist Party's nomination for the presidential elections, was among those who tried to draw political capital from this visit by calling Sarkozy 'Bush's poodle'.[12] Clearly, the relationship with the USA cannot be considered solely as a foreign policy issue in France.

Cooperation and shared values at the height of the crisis

During the 2000s, the media harped on the political disagreements between France and the USA so insistently that it is sometimes forgotten how developed cooperation has been at other levels. Despite quarrels regarding the type of action to be taken, the perception of the threats was the same,[13] and the need to work together was never seen to be stronger. At the height of the crisis, when France sought to prevent the USA gaining the support of the UN Security Council for the invasion of Iraq, the secret services of the two countries liaised more closely than ever on terrorism (Priest, 2005; Stein, 2005). A discreet, international counter-terrorism intelligence centre code-named 'Alliance Base' was set up in Paris by the CIA and French intelligence in 2002, which remained active even when the Franco-American dispute was at its most bitter in 2003. In the same year, France agreed to become the main contributor to the NATO Reaction Force.

Despite their differences on a broader strategy for the Middle East, French and American politicians agreed on the need to prevent Afghanistan from falling back into the hands of the Taliban.[14] From 2002, France had special forces under direct American command in Afghanistan, operating outside of the NATO framework. Some 5000 French troops participated in the stabilisation operation, engaged in high-risk operations against the Taliban and their allies. French involvement also included air sorties against caves where Al-Qaeda supporters had gathered, which American planes could not undertake because it would have obliged them to fly dangerously low. In late 2006, France had over 1000 troops in Afghanistan and was in charge of security in and around Kabul, whilst the USA handed over the Eastern part of Afghanistan to NATO command.[15]

The close economic ties between the two countries have remained undisturbed by the political turmoil. No substantial economic backlash occurred because of the high degree of economic integration (French Economic Mission, 2005). On average, commercial transactions to the value of over $1 bn take place between the two countries every day of the year. France is the ninth largest trading partner for manufactured goods with the USA, and the sixth largest for trade in services. Three thousand French companies have offices in the USA and employ about 600,000 American workers, directly or indirectly; $150 bn of foreign direct investment into the USA comes from France.[16]

Disagreement on foreign policy is not to be associated with anti-Americanism in general. In terms of culture and values, the French and the Americans are far more alike than they tend (and like) to think.[17] The French listen to American music, go to see American movies and dream of sending their children to American universities. Differences between both countries are no bigger today than they were in the 1940s and 1950s when the Western system of alliances was put in place (Asmus, 2006).

At the more general level, the impact of the Europeanisation of French foreign policy on the bilateral relationship will have to be addressed, as well as the effect of French-US disagreements on France's hopes for a European foreign policy. This means addressing squarely the problems of the main transatlantic organisation – NATO – which defines the terms of the relationship in ways which date from the Cold War but which need to be improved to meet the necessities of our times.

France, NATO and the new world order

Whatever their differences during the Cold War, Western countries were ultimately forced to agree on the fundamentals in the face of a common threat. Even though France always maintained more independence toward the USA than did Germany, for example, French politicians knew where their interests lay and where to look in times of crisis. Although France left the integrated military command structure in 1966 and thereby forced NATO to move to Belgium, it remained strongly integrated in NATO's political structure and, above all, in the Atlantic Council. In the French view, the latter remained an essential instrument for transatlantic dialogue.

Today, Western countries no longer have a clearly defined common enemy. This increases the temptation to indulge in the luxury of open disagreement. This does not mean that differences are stronger than they were, only that they have become more apparent. In this sense, the Iraq controversy could not have come as a complete surprise. Mutual dependency has enormously diminished and the logic of NATO's internal structure does not hold any more. This begs the question of how to overhaul transatlantic institutions and adapt to the new context.

An organisation inherited from the Cold War

NATO's command structure was developed in a way which allowed the Allies to react most efficiently to the threat posed by the Soviet Union. Its division into regional commands corresponded to a static, traditional approach to warfare, having the aim of stabilising the military fronts. It ensured that most countries were directly in charge of the defence of their own territory, whilst allowing for an international presence. The command structure reflected the distribution of power and the differences in military capability within NATO in a logical way. Since the Europeans had entrusted the Americans with their security after the Second World War, and since most NATO assets depended on US military infrastructure, it was natural to choose an American commander-in-chief as Supreme Allied Commander Europe (SACEUR). The latter also served as commander-in-chief within the US military in Europe. The dependence on the USA was overwhelming because of the extreme feebleness of post-war Europe. This justified the loss of sovereignty that resulted from entrusting the main responsibility for Western European defence to an American Supreme Commander directly subordinated to Washington through the 'double hatting' system (Parmentier, 2000). Further, the dependence of Europeans on the Americans meant that consultation within NATO was often no more than a formality.

After 1966, France became convinced that the diminishing Soviet threat was not worth the diminution in her sovereignty, but was most often alone in speaking out. American predominance was seen as the condition of democratic Europe's survival. But the ending of the Cold War fundamentally altered the world order. The enemy is no longer a group of communist states with a strong conventional army. With the ending of confrontation between two military blocs, the new security context is characterised by individual threats, regional conflicts and systemic problems. Today's main dangers are failed states, proliferation of weapons of mass destruction, terrorism, humanitarian or ecological catastrophes, and pandemics. Some issues are linked to small groups of people who are difficult to track and against whom traditional weapons are of little use.

The lack of adaptation

NATO's refusal to adapt to the realities of the post-Cold War order had the consequence that it has been sidelined militarily in Kosovo, strategically after 9/11, and politically during the war on Iraq. NATO's image suffered greatly during the Kosovo conflict. The organisation turned out to be too multilateral an instrument to suit the purposes of the USA (which now viewed it with suspicion), yet too dominated by Americans to suit the needs of Europeans. The result was that the USA did not use it after 9/11, even though NATO's major defence provision – article 5 of the Washington Treaty – was invoked for the first time on 12 September. The strategic vacuity of the organisation became plain to see. The phrase used by the then Defence Secretary Rumsfeld – 'the mission determines the coalition' – was directly contrary to the spirit of a standing alliance such as NATO and so was strongly criticised by French public opinion.[18]

The American perception of NATO has changed from considering it the main tool for solving European problems (as in the 1990s) to seeing it as an excessive constraint on foreign policy. The crisis within the Alliance over Iraq that was triggered by the French and Germans only revealed once more what Bosnia had shown a few years earlier. Even before the American intervention in 1995, the Alliance had proved incapable of reconciling the different viewpoints of its members. At the height of the Iraq crisis, NATO Secretary General Lord George Robertson stated: 'finally, we had to accept that consensus among 19 NATO members was impossible, not for capricious reasons but because of substantive differences of policy' (Robertson, 2003). Whilst in public NATO member countries have stressed their common ground, they have done nothing to adapt the organisation to meet the real challenges. It is significant that the Allies talk more about shared values than mutual interests. Divergences over a common strategy are too large to be easily reconciled: it is easier to stick to broad principles and generalities.

A symbolic turning-point occurred at the end of 2001 when the USA chose to build an ad hoc 'coalition of the willing' rather than rely on a permanent alliance. It was a breaking point in the history of NATO, and a return to a more traditional American approach to foreign policy. Alliances are not part of the US tradition, with the last fifty years being more the exception than the rule (Daalder and Lindsay, 2005). In his First Inaugural Address of 4 March 1801, Thomas Jefferson promised 'peace, commerce, and honest friendship with all nations, entangling alliances with none'. In 1949, the founding of the transatlantic Alliance led to a heated debate in Congress that feared that America might be giving up its traditional independence. The equilibrium of fear over the next fifty years turned the Alliance into a lesser – and necessary – evil. With the communist danger gone, the USA is giving consideration to the restoration of a foreign policy based on varied options, rather than the automatic alignment that a permanent alliance requires and which the USA currently sees as being too constraining. This is an attitude that the French – more perhaps than any other European nation – are able to understand because alliances have repeatedly failed France throughout modern history. Since de Gaulle, the French have had an ambivalent relationship with NATO, fearing that it might be America's Trojan horse in Europe and refusing the perceived loss of sovereignty that came with an integrated command structure.

The necessity of reform

It would be idle to try and re-create the conditions of the past. NATO will no longer constrain the USA in the way it could have done if a conflict with the Soviet Union had taken place during the Cold War. In the French view, the task now consists in adapting the organisation to a new reality, and in taking advantage of the fact that it has become optional – both for the USA and for the other Allies. Two outcomes are required: (a) to transform the Alliance into an '*à la carte*' organisation, usable by its members in different configurations, and (b) to ensure that *all* members (not just the USA) can use the organisation in this flexible manner. Flexibility cannot be a one-way street. This evolution would provide the best way to reconcile the viewpoints of France and the USA, as France is the European country least beholden to the automaticity of the NATO system, by virtue of its having left the integrated military command in 1966.

If NATO is not to become a mere 'relic of the past' (to quote American Defence Secretary William Cohen),[19] an overhaul of the entire organisation is needed. This is the key to the improvement of the US-French relationship, which has so often focused in the past on the very different conceptions held by the two countries of the transatlantic organisation's role and structures. What is needed is an instrument that can be used by NATO members when they need it. The organisation has unique features, including a command and communication system which enables different nations to cooperate effectively during an international crisis when military intervention is necessary. The Europeans need this capability, and can use NATO assets of which they are co-owners to achieve it. Implementing the arrangements known in NATO as 'Berlin Plus' would increase cooperation.[20] The Franco-American relationship never works more effectively than when it is pragmatic and issue-based.

NATO operations need to be controlled politically by the member states who put their men and women in harm's way. This cannot be done, as was the case in Kosovo, through the NATO Council interfering in military matters. The price paid in efficiency terms would be too heavy, especially if the operation is high risk (as in Afghanistan). What is needed is that the NATO Military Committee (MC) be made the highest military authority in the Alliance, with all nations represented on an equal footing. This reform was envisaged in the Washington Treaty, but proved impossible to implement due to the need to give the USA the leading military role at all times. SACEUR should report to the MC so that the political ends which member nations legitimately pursue are communicated to the commanders in the field in ways which are compatible with military efficiency. A regional command cannot be the supreme authority in an alliance of free nations. A process of streamlining NATO's decision-making has also to be implemented. This could be achieved through the creation of small groups playing an influential role within the framework of the MC. Countries which contribute more to the military effectiveness of the Alliance should be recognised as such, and criteria of effectiveness should be agreed upon by all nations for this purpose.

NATO can no longer act as if European construction were a purely external factor to which the Alliance could remain impervious. Obviously, the ultimate responsibility for defence rests with sovereign states. NATO cannot be transformed into a Euro-American body where the Europeans were represented by a single representative. But NATO circles should not believe that the organisation's credibility can be maintained if the budding, but rapidly expanding, European security effort is ignored. Fears of a 'European caucus' which would exclude America are greatly exaggerated. It would clearly be more difficult to isolate the USA if Europe had representation in NATO, than if European policy in the fields of defence and security was decided in complete isolation from the Atlantic Alliance.

Finally, communication between member states would be improved by a better division of labour. The negative impression formed by the USA that Europeans take advantage of American assets (without contributing much themselves) must be overcome. On the other hand, the European perception of NATO as a tool to relieve America's burden following military conflict needs to change. This factor is particularly problematic for America's allies, especially for one which has taken part in all these efforts, France.

Redefining the US-EU relationship

Proposals for reform of the US-EU relationship beg the question of the purpose of Europe. How far do the French and their partners want to go geographically but especially functionally? Are French leaders federalists or not? And what does federalism entail in terms of pooling of sovereignty? These questions need to be addressed directly. The character of the Franco-American relationship will be deeply influenced by choices on the future of the EU. It may continue as a mainly bilateral relationship or be replaced by a multilateral dialogue with two main voices – that is, if Europe manages to speak with one voice. The USA cannot be expected to make the EU a partner if the Europeans do not define the mechanisms which will allow the Americans to interact with them in a steady and efficient manner. However, the form to be given to the Europeanisation of foreign policy was put into disarray by the French (and Dutch) rejection of the European Constitutional Treaty in 2005. Furthermore, although the transatlantic relationship was largely dominated by security issues during the Cold War, its coverage is far broader today. The security element remains very important, but is not as overwhelming as in the past. In consequence, the transatlantic partners need to deepen the consultation process to include EU representation as such, along with other member states.[21] The EU and the USA need a permanent dialogue in order to work together. Even though the relationship between the EU and NATO is considered a key topic in administrative circles in Brussels, it is not conceived as an important political question. If the architecture for the political relationship between the USA and Europe is properly designed, then its technical consequences – in particular, the arrangements between the EU and NATO – will fall into place.

Yet it is up to the Europeans to organise themselves in ways that make it possible for them to be taken seriously in Washington. The six-monthly rotating presidency and the arrangements regarding the High Representative complicate the transatlantic dialogue, making it difficult for the US administration to know who is responsible for what in the European Union. From the American point of view, it can only be regretted that Europeans failed once more to improve the decision-making process by rejecting the Constitutional Treaty which provided for a three-headed presidency for one and a half years. European foreign policy would have gained in coherence with a single person, the European Minister of Foreign Affairs, at its head. This would have provided the single interlocutor for which the Americans have been asking for so long.

We now need to pick up the pieces. The political elements in the treaty are not in question, since all EU member states agree on their provisions. Implementing these provisions is a necessary prerequisite for a balanced relationship with the USA, which will no longer be in a position to complain that they do not know the telephone number to dial Europe, to use Kissinger's famous expression. But Europeans still need to solve the question of the limits of Europe. More specifically, the member states need to determine the geographical, legal and functional borders of the EU.

Conclusion

The Franco-American relationship can only be improved in the larger context of the EU-USA relationship. Both sides now understand that it is better to leave their differences behind. Like an old couple, France and the USA have maintained a passionate but tormented relationship. 'I find it an old record that gets replayed about every five or seven years', as Donald Rumsfeld put it (US Department of Defense, 2003a). Without their quarrels, the relationship would just not be the same.[22] Many challenges lie ahead, in which France and the USA must work side by side. Now that Iraq is seen in a different perspective in the USA, the time has come to concentrate on new areas of cooperation. France and the USA are fighting together in Afghanistan, in the Balkans, in Kosovo. Solutions need to be found together for the Middle East. Palestine, Lebanon and Syria constitute particular challenges. On Iran, the USA will need to work hand in hand with France, Germany and the United Kingdom. North Korea poses issues that will challenge the United Nations for some time yet. In all these areas, collaboration between France and the USA remains essential and is working. After all, a little-known fact is that, whatever the disagreements, France has voted more often in the UN *with* the USA than has any other country.

Notes

Thanks are due to Ruth Lambertz for her help with the preparation of this text.
1. It is well known in both countries that their values are at the origin of the preamble of the United Nations Charter (United Nations, 1945). These principles are also found in the preamble to the North Atlantic Treaty (NATO, 1949).
2. For discussion, see Mead (2002) and Girardet (1986).
3. For examples, see *Le Monde Diplomatique*.
4. According to a poll conducted in February 2003, 59 per cent of Americans had a favourable image of France and 63 per cent had a favourable image of Russia. In 2002, 79 per cent of Americans had a favourable opinion of France (Gallup Organisation, 2003).
5. When polled in June 2005, 35 per cent of American respondents expressed a favourable opinion of France as compared to 50 per cent in 2002, whilst 25 per cent saw France in an unfavourable light as compared to 10 per cent in 2002 (French-American Foundation, 2005).
6. In June 2005, 31 per cent of French respondents felt sympathetic towards the USA (39 per cent in 2002), 51 per cent felt indifferent (44 per cent in 2002), and 17 per cent were critical (16 per cent in 2002) (French-American Foundation, 2005).
7. For a comprehensive database on terrorist activities in France since the 1950s, see the website of the Foundation for Strategic Research (Paris) at https://bdt.frstrategie.org. For discussion, see Parmentier (2006a).
8. Since Hawaii become a federal state only in 1959, the Japanese attack on Pearl Harbour in 1941 was an aggression of a very different nature, as it was against purely military installations.
9. Polled in June 2006, 36 per cent of French respondents considered the USA's actions in Iraq to be a 'danger for world peace' (Pew Global Attitudes Project, 2006).
10. When asked which government function they considered more important, 34 per cent of Americans and 62 per cent of French considered it more important to ensure that no one is in need, whilst 58 per cent of Americans and 36 per cent of French considered it more important for individuals to be free to pursue their goals (Pew Global Attitudes Project, 2003).
11. On the tendency of the Republican majority to behave like a parliamentary party, see Ornstein and Mann (2006). The bi-partisan system was not yet dreamt of at the time the American constitution was written. Thus the founding fathers could not foresee that its 'checks and balances' could be overruled if the executive and the legislative body were in the hands of the same party.
12. Laurent Fabius at a Socialist meeting in Lens on 16 September 2006.
13. See German Marshall Fund of the USA (2004).
14. Interview with Jean-David Levitte, Ambassador of France to the USA, in *San Diego Union-Tribune*, 5 May 2006.

15. For details, see the website of the International Security Assistance Force (ISAF): http://www.jfcbs.nato.int/ISAF/index.htm.
16. Nicolas Sarkozy in a speech to the 'Daughters of the American Revolution' on 12 September 2006.
17. See German Marshall Fund of the USA (2004, 2006).
18. Donald Rumsfeld at a press conference after NATO's defence ministers' meeting in Brussels on 18 December 2001.
19. Speech to NATO defence ministers on 5 December 2000 in Brussels (BBC News, 2000).
20. 'Berlin Plus' is a comprehensive package of agreements between NATO and the EU. It includes consultation procedures and a 'Security Arrangement', assuring access to NATO planning capabilities, assets and capabilities for EU-led 'Crisis-Management Operations'.
21. This could take different forms, from a EU representative within NATO – or even at the UN – to a regular EU-US summit. For discussion, see Parmentier (2006b).
22. When asked in interview whether he thought that the quarrel within NATO had gone too far, Secretary Rumsfeld said 'there's never been a five-year period that I can remember where there hasn't been something of the kind and we've survived it all' (US Department of Defense, 2003b).

References

Asmus, R.D. (2006) 'A dissenting voice on the values and interest gap', in M. Zaborowski (ed.), *Friends Again? EU-US Relations after the Crisis*, Paris: Transatlantic Books / European Union Institute for Security Studies, pp. 55–62.

BBC News (2000) 'US sounds alarm over EU force', http://news.bbc.co.uk/1/hi/world/europe/1055395.stm, consulted 26 March 2007.

CNN (2001) 'You are either with us or against us', http://archives.cnn.com/2001/US/11/06/gen.attack.on.terror/, consulted 27 March 2007.

Colombani, J.-M. (2001) 'Nous sommes tous Américains', *Le Monde*, 13 September.

Daalder, I.H. and J.M. Lindsay (2005) *America Unbound: the Bush Revolution in Foreign Policy*, Washington: Brookings Institution Press.

French Economic Mission (2005) 'France and the United States: a strong economic relationship', *Les Publications des Missions Economiques*, Washington DC, http://www.missioneco.org/etatsunis/documents_new.asp?V=1_PDF_109221, consulted 28 March 2007.

French-American Foundation (2005) 'France – Etats-Unis: regards croisés', http://www.french-american.org/upload/flb/107/Synthese_FAF_Juin_2005_FAF_11350034231 61.pdf, consulted 28 March 2007.

Friedman, T.L. (2003) 'Our war with France', *New York Times*, 18 September.

Gallup Organisation (2003) 'Americans uncertain about Iraq threat. Poll conducted from February 3–6', www.gallup.com, consulted 28 March 2007.

German Marshall Fund of the USA (2003) 'Transatlantic trends 2003', http://www.transatlantictrends.org/doc/2003_english_key.pdf, consulted 20 March 2007.

German Marshall Fund of the USA (2004) 'Transatlantic trends 2004', http://www.transatlantictrends.org/doc/2004_english_key.pdf, consulted 20 March 2007.

German Marshall Fund of the USA (2006) 'Transatlantic trends 2006', www.transatlantictrends.org, consulted 1 May 2007.

Girardet, R. (1986) *L'Idée coloniale en France de 1871 à 1962*, Paris: Hachette.

Ignatius, D. (2006) 'Bush's new ally: France?', *The Washington Post*, 1 February.

Luce, E. (2006) 'Iraq war decimates Republican vote', *Financial Times*, 9 November.

Mandelbaum, M. (2005) *The Case for Goliath. How America Acts as the World's Government in the Twenty-first Century*, New York: Public Affairs.

Mead, W. R. (2002) *Special Providence: American Foreign Policy and How it Changed the World*, London: Routledge.

NATO (1949) 'North Atlantic Treaty', http://www.nato.int/docu/handbook/2006/hb-en-2006.pdf, consulted 27 March 2007.

Ornstein, N.J. and T.E. Mann (2006) 'When Congress checks out', *Foreign Affairs*, 85(6) (November 30): 67–83.

Parmentier, G. (2000) 'Redressing NATO's imbalances', *Survival*, 2: 96–112.

Parmentier, G. (2006a) 'Terrorism in France: its main features and its evolution since the 1970s', in Y. Alexander (ed.), *Counterterrorism Strategies: Successes and Failures of Six Nations*, Washington DC: Potomac Books.

Parmentier, G. (2006b) 'Europe must play a bigger part in NATO', *Financial Times*, 17 March.

Pew Global Attitudes Project (2003) 'Views of a changing world: Pew Global Report', http://pewglobal.org/reports/display.php?ReportID=185, consulted 28 March 2007.

Pew Global Attitudes Project (2006) 'America's image slips, but allies share US concerns over Iran, Hamas', http://pewglobal.org/reports/display.php?ReportID=252, consulted 1 May 2007.

Priest, D. (2005) 'Help from France key in covert operations; Paris's "Alliance Base" targets terrorists', *Washington Post*, July 3.

Robertson, George (2003) 'Building a transatlantic consensus', speech at the European Institute, Washington DC, 20 February, http://www.nato.int/docu/speech/2003/s030220b.htm, consulted 28 March 2007.

Stein, D. (2005) 'Meet the USA's unlikely ally in the terror wars', *Congressional Quarterly Homeland Security*, 28 October, http://www.cq.com/public/20051028_homeland.html, consulted 29 May 2007.

United Nations (1945) 'The UN Charter', http://www.un.org/aboutun/charter, consulted 27 March 2007.

United Nations (2001) 'Security Council Resolution 1368 (2001)', http://daccessdds.un.org/doc/UNDOC/GEN/N01/533/82/PDF/N0153382.pdf?OpenElement, consulted 20 March 2007.

US Department of Defense (2003a) 'Secretary of Defense Donald Rumsfeld Interview with Washington Times, Editorial Board', Department of Defence News Transcript, *Defenselink* (October 23), http//www.defenselink.mil/transcripts/2003/tr20031023-secdef0819.html, consulted 30 March 2007.

US Department of Defense (2003b) 'Secretary Rumsfeld Interview with Regis le Sumier, Paris Match Magazine', Department of Defence News Transcript, *Defenselink* (November 20), http://www.defenselink.mil/transcripts/2003/tr20031120-secdef0982.html, consulted 27 March 2007.

Zoellick, R.B. (1999) 'Congress and the making of US foreign policy', *Survival*, 41(4): 20–41.

As Jacques Marseille (1984) showed for the colonial period, although the interests of French capitalism and colonial empire had diverged long before Raymond Cartier (1956) argued that colonialism was no longer in France's economic interest, certain influential sectors of French capital did very well out of empire and lobbied effectively for the maintenance of the French presence. However, it was not economic considerations but the notion of France's world power status and the consequent need for *rayonnement* (the projection of French power overseas) that were the primary determinants of French African policy. It was these shared assumptions that provided the basis for a common understanding among French political leaders of Africa's significance to France that transcended traditional divisions between Left and Right. Successive presidents of the Fifth Republic from de Gaulle to Chirac all shared the belief that France should maintain a *pré carré* (privileged sphere of influence) in Africa. Moreover, sub-Saharan Africa was a region where it was still possible for a medium-sized power such as France to continue to wield influence. As Giscard's Foreign Minister, Louis de Guiringaud, put it in 1981: 'Africa south of the Sahara is a group of countries that is manageable in size for France: neither the size of the population nor the scale of the economic problems are out of proportion with the means that France is able to devote to a prolonged action outside her own frontiers' (Guiringaud, 1982: 443).

The cultivation of this special relationship with Africa under the Fifth Republic was facilitated by four factors. First, de Gaulle's appropriation of African policy as a presidential *domaine réservé* (exclusive field of action) was adopted and perpetuated by his successors. In practice, the day-to-day running of African policy was delegated to the *cellule africaine* (Africa unit) at the Elysée Palace, which was headed during de Gaulle's presidency by his close ally and 'fixer' Jacques Foccart who had developed a dense network (*réseau*) of close and highly personalised relationships with political leaders in French-speaking Africa.[2] De Gaulle was happy for Franco-African relations to be handled in this manner, away from the public gaze. After the trauma of two wars of decolonisation, the colonial empire represented part of the 'baggage' of the past that de Gaulle now wanted France to forget, as he sought to project the image of a new, modern France that had put the outmoded practices of empire behind it. De Gaulle's successors maintained this system. Despite promises of reform before his election, President Mitterrand continued to conduct Franco-African relations through a network of unofficial and semi-official personalised relations. Thus, for most of his presidency the *cellule africaine* was headed by his son Jean-Christophe who, like Foccart, had his own network of close contacts and friends among French-speaking Africa's political leaders. With the election of Jacques Chirac to the presidency in 1995, Foccart made a final comeback as presidential adviser on African affairs. The consequence of this has been that the president and his close advisers, rather than the Foreign Ministry, have been the key drivers of French African policy under the Fifth Republic.

Second, and notwithstanding what we have just said about African policy as a presidential *domaine réservé*, a multiplicity of other, subordinate actors had a finger in the pie of African policy, including the ministries of foreign affairs and cooperation (merged in 1998), defence, finance and the interior, as well as the Agence Française pour le Développement, the secret services and the Bank of France. While each of these actors played a role in maintaining the French sphere of influence in Africa, it was the French franc zone that was the linchpin of the relationship. Its structure and modus operandi were established at the end of the Second World War: free convertibility and fixed exchange rate of the currency, the CFA franc, guaranteed by the French Treasury; centralisation of the currency reserves of the fourteen member countries, with a requirement that 65 per cent of the reserves be held in and managed by Paris; and strict rules governing the operation of the zone, for example in relation to budgetary deficits. The system remained intact after decolonisation, with the result that, through the franc zone, Paris retained a high degree of monetary control over its former colonies in sub-Saharan Africa.[3]

Third, Franco-African relations were often highly personalised. Under the Fourth Republic, many of the political leaders of French-speaking Africa had been elected to the National Assembly in Paris and during this time forged alliances, and sometimes friendships, with French political leaders. Once independence was gained, many of these close links continued, with the result that French political leaders were often predisposed to intervene in support of African leaders who were seen as friendly to France. Moreover these personalised links were not confined to the summit of the French state. France's decision to maintain an elaborate network of military, economic and cultural ties with French-speaking Africa after political independence meant that these close links between France and Africa penetrated deep into French and to some extent African civil society. For example, defence and military assistance agreements provided for the permanent posting of some 8000 troops in France's African *pré carré*, for the seconding of French military advisers to African governments, and brought French and African military personnel into regular contact for planning and training exercises. Moreover, the concentration of French aid on French-speaking Africa mobilised large numbers of private and public sector actors, as much of this aid traditionally went to French firms for the construction of infrastructure projects (Adda and Smouts, 1989: 40, 44). Finally, twenty-five years after independence, some 16,000 French *coopérants* (volunteers) continued to be posted to French-speaking Africa (Adda and Smouts, 1989: 46),[4] so that very many households throughout France had some contact with Africa, either because a family member had been to Africa or because they had a personal acquaintance who was working or had worked there. The importance of these personal links in underpinning the 'special relationship' between France and Africa cannot be overemphasised.

It is important to stress that the emergence of this Franco-African special relationship was facilitated by the Cold War context of international relations. A central plank of de Gaulle's foreign policy was to assert an independent French identity and presence on the global stage. This meant proclaiming French autonomy of action vis-à-vis the USA while remaining part of the Atlantic Alliance and presenting France as the champion of Third World, and especially African, interests in the context of a global system dominated by the two superpowers.

François-Xavier Verschave coined the term *la Françafrique* to describe this multi-tiered special relationship between France and Africa with its particular combination of presidential dominance over policy and a complex matrix of other state and non-state actors with a stake in African policy (Verschave, 1998). It is in many ways a neo-colonial relationship, in so far as it has perpetuated and entrenched relations of dependency between France and its former colonies. But Jean-François Médard makes the point that describing it in this way does not enable us fully to appreciate the particular nature of the ties between them; he prefers to characterise it as a system 'based on international clientelism, which can be considered a transposition to the international level of a traditional clientelistic relationship, a relationship of personal dependency based on an exchange between two persons, the patron and the client controlling unequal resources' (Médard, 2005: 39). The point here is that the client is not a mere puppet but has a degree of autonomy and can influence its patron: President Omar Bongo of Gabon is a good example of this (Bayart, 1984: 60–1). Verschave has documented how this system, which gave both parties a stake in its maintenance, led not only to lack of transparency and an absence of accountability, but also to widespread abuses and corruption (Verschave, 1998, 2000; *Dossiers noirs*, 1995–96). One might add that it is also one of the key reasons for the slowness of French African policy to adapt to the new, post-Cold War world order.

Pressures for a change in policy

The Franco-African special relationship began to come under pressure from a number of quarters in the early 1990s. The end of the Cold War marked the close of an era in which France had been able to carve out a political and diplomatic 'space' in west and central Africa in which it enjoyed relative autonomy of action vis-à-vis the USA while at the same time remaining within the Atlantic Alliance and playing the role of guarantor of Western interests in this part of the world. With the end of the Cold War, Africa no longer had the same strategic interest for the West. Moreover, the attention of the EU member states, including France, turned to East and Central Europe as preparations for the admission of the former Communist bloc countries to the EU began. At the same time, against the background of the worsening economic situation in many African countries, there were growing concerns in Paris, especially at the Treasury, about the cost of African policy (Hibou, 1995). Articles critical of African policy began to appear in the French quality press for the first time and several books highly critical of French aid policy were published (Adda and Smouts, 1989; Chesnault, 1990; Duteil, 1990; Hoche, 1990; Brunel, 1993). Finally, many of the key actors in the Franco-African special relationship were disappearing from the scene: the doyen of *la Françafrique*, Houphouët-Boigny, died in December 1993; Mitterrand fell seriously ill and came to the end of his presidential mandate in 1995; and Foccart – despite his comeback as Chirac's special adviser on African affairs in 1995 until his death in 1997 – was no longer the force he had once been. A change of political generations was taking place and the new French and African leaders that were emerging did not share the same assumptions about, and attachment to, the Franco-African 'special relationship' as their predecessors.

The first concrete sign of a change in French policy actually came at the 1990 Franco-African summit in La Baule, where President Mitterrand made a speech in which he told France's traditional allies in Africa that things could not continue as in the past and that France would henceforth give priority in its aid allocations to those countries undertaking political reform. Mitterrand realised that in the post-Cold War context France could no longer be seen to be propping up African dictatorships and he warned his African counterparts that progress towards democratisation was unavoidable.[5] But it soon became clear that there was a considerable gap between words and actions, as those countries where the pace of change was slowest, such as Cameroon, Chad and Gabon, continued to be among the largest beneficiaries of French aid, whereas countries such as Benin which had led the reform process did not benefit (Ministère de la Coopération, 1995: 19–20; Cumming, 2001: 106). Indeed it has been suggested that French policy at this time was in practice 'often contradictory and even more often, covertly in favour of the autocrats' (Médard, 2005: 51).

The watershed in the Franco-African special relationship came in 1993–94. First, in September 1993 Prime Minister Balladur announced that budgetary aid to franc zone countries would henceforth be conditional upon their having previously signed an accord with the International Monetary Fund and the World Bank. The effect of this measure, known as the 'Abidjan' or 'Balladur' doctrine, was to align French aid policy in sub-Saharan Africa with the neoliberal approach to economic policy and structural adjustment of the Bretton Woods institutions.[6] As France continued to resist the pressures of economic globalisation at home, it was sending a clear message to African political leaders that they would henceforth be exposed to the full rigours of economic globalisation. There would, for example, be no more special favours like the bail-outs to pay civil servants that Paris had provided in the past to tide them over when the public coffers were bare at the end of the month. In January 1994 the French government announced the 50 per cent devaluation of the CFA franc, which had been tied to the French franc at a fixed rate since 1948. The long-awaited measure, which had been delayed largely because of strong objections from Houphouët-Boigny, was finally pushed through just a month after his death (Leymarie, 1994: 24). A key feature of the franc zone was the fixed parity with the French franc, which was seen as a pillar of the Franco-African special relationship. Its abandonment represented a further admission by France that it could not, or would not, protect its African clients from the pressures of globalisation. The devaluation was seen by African political leaders as a betrayal.

Second, shortly after this, in April 1994, the Rwandan genocide began. Some 500,000 to 800,000 Hutus and moderate Tutsis were killed as France, along with the other Western powers, failed to intervene and prevent the killings. The genocide implicated France in particular, however, because it had been the principal military backer of the Habyarimana regime since 1990 and had ignored several warnings about developments in the country in the run-up to the genocide (Krop, 1994; Saint-Exupéry, 1998b: 4; Prunier, 1995; Melvern, 2006; Wallis, 2006). Rwanda was seen by French presidential advisers as the frontline between French-speaking and English-speaking Africa. Support for the ramshackle Rwandan army was thus motivated by the perceived need to prevent the takeover of the country by the English-speaking Rwanda Patriotic Front (RPF), which had invaded the country from Uganda (Ba, 1997: 29; Saint-Exupéry, 1998a: 4). Four months later, with the genocide largely over, France obtained United Nations (UN) approval for Operation Turquoise, which it presented as a humanitarian intervention to provide help for refugees from the genocide. However, many independent observers saw the intervention as motivated by an effort to create a secure zone in the south-west of the country to provide those responsible for the genocide with a safe escape route into eastern Zaire (Saint-Exupéry, 1998c: 5). In any case, French policy in Rwanda was a manifest failure as France was unable to prevent the RPF takeover of the country, the *génocidaires* who escaped into Zaire provoked instability throughout the region, which was to lead to the downfall of another French ally, President Mobutu of Zaire, and French African policy was subjected to unprecedented scrutiny and criticism in the domestic and international press. Moreover, its support to the last of the discredited Mobutu left France isolated in the international arena. By the time France finally gave up on Mobutu in May 1997, the USA and all other European powers had abandoned him. With France no longer in a position to mediate between Mobutu and Laurent Kabila's rebel forces (because of its support for the former), Nelson Mandela took on the role of mediator to avert a civil war. The regional wars that ensued caused the deaths of at least four million people (Astill, 2003). As for France, its catastrophic failures in Rwanda and Zaire discredited French military policy in Africa and undermined its claim to be an 'African' power that had a special relationship with the continent (McNulty, 1996: 497).

The search for a new African policy

Following the end of the Cold War, President Mitterrand's La Baule speech represented a first signal of a change in policy, but old reflexes and practices continued largely unchanged in the early 1990s. In response to the new international situation, France sought initially to make adjustments to, rather than radically overhaul, its African policy (Cumming, 2001: 104–10, 340–1). It was only after the debacle of Rwanda and Zaire, when it became clear that African policy was not only failing to achieve its aims but actually undermining France's international reputation, that a serious reassessment of French African policy began. Support for the Franco-African 'special relationship' that had previously been the subject of a political consensus extending across the political spectrum from the Left to the Right now began to fragment rapidly as the political dividends, both international and domestic, resulting from the policy evaporated. At the start of the Chirac presidency in 1995, Prime Minister Alain Juppé tried to push through a merger of the foreign affairs and cooperation ministries. As one of the linchpins of the Franco-African special relationship which had traditionally been considered by French-speaking African presidents as 'their' ministry, the latter was closely associated in the minds of many with the abuses and corrupt practices of *la Françafrique*. Its abolition was therefore highly symbolic. For its advocates it marked an overdue step in the direction of the 'normalisation' of Franco-African relations, in the sense of putting them on a more regular state-to-state footing, whereas its opponents saw it as symbolising French disengagement from Africa and the end of the Franco-African special relationship. In fact it was neither. In pushing for the reform, its advocates sought neither to withdraw from Africa, nor fully to normalise the relationship, but rather to reorient and modernise policy-making structures so as to better serve French interests (Chafer, 2002: 362–3). Chirac blocked the reform after lobbying from several African presidents, only for it to be implemented two years later by the new Socialist Prime Minister, Lionel Jospin, following the Right's defeat in the 1997 parliamentary elections.

Similarly, developments in military policy after the Rwanda and Zaire debacle indicated a reorientation of policy so as better to serve French interests. There were no new French military interventions in Africa after Operation Turquoise in 1994 and, as we shall see below, France even refused to intervene to save its ally, President Konan Bédié of the Côte d'Ivoire, following a military coup in 1999. The French government also announced a reduction from 8000 to 6000 in the number of troops stationed in Africa. The two bases in the Central African Republic were closed completely and Libyan troops took over from French troops, while the other five bases in Africa were reduced in size (Couve, 1997; Isnard, 1997). The rejection of old-style military interventions and the troop reductions were accompanied by a significant change in the political discourse of military policy. The French military presence in Africa was no longer to be seen as promoting French interests but rather as serving 'primarily African ends, as well as the common international goals of peace and stability' (Utley, 2005: 38). 'Hard' power was now to be presented as 'soft' power.

At the same time, other significant changes were taking place. The French aid budget, the large majority of which was spent in sub-Saharan Africa, underwent a sustained decline in the 1990s, from 47 billion francs (0.64 per cent of gross national income) in 1994 to 29.2 billion francs (0.32 per cent) in 2000 (Observatoire Permanent, 2001: 15). Elf, the oil company established under de Gaulle with a brief to secure French access to oil and which had been a key pillar of the *réseaux* in *Françafrique*, was privatised. The company had used a variety of corrupt practices to maintain access to African oil reserves and secure French interests in the countries in which it operated. It had also been a major source of funding for the Gaullist party (Vallée, 2000; Le Floch-Prigent, 2001: 60–1; Routier, 2001: 54–5; Smith, 2005: 163–8). However, it became mired in a series of scandals in the 1990s, notable among which was the effort to topple President Lissouba of the Congo, whom it had not forgiven for trying to loosen its stranglehold over his country when he became president in 1992 (*Africa Confidential*, 1997; Verschave, 2002: 208–9). Chirac enlisted Angolan support to remove Lissouba and succeeded in replacing him with the previous president, Sassou Nguesso. However, the resulting civil war, 'covertly encouraged by Elf and the French presidency, caused more than 100,000 deaths' (Médard, 2005: 51). Following these scandals the company was merged with the Belgian oil company TotalFina, marking its evolution away from being a vehicle of French state power and patronage towards becoming a more conventional commercial enterprise.

Faced with accusations from supporters of the Franco-African special relationship that France was abandoning Africa, Prime Minister Jospin moved to reassure his critics by promising that France aimed 'not to do less but to do better' (Jospin, 1997). Various steps were taken to move away from the traditional French unilateral approach to Africa and share the burdens and risks of African policy. Just as the Abidjan doctrine sought to share the economic cost of supporting Africa with the IMF and World Bank, so the RECAMP (Reinforcement of African Peacekeeping Capabilities) initiative sought to share the burdens and risks of French military policy on the continent. Launched by France in 1997, the RECAMP programme provided African forces with training and financial and logistical support to enable them to take greater responsibility for peacekeeping and the maintenance of security on the continent (Gregory, 2000: 442). In the following year, at the Saint-Malo Franco-British summit, both governments announced their intention of co-operating more closely on African policy. Finally, France sought to distance itself from the notion of a French *pré carré* in Africa by developing a policy for the whole of Africa. For example, every African president – excluding Colonel Qaddafi but, to the UK's dismay, including Robert Mugabe – was invited to attend the 2003 Franco-African summit in Paris. And France, along with the UK, became one of the key sponsors of the New Partnership for Africa's Development (NEPAD), a multilateral initiative that aims to mobilise resources for a new development partnership between the West and the whole of Africa.

Thus, France's new African policy sought to take account of the rigours of globalisation – indeed promoted the fuller integration of Africa into the globalisation process – by pushing African leaders to undertake reform. It also sought to 'multinationalise' support for Africa, and thus to share the burden – and risks – of supporting Africa, for example by channelling a higher proportion of its aid budget through the EU and through the 'Africanisation' of peacekeeping. This new policy was underpinned by a rhetoric of 'soft' power that distracted attention from the fact that African policy continued in practice to be underpinned by the instruments of 'hard' power.

France's 'little Iraq': the Côte d'Ivoire quagmire and the search for a new role in Africa

French attempts to maintain influence in Africa by redefining its role on the continent and undertaking a hesitant process of policy adaptation were knocked off course by developments in its former African showcase, the Côte d'Ivoire. General Guei overthrew the increasingly unpopular President Henri Konan Bédié in December 1999 and subsequently sought to legitimise his seizure of power in a presidential election that most of the Côte d'Ivoire's political parties, apart from Laurent Gbagbo's Front Populaire Ivoirien, boycotted. Despite being defeated in the election, Guei proclaimed himself the victor, provoking a popular uprising on 25–26 October 2000. As a result, Guei and his military junta were chased from power and Gbagbo was proclaimed president. In September 2002, a mutiny broke out in Abidjan, rebel forces took control of the north of the country and prepared to march on the capital. Gbagbo requested French military intervention in support of his government, as he was entitled to do under the terms of the Franco-Ivoirian defence agreement, but this was turned down (Smith, 2005: 13). Fearing for the future of more than 20,000 French citizens and many more foreign nationals in the country, France did however send troops to the centre of the Côte d'Ivoire to establish a demarcation line between government and rebel forces and prevent the latter from marching on the capital. France then became further embroiled in the crisis in January 2003 when it called the belligerent parties to a conference in Linas-Marcoussis near Paris, at which it imposed on the Gbagbo government a power-sharing agreement that provided for the appointment of government ministers from the rebel forces. The agreement revealed the depth of the confusion at the heart of

French policy, since it had previously recognised Laurent Gbagbo as the leader of the Côte d'Ivoire yet now appeared to accord equal legitimacy to the rebels. Moreover, in a powerful symbol of France's implication in the Ivoirian crisis, it was the French Foreign Minister Dominique de Villepin who announced the power-sharing agreement. Immediately afterwards, anti-French demonstrations broke out in Abidjan and symbols of the French presence in the country, such as the French cultural centre and *lycée*, were destroyed.

France subsequently sought and obtained support for its intervention from the Economic Organisation of West African States (ECOWAS) and from the UN, in an effort to give international legitimacy to its attempts to arbitrate between the warring parties. However, it was seen as partisan by both sides, having lost the confidence of the Gbagbo government from the moment it refused to intervene and of the rebels when it established the demarcation line separating them from government forces and preventing them from marching on Abidjan. In November 2004, France became even more deeply embroiled in the conflict, and suffered a further loss of credibility in its effort to arbitrate between the warring parties when President Chirac ordered French forces to destroy the entire Ivoirian air force in retaliation for an attack on a French military base that caused the deaths of nine soldiers (Marshall, 2005: 25). Mass anti-French demonstrations followed in Abidjan, during which French troops opened fire on the crowd causing some 67 deaths and wounding 1256 others (Smith, 2005: 17).

Because of the nature of France's involvement, the Ivoirian crisis proved another disaster for its African policy and has been labelled as 'France's little Iraq' (Adams, 2004). First, it undermined tentative French moves away from its traditional unilateral approach to Africa. Whatever attempts France may have made after the Rwanda debacle to 'multilateralise' its African policy, there was no hiding the fact that this was a French intervention and that key decisions, such as the one to recognise the Gbagbo government and later to destroy the Ivoirian air force, were taken unilaterally by France. Having decided to reduce its military presence in Africa, France was actually forced, at the height of the crisis, to increase that presence to 4000 troops in the Côte d'Ivoire alone. Second, the Ivoirian crisis further undermined French credibility in Africa. France failed to develop a coherent strategy for dealing with the crisis in the Côte d'Ivoire, constantly appearing unsure of what to do. The decision not to intervene to save President Konan Bédié, to ignore international advice and recognise Gbagbo's election victory but then to force him to share power with the rebels – thereby effectively recognising the legitimacy of the rebellion – and the subsequent attacks on his regime for its 'fascist tendencies' (Le Pape and Vidal, 2002: 321; Smith, 2004) have created an impression of confusion at the heart of French policy. They have also reinforced the image of France on the continent as an unreliable ally. Third, the crisis has provoked a new wave of anti-French feeling in its African *pré carré*: 'Chirac go home, Bush welcome', *'Vive la Côte d'Ivoire indépendante'* proclaimed the banners on the streets of Abidjan in November 2004. Such sentiments are not confined to the Côte d'Ivoire: French support for African dictators, its failure to promote human rights and development and general interference in African affairs are increasingly condemned loudly and widely across the continent (Ould Mohamedou, 2005; Lecoutre and Kambudzi, 2006; Leymarie, 2006).

Tentative French attempts to redefine its role in Africa and modify its African policy were further derailed by the terrorist attacks of 11 September 2001. Following these attacks, the USA proclaimed itself the leader of the global 'war on terror', a war in which Africa was now part of the front line (after the 1998 attacks on the US embassies in Nairobi and Dar es Salaam). The resulting increase in American interest in Africa posed a challenge to established French interests in west and central Africa. During the Cold War, the USA had effectively subcontracted to France the role of guarantor of Western interests in this part of Africa. But in a world order dominated by one superpower preoccupied by the war on terror, what role could France now play on the continent? After his presidential election victory in 2002, Chirac promised to 're-engage' with Africa. It is not at all clear what this renewed French activism actually meant in practice, apart from a few high-profile presidential visits to Africa in 2002–03 (Chafer, 2005: 17–18) and a resurgence of French unilateral interventionism on the continent, notably in Chad, the Central African Republic and Togo. In any case no new vision for Franco-African relations or for France's role in Africa emerged (Banégas et al., 2007: 8).

A further complicating factor in French efforts to redefine its role in Africa is France's deteriorating image in Africa. This is linked to a growing intolerance on the continent of French interventionism; indeed the Ivoirian conflict can be interpreted at one level as a struggle for a 'second independence' from France (Bayart, 2005; Banégas and Marshall, 2003: 6; Marshall, 2005: 39). Moreover, France's image has been tarnished by the visa and the charter flights issues. Many Africans used to study in France, but the interminable queues outside French consulates to apply for a visa, the difficulty of obtaining a visa and the obligation to sign an undertaking to leave France on completion of their studies (introduced by Interior Minister Charles Pasqua in 1993) have led increasing numbers to enrol in universities in the USA, Canada and the Middle East rather than France. Whereas the independence and immediate post-independence generations of African students were imbued with French culture and felt a special affinity for France, the new generations of Africans do not share such feelings; in the era of globalisation they feel free to choose their own attachments (Ngoupandé, 2002: 33–46; Lecoutre and Kambudzi, 2006; Marshall, 2005: 27). Equally damaging have been the charter flights organised by the Interior Ministry to return illegal immigrants to Africa. These have been widely reported in Africa and have been experienced there as another humiliation inflicted on Africans by France (Royer, 2003: 20). To make matters worse, in 2006 a French judge, Jean-Louis Bruguière, who belongs to the UMP and is close to Nicolas Sarkozy, issued arrest warrants for nine associates of the Rwandan president, Paul Kagamé, for their alleged role in the incident that triggered the 1994 genocide: the shooting down of the then president's plane. He also asked for the case to be heard by the UN International Criminal Tribunal for Rwanda, a request that was turned down by the tribunal. Kagamé responded by accusing the French of arming the regime that carried out the 1994 genocide (*The Economist*, 2006: 39; *Africa Confidential*, 2006: 3). Taken together, these developments mean that most of the younger generation of Africans feel no sense of a special relationship linking Africa to France.

French African policy in transition ... or desperately seeking an African policy?

France was slow to adapt its African policy to the new world order created by the end of the Cold War. When it finally did begin to make serious efforts to modify its policy after the Rwanda-Zaire debacle, no new vision for Franco-Africa relations emerged. Instead, France seemed to hesitate between disengagement and 'normalisation', with the result that it usually appeared to be reacting to events rather than having any clear strategy for dealing with the challenges facing Africa in an era of accelerating globalisation. This is perhaps not surprising, given that 'the main aim of French policy towards Africa has never been to respond to African challenges' (Médard, 2005: 44); rather, France has traditionally viewed Africa as an arena for French *rayonnement*. As the political dividends, at both domestic and international level, from this policy have declined, so the shared assumptions and political consensus that underpinned it have fragmented and dissolved. Whereas the Franco-African special relationship was for many years after decolonisation perceived positively by French public opinion – albeit because much of the reality of Franco-African relations was hidden from public view – it is now viewed negatively. Media coverage of African policy in the wake of the Rwanda genocide and the various court cases involving corrupt practices by politicians and former Elf executives mean that Africa no longer brings domestic political returns, with the result that politicians from across the political spectrum are desperate to distance themselves from *la Françafrique*. The images on television screens in November 2004 of French citizens being forced to flee the Côte d'Ivoire by the attacks on them and their property – following large demonstrations against the French presence in the country – reinforced these negative perceptions of Africa in France. Successive French policy failures, notably in Rwanda, former Zaire and the Côte d'Ivoire, have further deteriorated France's already tarnished image on the continent.

At the same time many of the vectors of French influence on the continent have declined. The number of French *coopérants* in Africa has more than halved, there are now far fewer French citizens living in Africa, business links with Africa have declined, the French military presence (apart from in the Côte d'Ivoire) has been reduced, French aid to Africa has undergone a steady decline and the franc zone is no longer a vehicle for French power and patronage, since major policy decisions relating to the zone now require the approval of the European Central Bank. The complex web of *réseaux* that bound large sections of France's political and economic elites to Africa's political elites have fragmented. Whereas in the early years Foccart saw himself as serving the French state while at the same time pursuing his own business interests (this was possible as they frequently overlapped), his successors in the various competing networks that now link France to Africa serve only their own interests. In Verschave's polemical but evocative epithet, *la Françafrique* has evolved into *la Mafiafrique* (Verschave, 2004; Smith and Glaser, 1997; Rueff, 2004: 117–18). French influence and power in Africa are also increasingly challenged by the USA, which has renewed its interest in the continent in the aftermath of the terrorist attacks of September 2001, by China, which brings investment, business opportunities and development projects without the conditionalities that the West imposes, and by a more activist British African policy that portrays Africa as a 'scar' on the conscience of the world and has sought to move the twin challenges of African development and poverty reduction up the Western policy agenda (Cumming, 2005: 55–73). Finally, its position as an 'African' power is under threat within Africa itself, where France is increasingly perceived by political leaders as a difficult and unreliable ally and by ordinary Africans and opposition groups as propping up unpopular, corrupt and dictatorial regimes in the pursuit of its own interests.

Conclusions

The result of these developments is that France no longer appears as a self-confident 'African' power. The overriding impression is of policy confusion, of a France that no longer has a distinctive African project or any clear vision of its future role in Africa. It claims to be committed to African development, yet reduced its aid to Africa between 1995 and 2002, though with aid increasing since (Frémeaux, 2007: 9). It resists globalisation at home and continues to talk of its special relationship with Africa, yet promotes globalisation in Africa. It appears to hesitate between 'normalisation' and disengagement in its relations with the continent. It proclaims the need for a multilateral approach to Africa, yet has displayed many of its old unilateralist impulses in the Côte d'Ivoire. It talks the language of 'soft' power, of promoting African security and peace-building, yet – quite apart from Operation Licorne in the Côte d'Ivoire – over 4000 French troops remain permanently stationed in Africa. In sum, France has often appeared an unreliable ally and African political leaders have responded by seeking new allies and friendships. To be sure, the international context and domestic political consensus on which the Franco-African special relationship depended have now gone. France can no longer claim, as Louis de Guiringaud did in 1979, to be able to 'change the course of history [in Africa] with 500 men' (quoted in D'Epenoux and Hoche, 1979: 38). And President Chirac was probably the last of the generation of French political leaders to have close personal links with African presidents. In this respect we are witnessing the end of an era.

However, it is possible to argue that this policy 'confusion' is not actually a problem, in so far as French African policy has continued to serve national interests effectively. France continues to be – and continues to be seen as – an active presence on the continent and many French companies continue to do good business in Africa. For example, companies such as Bolloré (whose chairman is a good friend of President Sarkozy), Bouygues and France Télécom have done well out of the privatisation of public utilities and continue to win contracts for major infrastructure projects in Africa. At the same time, France's most important trading partners on the continent are now South Africa and Nigeria. There is thus a growing divergence between French diplomatic and military efforts on the continent, which have hitherto remained focused on its traditional *pré carré*, and its economic and business interests, which increasingly lie elsewhere. In his major campaign speech on international affairs, Sarkozy made no mention of the Franco-African special relationship but promised that one of the key objectives of his foreign policy would be to 'promote [French] economic and commercial interests' (Sarkozy, 2007: 152). Before his election he also criticised France's old-style, 'paternalist' relationship with Africa based on personalised links with African presidents and proclaimed the need for reform: 'Dialogue must take place on the basis of equality … I reject the notion of France giving lessons' (Schneider, 2006). It will be interesting to see whether President Sarkozy continues the refocusing of French African policy that was interrupted by the eruption of the crisis in the Côte d'Ivoire and the re-election of Chirac as president in 2002, so that France's diplomatic and military efforts are more closely aligned to its economic and business interests on the continent. Or alternatively, whether he develops an African policy that focuses on meeting African needs and seeks to address the challenges of Africa in the new, globalised international order of the twenty-first century. The former may be in France's interest in the short to medium term, but it may be that, in an increasingly unpredictable world, the latter is more in its long-term interest.

Notes

1. General Boulanger, for example, believed that taking colonies in Africa was a distraction from what he believed should be France's key foreign policy priority, the retaking of Alsace-Lorraine, which France had lost to Germany in 1871.
2. The term *réseau* has a specific meaning in this context. Smith and Glaser (1997: 25) define it as 'an informal, indeed secret, association of individuals, some of whom are civil servants, who pursue common objectives, the realisation of which implicates the State and, ultimately, the Nation or some other high idea'.
3. Following the adoption of the euro in place of the French franc, the CFA franc is now pegged to the euro.
4. Many of these *coopérants* were young people who did not wish to do military service but who chose instead to work for two years as civilians in Africa, often as teachers but also for example as health workers, technicians or on development projects.
5. Less noticed at the time was his proviso that each country would democratise at its own pace; see Barrin (1990) and Wauthier (1990).
6. Edouard Balladur's letter to franc zone heads of state laying out the new policy was published in *Le Monde*, 23 September 1993.

References

Adams, R. (2004) 'France's little Iraq', *Guardian*, 21 December.

Adda, J. and M.-C. Smouts (1989) *La France face au sud. Le miroir brisé*, Paris: Karthala.

Africa Confidential (1997) 'And across the river', *Africa Confidential*, 20 June, 3–4.

Africa Confidential (2006) 'La grande rupture', *Africa Confidential*, 1 December, 3.

Astill, J. (2003) 'Conflict in Congo has killed 4.7m, charity says', *Guardian*, 8 April 15.

Ba, M. (1997) *Rwanda. Un Génocide français*, Paris: L'Esprit frappeur.

Banégas, R. and R. Marshall (2003) 'Côte d'Ivoire: un conflit régional?', *Politique africaine*, 89: 5–11.

Banégas, R. et al. (2007) 'La fin du pacte colonial', *Politique africaine*, 105: 7–26.

Barrin, J. de (1990) 'M. Mitterrand lie l'octroi de l'aide française aux efforts de démocratisation', *Le Monde*, 22 June.

Bayart, J.-F. (1984) *La Politique africaine de François Mitterrand*, Paris: Karthala.

Bayart, J.-F. (2005) 'La politique africaine de la France est régressive', *Le Figaro*, 6 July.

Brunel, S. (1993) *Le Gaspillage de l'aide publique*, Paris: Seuil.

Cartier, R. (1956) 'En France noire avec Raymond Cartier', *Paris-Match*, 11 August, 38–41; 18 August, 34–7; 1 September, 39–41.

Chafer, T. (2002) 'Franco-African relations: no longer so exceptional?', *African Affairs*, 101: 343–63.

Chafer, T. (2005) 'Chirac and "la Françafrique": no longer a family affair', *Modern and Contemporary France*, 13(1): 7–23.

Chesnault, V. (1990) 'Que faire de l'Afrique?', *Le Monde*, 28 February, 2.

Couve, P. (1997) 'La France fermera progressivement ses bases en Centrafrique', *Le Monde*, 2 August.

Cumming, G. (2001) *Aid to Africa*, Aldershot: Ashgate.

Cumming, G. (2005) 'From Realpolitik to the Third Way. British African policy in the new world order', in U. Engel and R.F. Olsen (eds), *Africa and the North*, London: Routledge, pp. 55–73.

D'Epenoux, C. and C. Hoche (1979) 'Giscard l'Africain', *L'Express*, 22 December, 34–8.

Dossiers noirs de la politique africaine de la France (1995–96) *Dossiers noirs de la politique africaine de la France*, vols 1–6, Paris: L'Harmattan.

Duteil, M. (1990) 'Afrique: la faillite', *Le Point*, 4 June, 36–8.

The Economist (2006) 'The glory days are passing', *The Economist* (16 December), 39–40.

Frémeaux, P. et al. (2007) 'L'Etat de la France', *Alternatives économiques*, April, 6–12.

Gregory, S. (2000) 'The French military in Africa: past and present', *African Affairs*: 99, 435–48.

Guiringaud, L. de (1982) 'La Politique africaine de la France', *Politique étrangère*: 2, 441–55.

Hibou, B. (1995) 'Politique économique de la France en zone franc', *Politique africaine*: 58, 25–40.

Hoche, C. (1990) 'Afrique: naufrage d'un continent', *L'Express*, 27 April, 38–40.

Isnard, J. (1997) 'La France remanie son dispositif militaire en Afrique', *Le Monde*, 21 July.

Jospin, L. (1997) 'Allocution du Premier ministre devant la communauté française à Dakar', 19 December, http://www.defense.gouv.fr/actualites/dossier/d20/5_3.htm, consulted 27 March 2002.

Keiger, J. (2001) *France and the World since 1870*, London: Arnold.

Krop, P. (1994) *Le Génocide franco-africain*, Paris: J.-C. Lattès.

Lecoutre D. and A. Kambudzi (2006) 'Vers un divorce entre Paris et le continent africain?', *Le Monde diplomatique*, June, 6–7.

Le Floch-Prigent, L. (2001) *Affaire Elf, affaire d'Etat*, Paris: Gallimard.

Le Pape, M. and C. Vidal (eds) (2002) *Côte d'Ivoire. L'année terrible 1999–2000*, Paris: Karthala.

Leymarie, P. (1994) 'Monnaie dévaluée, peuples oubliés', *Le Monde diplomatique*, March, 24.

Leymarie, P. (2006) 'Ingérence à l'ancienne au Tchad', *Le Monde diplomatique*, June, 6–7.

Marseille, J. (1984) *Empire colonial et capitalisme français. Histoire d'un divorce*, Paris: Albin Michel.

Marshall, R. (2005) 'La France en Côte d'Ivoire: l'interventionnisme à l'épreuve des faits', *Politique africaine*, 98: 21–41.

Médard, J.-F. (2005) 'France and sub-Saharan Africa: a privileged relationship', in U. Engel and R.F. Olsen (eds), *Africa and the North*, London: Routledge, pp. 38–54.

Melvern, L. (2006) *Conspiracy to Murder: the Rwandan Genocide*, London: Verso.

McNulty, M. (1996) 'France, Rwanda and the genocide: a review of the literature', *Modern and Contemporary France*, 4(4): 497–503.

Ministère de la Coopération (1995) *Rapport d'activité 1994–95*, Paris: Ministère de la Coopération.

Mitterrand, F. (1957) *Présence française et abandon*, Paris: Tribune Libre 12.

Ngoupandé, J.-P. (2002) *L'Afrique sans la France*, Paris: Albin Michel.

Observatoire Permanent de la Coopération française (2001) *Rapport 2001*, Paris: Karthala.

Ould Mohamedou, M.-M. (2005) 'Variation sur l'usage du coup d'Etat en Mauritanie', *Le Monde diplomatique*, November, 8–9.

Prunier, G. (1995) *The Rwanda Crisis 1959–1994: History of a Genocide*, London: Hurst.

Routier, A. (2001) 'Le dossier Elf', *L'Histoire*: 251 (February), 54–5.

Royer, S. de (2003) 'La France reste l'"eldorado" des Sénégalais', *La Croix*, 18 December.

Rueff, J. (2004) *Côte d'Ivoire. Le feu au pré carré*, Paris: Editions Autrement.

Saint-Exupéry, P. de (1998a) 'France-Rwanda: "services", réseaux, familles', *Le Figaro*, 1 April, 4.

Saint-Exupéry, P. de (1998b) 'France-Rwanda: des mensonges d'Etat', *Le Figaro*, 2 April, 4.

Saint-Exupéry, P. de (1998c) 'Les ambiguités de "Turquoise"', *Le Figaro*, 2 April, 5.

Sarkozy, N. (2007) 'Mes objectifs en matière de politique internationale', extracts of a speech given on 28 February 2007, *Politique africaine*, 105: 149–52.

Schneider, V. (2006) 'Sarkozy veut nettoyer la "Françafrique"', *Libération*, 20 May, 10.

Smith, S. and A. Glaser (1997) *Ces Messieurs Afrique 2. Des réseaux aux lobbys*, Paris: Calmann-Lévy.

Smith, S. (2004) 'Mission impossible pour la France en Côte d'Ivoire', *Le Monde*, 3 December.

Smith, S. (2005) *Comment la France a perdu l'Afrique*, Paris: Calmann-Lévy.

Utley, R. (2005) 'Franco-African military relations: meeting the challenges of globalisation?', *Modern and Contemporary France*, 13(1): 25–40.

Vallée, O. (2000) 'Elf au service de l'Etat français', *Le Monde diplomatique*, April, 24.

Verschave, F.-X. (1998) *La Françafrique*, Paris: Stock.

Verschave, F.-X. (2000) *Noir Silence*, Paris: Les Arènes.

Verschave, F.-X. (2002) *Noir Chirac*, Paris: Les Arènes.

Verschave, F.-X. (2004) *De la Françafrique à la Mafiafrique*, Brussels: Tribord.

Wallis, A. (2006) *Silent Accomplice. The Untold Story of France's Role in the Rwandan Genocide*, London: I. B. Tauris.

Wauthier, C. (1990) '"Démocratie", "développement" ces mots piégés…', *Le Monde diplomatique*, July, 4.

4
France in East Asia: the Europeanisation of French Foreign Policy

Reuben Wong

Introduction

This chapter focuses on the interaction of French national policy with collective European foreign policy in one important part of the world – the *Extrême Orient* ('Far East' or East Asia). It argues that in at least two areas of European Union (EU) policy in East Asia – political/security relations and human rights – French policy has converged significantly with EU norms to an extent unimaginable under the traditional Gaullist understanding of French foreign policy. Through a dynamic and itera-tive process in which French and European foreign policy objectives, procedures and actions co-evolve, a negotiated and convergent policy towards East Asia has developed. The case studies are political relations with Japan, and human rights policy towards China. The period in ques-tion is 1985 to 2005, so covering a decade of each of the Mitterrand and Chirac presidencies.

The dominant academic approach to French policy is to explain it as a medium power with Gaullist great-power ambitions, reflexes and clear foreign policy goals of security and independence (Doise and Vaïsse, 1992; Gordon, 1993; Grosser, 1989). Foreign policy-making in France is portrayed as the product of a rational state with a clear sense of its 'national interests' (Kessler, 1999). Does participation in EU foreign pol-icy make a difference to the foreign policy of EU member states? No, according to the dominant intergovernmentalist view, exemplified by Stanley Hoffmann. Foreign policies are the domain of sovereign states and the EU can never have a foreign policy, properly speaking, as it is made up of a *collection* of states (Hoffmann, 1966, 2000; Bull, 1983). As such, individual states within the EU can at best be constrained by EU structures, but will never allow these structures to set their policy.

The Gaullist approach posits that member states such as France (and the UK) with a strong attachment to an independent foreign policy will resist pressures to conform to European institutions.

As the Gaullist approach is increasingly unable to explain the actions and policies of France – even in the *domaines privés* (traditional colonial spheres of influence) – other works emphasise the input and impact of EU foreign policy-making mechanisms. According to this second view, French foreign policy-making has been fundamentally altered by Europe. There is a coordination reflex among EU foreign policy-making elites, and this is set to increase over time with the further institutionalisation of foreign policy coordination with the Common Foreign and Security Policy (CFSP) since 1992, and the European Security and Defence Policy (ESDP) since 1998 (La Serre, 1996; Lequesne, 1993; Blunden, 2000; Øhrgaard, 1997). A third approach is to ignore the member states' foreign policies altogether and to study the actions of the EU in the world. This approach assumes that member states' foreign policy interests are increasingly subsumed by and expressed through the EU. Thus Hazel Smith (2002) argues that the EU has been a significant and unmistakable actor in international relations for several decades and is recognised by other actors as such. European foreign policy is considered a separate entity, distinct from and far from being a mere summation of individual member states' foreign policies, being constructed through a complex process of intergovernmental negotiation (Smith, 2002; Nuttall, 2000; Piening, 1997; Regelsberger et al., 1997).

This chapter is partial to the second view above. It employs the concept of 'Europeanisation' to analyse French foreign policy, arguing that French policy in East Asia has undergone significant convergence with the policies of other EU member states and the European Commission. French national resources are increasingly inadequate for a consistent, comprehensive policy towards whole geographic regions. Indeed, French capabilities are increasingly inadequate even to meet national objectives in large countries such as China and Japan. The key proposition is that membership of the EU has an important and growing impact on each member state's foreign policy. States that join the European Union must adapt to pressures for change in their foreign policies. The overlapping and interrelated forces of Europeanisation in foreign policy – policy convergence, national projection and identity reconstruction – interact with often surprising results. The ensuing foreign policy of each member state is the end product of a complex series of negotiations between governments, EU institutions (Commission, Council and Parliament), officials and member state representatives, as well as a process of policy learning and emulation between individual member states.

The novelty of 'Europeanisation' in foreign policy studies is a function of the debate on the existence of a common European foreign policy (Wong, 2005, 2007). The problem with the EU is that it is not a unified state actor, nor does it have clear and consistent external objectives. Instead of a coherent and authoritative decision-making centre, we observe persistent national foreign policies that operate under or alongside – and sometimes at variance with – foreign policies defined by EU institutions. As the EU is not a single unified actor, European foreign policy is usually understood and analysed as the sum and interaction of the three strands of Europe's external relations system, comprising: (1) the national foreign policies of the member states; (2) European Community (EC) external trade relations and development policy; and (3) the CFSP (Hill, 1993; White, 2001; Tonra and Christiansen, 2004).

The concept of Europeanisation of foreign policy in the scholarly literature is often employed to explain the top-down adaptation of national structures and processes in response to the demands of the EU, or what some call 'EU-isation' (Tsardanidis and Stavridis, 2005; Miskimmon and Paterson, 2003). Under the CFSP, Europeanisation can be understood as a process of foreign policy convergence. It is a dependent variable contingent on the ideas and directives emanating from actors (EU institutions, statesmen and so on) in Brussels, as well as policy ideas and actions from member state capitals. Europeanisation is thus identifiable as a process of change manifested as policy convergence (both top-down and sideways) as well as national policies amplified as EU policy (bottom-up projection). In this chapter, Europeanisation is understood as three distinct but interrelated processes which are dependent on the agents, targets and directions of change. As a top-down process ('downloading'), Europeanisation is the process of change in national foreign policies caused by participation over time in foreign policy-making at the European level. As a bottom-up process ('uploading'), it is the projection of national preferences, ideas and policy models up to EU level. A third aspect is the redefinition of national interests and identity in the context of 'Europe' (Aggestam, 2004; Hill, 1996). Europeanisation is thus a bi-directional process leading to a negotiated convergence of policy goals, preferences and even identity between national and supranational levels (Wong, 2007).

Japan and China are interesting case studies because they demonstrate the convergence between national and supranational EU foreign policies; between one important member state (France) and Brussels in the formulation and evolution of European policies towards two of the most important target states in East Asia.

Political and strategic relations with Japan

The France-Japan relationship has been a microcosm of the larger EC-Japan relationship. In the 1970s and 1980s, France (together with Britain and Italy) uploaded anti-Japan protectionism to European policy. Japan in the late 1980s and early 1990s was a target of the internal French debate on globalisation, the reform of the welfare state and the need for a Single European Market (SEM) to increase competitiveness. Modernising French industry to meet the challenges of economic globalisation (of which Japan was a particular symbol) provoked a protracted domestic debate (Kresl and Gallais, 2002: 1–16). French attitudes and policies towards Japan have often been hamstrung by fascination, suspicion and misunderstanding. Some scholars characterise France-Japan ties as an 'emotional love-hate relationship', with Japan being wary of France as the European country that could most easily turn 'anti-Japanese' (Wilkinson, 1990; Rigaudis, 1998; Bridges, 1999: 47). Yet, French economists and even politicians like Jacques Chirac have held up Japanese society and economic organisation as a model for France (Sautter, 1996). For most of the Cold War, Gaullist France's preoccupations with national independence and security issues, and Tokyo's heavy security dependence on the USA, prejudiced Paris to view Japan as a country of little political significance, 'being closely allied with, and subordinate to the United States' (Iwanaga, 2000: 213; Wong, 2006: 105).

President Georges Pompidou (1969–74) made the first French attempt to cultivate a serious relationship with Japan. Foreign Minister Maurice Schumann was scheduled to visit Tokyo in January 1972 to prepare a state visit by President Pompidou, but the latter died before the visit could occur (Domenach, 1990: 229; Pompidou, 1973). Prime Minister Miki was among the five world leaders invited by President Giscard d'Estaing (1974–81) to the inaugural 'Western' summit meeting of the world's economic powers in Rambouillet in 1975 (what was to become the G7). However Giscard did not consider Japan a bilateral priority (Seizelet, 2001: 179; Matsuura, 1998: 85). It required Marshal Tito's funeral in 1980 for a Japanese Prime Minister to visit Europe again.

A brief flowering in France-Japan political relations occurred between 1981 and 1983 under François Mitterrand, the first French President to make a state visit to Japan (Domenach, 1990: 230).[1] Yet Mitterrand's 1982 visit and Emperor Hirohito's return visit in 1984 (the first by a reigning Japanese monarch) failed to reverse the tide of deteriorating relations dominated by bilateral and EC-Japan trade disputes (Matsui, 1989: 198–200). While Britain and Germany were developing strong political ties with Japan from the mid-1970s, France was viewed in Japan as a 'hostile power' for its protectionist measures.[2]

Common EC protectionist policies

The first common EC policies vis-à-vis Japan involved conflictual, lowest common denominator outcomes. A major reason for launching the SEM in 1986 was to enable European economies to enjoy economies of scale to compete better with the USA, Japan and rivals from Hong Kong, Singapore, South Korea and Taiwan. The creation of the single market was presented as the solution to revitalise, re-industrialise, and regain global competitiveness for a Europe of sclerotic companies in the face of American economic prowess and the onslaught of the *défi japonais* (Japanese challenge) (Lehmann, 1992).

Up to 1988, the European Commission led the charge in confronting Japan on trade disputes. It accused Japan of unfair trading practices such as government subsidies for Japanese industries that were inconsistent with the General Agreement on Tariffs and Trade (GATT), setting discriminatory standards for foreign products, and tolerating a complicated and anti-competitive distribution system. In the 1980s, threats by the European Commission to launch a complaint against Japan under article 23 of the GATT challenging Japan's economic system and 'social dumping' led to Japan agreeing to moderate the export of ten 'sensitive items' to Europe, including video cassette recorders (VCRs), colour televisions, forklift trucks and machine tools (Nuttall, 1996: 106–7). In the 1983 VCR dispute, France imposed an obstructionist customs policy which required all Japanese VCRs to be checked by a handful of customs officials in Poitiers. This made VCRs a much rarer and more expensive commodity in France than in other EC countries (Ishikawa, 1990; Bridges, 1992). On this occasion, the EC chose the 'lowest common denominator' approach, upholding the French action and adopting as common policy the position of the most protectionist EC member states.

Uploading confrontational policies against Japan

At the worst of times, France uploaded anti-Japan protectionist policies to the European level. France was a constant troublemaker for Japan because of its influence within the EC. It did this to spectacular effect in the 1980s and early 1990s through quotas, threats of trade wars, and excluding Japan from EU fora. France-Japan relations in the 1980s and 1990s were dominated by economic conflicts. More often than not, political ties were driven by and derived from economic ties. In the 1980s, the French government and French car corporations were notorious in Brussels for acting through the European Association of Car Companies and 'driving European policy' on car import restrictions on Japan (Lehmann, 1992; Wong, 2006: 117). France also levied national quotas limiting Japanese car imports to 3 per cent of the French market.

Up to 1991, the French response to the 'Japanese challenge' was to champion the hard-line cause within the EU. President Mitterrand adopted a 'hands-off' policy towards Japan. He did not intervene in bilateral conflicts, but allowed his party protégée and ally Edith Cresson to dominate political relations with Tokyo. In 1988–91, bilateral quarrels resulted in France being perceived in Japan as the 'most racist and hostile' European country. The 'Cresson effect' so dominated relations with Tokyo that her short but tumultuous term as Prime Minister over 1991–92 was marred by bilateral diatribes and threats of trade wars. In June 1991, Peugeot's Tokyo showroom was the target of anti-French graffiti while demonstrators marched outside the French Embassy (Wong, 2006: 125–6).

The economic problems spilled over into the political and security fields. France was also causing problems to Japan via its membership of the G7, North Atlantic Treaty Organisation (NATO) and the United Nations Security Council (UNSC) (Seizelet, 2001). At the G7 Williamsburg summit in 1983, Prime Minister Nakasone had to work hard to convince a reluctant Mitterrand to agree to the wording of the final communiqué on the 'indivisibility of Western security', the first time Japan linked its security in such a public way with the West as a whole against the Soviet Union (Nakasone, 2002: 54–5). France had opposed Japan's proposal of an informal arrangement with NATO, prompting Nakasone to intensify consultations directly with the EC's 'big three' member states. During the first NATO-Japan Security Conference in 1990 involving government officials and academics from both sides, France refused to attend because it felt that such a conference violated NATO's charter. Likewise, Foreign Minister Taro Nakayama floated the possibility of Japanese involvement as observer in meetings of the Organisation for Security and Cooperation in Europe (OSCE) in Prague in May 1990, but shelved the idea because of French opposition (Drifte, 1998: 86).

By the early 1990s, however, France found itself having to adjust and conform to changed circumstances. Encouraged by Japanese incentives, the European Commission's new attitudes and trading policies vis-à-vis

Japan, and policy learning from other EU states (chiefly Britain and Germany), both the French government and French industry stepped back from confrontation. In April 1988, the EC Council determined that market access would henceforth be sought in parallel with cooperation with Japan. This was prompted by a change of heart in Thatcher's Britain. The UK had resolved its outstanding trade problems with Japan, and when it changed sides in 1988, the weight of opinion in the EC moved from confrontation towards a cooperative dialogue with Japan. In 1991 the European Commission again ruled in favour of free trade, backed in particular by Britain (which stood to benefit as it hosted a Nissan assembly line). Overcoming French, Italian and Spanish opposition, the EC undertook to remove all restrictions on Japanese car imports from January 1993 in return for which Japan would monitor exports until the end of 1999. The 'car deal' in July 1991 was thus a significant step forward from the 1983 deal struck between the EC and Japan on VCRs (Wong, 2006: 113–18).

France-Japan rapprochement

Political relations between Paris and Tokyo improved towards the tail-end of Mitterrand's presidency, when France received Emperor Akihito on a state visit in October 1994. The changes were even more dramatic under President Chirac. Japan was ranked among the world's 'seven great powers with global influence' (Dorient, 2002: 180), and French diplomacy under Chirac took the initiative, both unilaterally and through the European framework, to create 'strategic alliances' with major powers like Japan in a bid to balance the sole post-Cold War 'hyper-power', the USA. Chirac's first Foreign Minister, Hervé de Charette, explained in 1996 that Japan was the second economic power and the largest Official Development Assistance donor in the world. It thus played a primary role in Asia that dovetailed with Chirac's designation of Asia as the 'new frontier' of French diplomacy. France wanted to give a 'special dimension' to bilateral relations with Japan (Charette, 1996). A France-Japan Forum was launched in September 1996, chaired by former prime ministers Raymond Barre and Yasuhiro Nakasone, to meet annually and generate initiatives for improving bilateral relations and exchanges.

The Mitterrand era conflicts had prompted Japan to seek better political and economic relations with France as a key actor in Europe, especially with the establishment of the SEM in 1992 and the euro in 1999. Britain's success in attracting Japanese foreign direct investment was emulated by French governments. By the end of the decade, French companies realised that the Japanese economy was neither invincible nor impenetrable, and were quick to take advantage of new opportunities offered by economic reforms and market openings in Japan, and the launch of the euro in 1999. Following the privatisation of Air France and France Télécom, the Renault-Nissan merger was defended in the National Assembly as complementary and offering 'real growth opportunities' (Wong, 2006: 123).

French willingness to work with Japan on security matters also made huge strides compared to the 1980s. In 1994, France started annual bilateral dialogues on a 'two-plus-two' basis, involving both foreign and defence ministries (Stares and Régaud, 1998: 122). French and Japanese troops cooperated in UN peacekeeping operations (PKO), notably in Cambodia and in Zaire in 1994. Japan represents a potentially lucrative market for French arms sales, since it has one of the highest military expenditures in the world. France tried to offer itself as a partner during the early 1990s at the height of Japan's internal debate about developing an autonomous defence industry, or *kokusanka*. The August 1994 Higuchi report on a security policy vision for the twenty-first century urged that joint research and development of weapons be pursued with European countries as well as the United States (Green, 1995: 148). The 'European card' was evident in the highly publicised international strategic alliance between the Mitsubishi group and Daimler Benz in April 1990 (which sent shock waves through the US aerospace community in Tokyo). US reservations about sharing military technology with Japan encouraged *kokusanka* attempts to build a jet fighter code-named the FSX; meanwhile the French aerospace company Dassault proposed building the jet based on its Rafale fighter.[3]

Chirac enjoyed a familiarity with Japan unique among Western leaders and his activism was a crucial factor in stepping up high-level contacts with Tokyo. Having visited Japan over 40 times in various capacities (as private citizen, Mayor of Paris, Prime Minister and so on), the 'Chirac factor' was instrumental in overcoming a history of difficult bilateral relations. In 1996 President Chirac and Prime Minister Hashimoto Ryutaro signed a long-term bilateral agreement *20 actions pour l'an 2000* ('Twenty measures for the year 2000'), to develop multi-dimensional bilateral cooperation. This document provided a model for the EU's own 10-year Action Plan for EU-Japan relations in 2001. The theme of political partnership initiated by Paris was reproduced in subsequent German and British bilateral agreements with Japan. Like the Franco-Japanese document, the 1996 Japan-Germany Partnership Action Plan and the September 1998 UK-Japan 'Action Agenda 21' were 'strategic partnerships' which rest on strong economic links and shared values on international issues (Hughes, 2001: 63; Umezu and Howell, 2000: 101). The rapprochement continued during the power sharing period of 1997–2002 when Socialist Prime Minister Lionel Jospin visited Tokyo in December 1999 and met with the Emperor and Prime Minister Obuchi to continue the charm offensive to woo Japan. Efforts to build strong political and cultural relations with Japan – thereby broadening the relationship from a near-exclusive focus on trade and economics – have included cooperation on issues ranging from stabilising international exchange rates to combating terrorism. In January 2001 at an Asia-Europe Meeting (ASEM) meeting in Kobe, the French and Japanese finance ministries released a controversial discussion paper ('Exchange Rate Regimes for Emerging Market Economies') appealing for greater euro-yen coordination to stabilise volatile exchange rates across Asia (*Financial Times*, 16 January 2001).

Popular French images of Japan have moved beyond the extremes of fascination and suspicion, to accepting Japan as a normal country. According to official surveys, the proportion of opinion-makers in France expressing confidence in Japan rose from 57 per cent in 1993 to 62 per cent in 1996 and 72 per cent in 1998 (French Senate, 1999). Chirac officiated at the inauguration of the *Maison de la Culture du Japon* in 1997 (fifteen years after agreement on the project was reached at Mitterrand's 1982 state visit). High-profile cultural festivals (1997 was 'Japan Year' in France and 1998 was 'France Year' in Japan) have contributed to a wave of *japonisme* (Matsuura, 1998: 61–71). Likewise, successful French management in Nissan and Japan's World Cup 2002 football team have helped rehabilitate the image of Paris in Japan.

In summary, during the Cold War, French political relations with Japan were framed within the larger context of EC-Japan relations. In the 1980s and early 1990s, France uploaded anti-Japan policies to the European level. In 1988–91, France resisted policy convergence with other member states and effectively blocked British attempts to promote EU political engagement with Japan. France acted within EC structures and used European policies to achieve or amplify national political and economic interests vis-à-vis Japan. France was able to do so because of disproportionate French influence in the EC, particularly in the European Commission. However, once a number of EC countries changed sides, the rapprochement heralded by the 1991 EC-Japan Declaration and the EC decision to scrap quotas, undercut the ability of Paris to upload its protectionist preferences (Commission of the European Communities and Japanese Government, 1991; Commission of the European Communities, 1995b). The election of a 'japanophile' president in 1995 further transformed France from being one of the most anti-Japanese EU member states to one of Japan's most vocal advocates. Today, Japan is perceived in French strategic thinking as a key actor in the Asia-Pacific region and the world (Godement, 2001). France has also welcomed Japanese participation in the evolving European security architecture through the OSCE. Yet, when the opportunity has arisen, Paris has tended to resist top-down Europeanisation to protect its own privileged political access to Tokyo.

China and human rights

The human rights agenda can be considered a special component of the EU-China political dialogue. It has been a major theme of EU-China relations since the Tiananmen Square crackdown in 1989 (Commission of the European Communities, 2004, 2006). Until the end of the Cold War, the European Commission and most member states did not emphasise human rights in their foreign policy or attach conditionalities to their aid or relations with third countries. Apart from the Netherlands and Nordic countries (especially Denmark and Sweden), few member states have stressed human rights in their relations with China (Foot, 2000: 48).

The June 1989 Tiananmen events politicised the EC's approach to economic relations with China. The European Commission – which had hitherto refrained from political comments– issued a statement expressing 'consternation' and 'shock' at the 'brutal suppression' in Beijing, and cancelled Foreign Trade Minister Zheng Tuobin's scheduled visit to Brussels (Shambaugh, 1996: 11). The introduction of sanctions and the relevance of the United Nations Commission on Human Rights (UNCHR) to EC-China relations shifted much of the discussion on China to the European Council and CFSP structures.

Common policy post-Tiananmen

From 1989 to 1997, the European policy on human rights in China lay principally in (1) the sanctions policy, (2) dialogue between member state governments and China, and (3) holding China accountable in multilateral fora, in particular in the UNCHR, by annually co-sponsoring with the USA a resolution criticising China's human rights record. Some activists consider this the most 'symbolically important' EU policy in monitoring and moderating human rights in China (Baker, 2002; Human Rights in China, 1998). The EC-12 held together in supporting sanctions from June 1989 to October 1990, the date when most of the sanctions were lifted (except the ban on military sales, which is officially still in force at the time of writing).

The UNCHR approach was adhered to each year from 1990 to 1996, except 1991 because the USA, Britain and France needed China's vote in the Security Council to endorse allied action against Iraq in the Gulf War. Although the resolution was always defeated by a no-action motion (except in 1995), the move was politically symbolic and significant in underlining the EC's commitment each spring to improvements in China's human rights record. However, commercial considerations undermined European resolve and discipline, with member states competing to get back into the Chinese market as early as the end of 1989. Almost a year before the EC officially lifted economic sanctions in October 1990, both Germany and France breached the sanctions policy on financial aid by extending soft loans to projects undertaken by German and French companies in China (Nesshöver, 1999: 93).

The Chinese case constitutes 'the most complex and multifaceted dialogue on human rights' which the EU has with any country (Patten, 2001). Although the EU has established an important human rights dialogue with China, it has suffered from coordination problems and conflicting interests between the European Commission, the Parliament, the General Affairs Council (GAC) and the member states (Commission of the European Communities, 2001: 11). Once the shock of Tiananmen faded away, the GAC and the larger member states tended to pay lip service to human rights in order to cultivate their political and economic relations with Beijing.

The French about-turn between the Mitterrand and Chirac presidencies

France under a Socialist president – François Mitterrand – initially took a high-profile and principled position on human rights after Tiananmen, but piped down considerably after the Beijing-Paris spat over Taiwan arms sales.[4] Tiananmen sparked a radical policy shift and dramatically ended French neglect of China. In its place a strident and confrontational human rights policy was adopted. This policy was informed by general public outrage at gross human rights abuses in China, the ideological influence of the French Left, and a strategic calculation to take advantage of Chinese weakness to step up relations with Taiwan. Mitterrand and Foreign Minister Roland Dumas took a vociferous leading position and used the EC to project and Europeanise French condemnation of the Chinese government in the aftermath of Tiananmen.

This confrontational position coincided with a tilt towards 'democratic' Taiwan, a move boosted by economic considerations – the protection of the French arms industry through sales to Taiwan.

France-China relations in 1989–92 reached their lowest point since 1964. From China's perspective, the French were particularly strident in their condemnation of China's human rights record. Not only the media and NGOs, but also 'political' personalities and well-connected human rights activists such as Bernard Kouchner, Danielle Mitterrand, and President Mitterrand himself denounced the Chinese government (Nathan and Link, 2001: 397). France imposed sanctions 'freezing' relations, reduced French diplomatic representation and suspended all political visits to China. At French insistence, the ban on high-technology arms sales and transfers to China was added as the tenth EC sanction at the June 1989 Madrid summit (Mengin, 1992: 48).

The right-wing victory in the 1993 parliamentary elections set the stage for a change in French human rights policy. The change was controversial in French intellectual and even government circles, but after 1996 Chirac's 'philosophical-semantic' approach gradually became established French policy. France under President Chirac made a dramatic about-turn in favour of shielding China's human rights record from EU and international scrutiny. In 1997, Foreign Minister Hervé de Charette remarked that it was 'preposterous for the West, which invaded and humiliated China in modern times, to "lecture" China, a country with a 5000-year old civilisation, on the Human Rights Declaration and the USA Constitution, which are merely 200 years old' (*Beijing Review*, 26 May–1 June 1997).

Disarray and compromise

The new French position was brought to bear at the 53rd UNCHR debate in April 1997 in Geneva. Unable to persuade its European partners and the Dutch EU Presidency to drop the resolution criticising China, France decided to withdraw its support from the ritual EU sponsorship of the resolution. Instead France led the 'Airbus group' (France, Germany, Italy and Spain) in defecting from the common position. It was left to Denmark to draft the resolution, whilst the USA and 14 other Western countries co-sponsored it. With the split in EU ranks, the vote was 27 in favour of China's no-action motion, 17 against and 9 abstentions, the most stunning repudiation of the UNCHR mechanism condemning China since the campaign started in 1990 (*Beijing Review*, 5–11 May 1997). The UNCHR debacle was celebrated as a spectacular victory by Chinese diplomacy. Meanwhile many Western governments heavily criticised Paris for 'kowtowing to Chinese pressure', putting short-term national economic interests over collective long-term EU interests and hence undermining the EU's credibility and France's own credentials as the birthplace of human rights (Wong, 2006: 95). The stage was then set for Chirac's state visit to China in May 1997, where a France-China joint declaration was issued. On human rights, it declared that both parties would 'respect diversity' and take into account the 'particularities of all sides' (French Foreign Ministry, 1997; *Beijing Review*, 2–8 June 1997).

After the EU debacle of 1997, a new approach to human rights in China was decided by the GAC and codified in the European Commission's strategy paper 'Building a comprehensive partnership with China' (Commission of the European Communities, 1998). The GAC agreed that in the 1998 UNCHR session, the EU would 'neither propose nor endorse, either by the organisation as a whole or by individual members' any resolution criticising China (*Beijing Review*, 6–12 April 1997). In effect, the French position had won the day and the 'hardliners' found themselves tied to an EU position projected by France. This Europeanised position *not* to co-sponsor (albeit with reservations expressed by the 'hardliners') the UNCHR resolution with the USA has been reached at the Council each March since 1998. Yet there was agreement to vote against China in the event of a resolution being put to a vote. The Council agreed that the EU should adopt the following (convoluted and inconsistent) approach at the UNCHR on China (EU General Affairs Council, 2001):

- EU members of the UNCHR will not sponsor or co-sponsor a resolution critical of China;
- However, if there is a resolution against China sponsored by other UNCHR member(s) and this is put to a vote, EU members of the Commission will vote in favour of the resolution;
- EU members will vote against a no-action motion, should one be presented, and the EU will actively encourage other UNCHR members to do likewise, since in the EU's view, the very notion of no-action is itself contrary to the spirit of dialogue.

Pressured by the pragmatic positions taken by Germany and France, most EU member states and the European Commission had towards the end of the 1990s toned down their critiques of the Chinese government, reaching a coordinated but weak common position of 'constructive dialogue'. Activist External Relations Commissioners are necessary to keep human rights on the agenda of EU-China relations. Chris Patten listed constructive engagement, multilateral cooperation, and the promotion of values (human rights, good governance and the rule of law) as three basic objectives of the EU in its relations with East Asia. But as External Relations Commissioner, he steered clear of antagonising Beijing, unlike during his term as the last British Governor of Hong Kong.

Aside from joint actions taken under the CFSP, individual EU governments regularly raise human rights concerns in their discussions with Chinese leaders. For example, the former German Foreign Minister Joschka Fischer mentioned China at the UNCHR in 1999 and 2002. The German federal government and the Bundestag have also repeatedly called upon the Chinese government to enter into a dialogue with the Dalai Lama with a view to granting Tibet substantial autonomy, and ending the suppression of Tibetan culture and religion (Auswärtiges Amt, 2002: 6).

In practice, the leading actor within the EU in promoting human rights in China has been the European Parliament (EP). Since 1987, it has made regular and public criticisms of the Chinese human rights record, especially on Tibet, arbitrary detention, capital punishment, religious and political freedoms. The GAC in May 1999 supported the EP's 1994 initiative to streamline a series of budget headings under a single chapter of the EU budget (B7-70) in the 'European Initiative for Democracy and Human Rights' (EIDHR). The EP's budgetary power over the EIDHR gives it added oversight of external relations. The EP thus holds the European Commission and GAC accountable for developments 'on the ground' for the continuation of the EU-China dialogue (Wong, 2006: 50). It has also conferred political prestige and international publicity on foreign personalities embodying human rights struggles. The EP infuriated Beijing in 1996 when it awarded Wei Jingsheng – then China's most celebrated dissident – the Sakharov Prize for Freedom of Thought (Nathan, 1999: 155). It invited the Dalai Lama to address a session in Strasbourg in October 2001.

Dealing with China on the subject of human rights remains a point of contention between member states who prefer making China publicly accountable at international fora, and those who prefer silent diplomacy or constructive engagement. While France and the 'Airbus group' defied the EU common position in 1997, they were nonetheless constrained by the general EU consensus at the GAC that China's human rights record is in need of improvement. The convergence (or compromise) of the member states' human rights policies on China since 1998 has watered down the positions of the more critical countries. A combination of the hard-line EP and Nordic governments' unilateral approaches combined with the conciliatory EU approach of 'constructive dialogue' pioneered by France and Germany, could be viewed as a way of engaging China through a mixture of negative measures and positive incentives (Alston, 1999: 578–80).

Conclusions

As regards Beijing, French Foreign Ministry officials could justifiably claim to have 'Europeanised' (namely, exported national policy to the European level) the EU's political dialogue with China by uploading in the 1990s French models of regular high-level political contacts with Chinese leaders (Bâtie, 2002). After Chirac's May 1997 state visit, France called on the EU to engage in a dialogue with China rather than confront it over human rights. The upgrading of the France-China political dialogue, set out in the 1997 joint declaration, provided a model for the EU-China dialogue. The 1996 Chirac-Hashimoto *20 actions pour l'an 2000* agreement provided a blueprint for the European Commission's own 2001 Action Plan. 'Europeanisation' in France's political relations with East Asian countries could thus be interpreted as a bottom-up process of France projecting its preferences upwards.

While there is good evidence to support claims of French agency in the EU's Asia policy, and success in exporting its preferences in East Asia to the European level, the preceding accounts of France-Japan and France-China relations show that the utility and impact of EU institutions on French foreign policy behaviour are more significant than is commonly imagined or admitted. The EU's role and presence in East Asia has grown, in contrast to the diminishing profiles of individual member states and ex-colonial powers in the region. From 1991, France was unable to act as a national actor in its own right (failing to win a separate national seat in the ASEAN Regional Forum (ARF), for example). It had to work through the European Union in the ARF, in ASEM, and in the EU's dialogues with ASEAN, Japan and China. EU member states have had to adjust to a slew of country and regional strategy papers produced in Brussels in relation to China, Japan and Asia (Commission of the European Communities, 1994, 1995a, 1995b, 1998, 2003, 2006).

The EU is progressively acting as a parallel actor alongside – and sometimes in place of – member states in the region. Europeanisation has thus affected foreign policy autonomy. The EU's human rights policy towards China at the UNCHR from 1998 could be interpreted as a 'levelling down' from the perspective of the more hard-line states (Denmark, Netherlands, UK), namely a 'drastic self-imposed reduction of sovereignty for those states that might choose to table or co-sponsor a resolution' (Clapham, 1999: 647). It also committed the more accommodating 'Airbus group' (France, Germany, Italy, Spain) to voting against a no-action motion. But Europeanisation also increased state autonomy by empowering states to pursue policies they could not engage in without the institutional protection offered by EU structures. In 1989, the EC-12 responded to the Tiananmen massacre with a collective sanctions policy. European governments had few policy alternatives in the face of outrage in their domestic constituencies, and were willing to risk Beijing's displeasure because they found strength behind an institutional edifice (Ferdinand, 1995: 31). By committing the member states to a collective sanctions policy on China, the EC served as an umbrella to reduce the costs of individual sanctions, promote credibility and reduce the likelihood of cheating.

France has tried to keep many of its activities with Japan and China outside the ambit of the EU, yet it is important to these countries because of its place at the heart of European integration. But whether on its own or within the EU, France is not capable of seriously challenging Japan's relationship with the USA. With or without the Europeanisation of French relations with Japan, the EU remains secondary to Japan's key foreign relationship. In brief, the underlying dynamic is a process of increasing engagement with China and Japan at the EU level, with national engagement taking its cue from EU-level initiatives and agreements.

Notes

1. Mitterrand was the first French president to visit all the major Asian countries – China, Japan, India and Indonesia (during his first term, 1981–88).
2. Queen Elizabeth visited Japan in 1975, Germany and Japan reached an agreement on scientific cooperation in 1974 and President Walter Scheel visited Tokyo in 1978. See Bouissou (2002: 213).
3. US-Japan trade tensions had spilled over into bilateral political relations. See Green (1995: 84, 149); Chinworth (1999: 286-310); Wong (2006: 127–8).
4. Paris had approved the sale of six Lafayette frigates and 60 Mirage fighters to Taiwan between 1990 and 1992. See Wellons (1994); Wong (2006: 82).

References

Aggestam, L. (2004) 'Role identity and Europeanisation of foreign policy: a political-cultural approach', in B. Tonra and T. Christiansen (eds), *Rethinking European Union Foreign Policy*, Manchester: Manchester University Press, pp. 81–98.

Alston, P. (ed.) (1999) *The European Union and Human Rights*, Oxford: Oxford University Press.

Auswärtiges Amt (2002) 'Relations between the People's Republic of China and Germany', http://www.auswärtiges-amt.de/www/en/laenderinfos/laender_ausgabe_html?type_id=14&land_id32, consulted 25 May 2004.

Baker, P. (2002) 'Human rights, Europe and the People's Republic of China', *China Quarterly*, 169 (March): 45–63.

Bâtie, H.D. de la (2002) *La Politique chinoise de l'Union Européenne: en progrès, mais peut mieux faire*, http:www.ifri.org/f/Centre%20asie/articles/hdb-ue-chine.htm, consulted 9 May 2002.

Blunden, M. (2000) 'France', in I. Manners and R. Whitman (eds), *The Foreign Policies of European Union Member States*, Manchester: Manchester University Press, pp. 19–43.

Bouissou, J.-M. (2002) *Japan: the Burden of Success*, London: Hurst and Company.

Bridges, B. (1992) 'Japan and Europe: rebalancing a relationship', *Asian Survey*: 32(3) (March): 230–45.

Bridges, B. (1999) *Europe and the Challenge of the Asia Pacific*, Cheltenham, UK and Northampton, MA, USA: Edward Elgar.

Bull, H. (1983) 'Civilian power Europe: a contradiction in terms?', *Journal of Common Market Studies*, 21: 149–70.

Charette, H. de (1996) 'Interview with the Foreign Minister by the journal "France/Japon/Eco"', 1 October 1996, http://www.doc.diplomatie.gouv.fr/BASIS/epic/www/doc/DDD/970113033.doc, consulted 10 August 2003.

Chinworth, M. (1999) 'The technology factor in US-Japan security relations', in M.J. Green and P.M. Cronin (eds), *The US-Japan Alliance: Past, Present and Future*, New York: Council on Foreign Relations, pp. 286–310.

Clapham, A. (1999) 'Where is the EU's human rights common foreign policy, and how is it manifested in multilateral fora?' in P. Alston (ed.), *The European Union and Human Rights*, Oxford: Oxford University Press.

Commission of the European Communities (1994) *Towards a New Asia Strategy*, COM (94) 427, 13 July.

Commission of the European Communities (1995a) *A Long-term Policy for China-Europe Relations*, COM (95) 279, 15 July.

Commission of the European Communities (1995b) *Europe and Japan: the Next Steps*, COM (95) 73 final, 8 March.

Commission of the European Communities (1998) *Building a Comprehensive Partnership with China*, COM (98) 181, 25 March.

Commission of the European Communities (2001) *Europe and Asia: a Strategic Framework for Enhanced Partnership*, COM (2001) 469 final, 4 September.

Commission of the European Communities (2003) *A Maturing Partnership: Shared Interests and Challenges in EU-China Relations*, COM (2003) 533 final, 10 September.

Commission of the European Communities (2004) *The EU's China Policy*, http://europa.eu.int/comm/external_relations/china/intro/index.htm, consulted 22 June 2005.

Commission of the European Communities (2006) *EU – China: Closer Partners, Growing Responsibilities*, COM (2006) 631 final, 24 October.

Commission of the European Communities and Japanese Government (1991) 'Joint Declaration on Relations between the EC and its Member States and Japan', The Hague, 18 July.

Doise, J. and M. Vaïsse (1992) *Politique étrangère de la France: diplomatie et outil militaire*, Paris: Imprimerie nationale.

Domenach, J.-L. (1990) 'La politique française au miroir de l'Asie', in F. de la Serre, J. Leruez and H. Wallace (eds), *Les Politiques étrangères de la France et de la Grande Bretagne depuis 1945*, Paris: Presses de la FNSP, pp. 228–44.

Dorient, R. (2002) 'Un septennat de politique asiatique: quel bilan pour la France?', *Politique Etrangère*, 1 (printemps): 173–88.

Drifte, R. (1998) *Japan's Foreign Policy for the 21st Century: From Economic Superpower to What Power?* London: Macmillan Press.

EU General Affairs Council (2001) *Human Rights – Conclusions*, General Affairs Council 2338th Council meeting, Brussels, 19 March.

Ferdinand, P. (1995) 'Economic and Diplomatic Interactions between the EU and China', in R. Grant (ed.), *The European Union and China: a European Strategy for the Twenty-first Century*, London: Routledge, pp. 26–40.

Foot, R. (2000) *Rights Beyond Borders: the Global Community and the Struggle over Human Rights in China*, Oxford: Oxford University Press.

French Foreign Ministry (1997) *Déclaration conjointe Franco-chinoise pour un Partenariat Global*, Pékin, 16 May.

French Senate (1999) *Japon: crise et douleureuses mutations*, report by the Delegation of the France-Japan Group in the Senate following an official visit to Japan in April 1999, on http://www.senat.fr, consulted 29 October 2002.

Godement, F. (2001) 'The US and Japan into the 21st century: new geopolitical thinking?', paper presented at Asia Pacific Security Forum, August, http:// www.inpr.org.tw/inprc/recent/event3_7.pdf, consulted 1 November 2002.

Gordon, P.H. (1993) *A Certain Idea of France: French Security Policy and the Gaullist Legacy*, Princeton, NJ: Princeton University Press.

Green, M. (1995) *Arming Japan: Defense Production, Alliance Politics, and the Postwar Search for Autonomy*, New York: Columbia University Press.

Grosser, A. (1989) *Affaires Extérieures: la politique de la France 1944–1989*, Paris: Flammarion.

Hill, C. (1993) 'The capability-expectations gap, or conceptualising Europe's international role', *Journal of Common Market Studies*, 31(1): 306–28.

Hill, C. (ed.) (1996) *The Actors in Europe's Foreign Policy*, London: Routledge.

Hoffmann, S. (1966) 'Obstinate or obsolete? The fate of the nation-state and the case of western Europe', *Dædalus*, 95(3) (Summer): 862–915.

Hoffmann, S. (2000) 'Towards a Common Foreign and Security Policy?', *Journal of Common Market Studies*, 38(2): 189–98.

Hughes, C.W. (2001) 'Japan in Europe: Asian and European Perspectives', in G.D. Hook and H. Hasegawa (eds), *The Political Economy of Japanese Globalisation*, London: Routledge, pp. 56–70.

Human Rights in China (HriC) Report (1998) *From Principle to Pragmatism: Can 'Dialogue' improve China's Human Rights Situation?*, New York: HriC.

Ishikawa, K. (1990) *Japan and the Challenge of Europe 1992*, London: Pinter.

Iwanaga, K. (2000) 'Europe in Japan's foreign policy', in B. Endström (ed.), *The Japanese and Europe: Images and Perceptions*, Richmond, Surrey: Japan Library/ Curzon Press, pp. 208–35.

Kessler, M.-C. (1999) *La Politique étrangere de la France: acteurs et processus*, Paris: Presses de Sciences Po.

Kresl, P.K. and Gallais, S. (2002) *France Encounters Globalisation*, Cheltenham, UK and Northampton, MA, USA: Edward Elgar.

La Serre, F. de (1996) 'France: the impact of François Mitterrand', in C. Hill (ed.), *The Actors in Europe's Foreign Policy*, London: Routledge.

Lehmann, J.-P. (1992) 'France, Japan, Europe, and industrial competition: the automotive case', *International Affairs*, 68(1) : 37–53.

Lequesne, C. (1993) *Paris-Bruxelles: comment se fait la politique européenne de la France*, Paris: Presses de la Fondation nationale des Sciences Politiques.

Matsui, A. (1989) *Mémoires d'un ambassadeur du Japon né en France: vers un renouveau*, Geneva: JR.

Matsuura, K. (1998) *La Diplomatie japonaise à l'aube du 21e siècle: réflexions sur les relations du Japon avec la France et sur son rôle international*, Paris: Publications orientalistes de France.

Mengin, F. (1992) 'The prospects for France-Taiwan relations', *Issues and Studies*, 28(3): 40–58.

Miskimmon, A. and W.E. Paterson (2003) 'Foreign and security policy: on the cusp between transformation and accommodation', in K. Dyson and K.H. Goetz (eds), *Germany, Europe and the Politics of Constraint*, Oxford: Oxford University Press, pp. 325–45.

Nakasone, Y. (2002) *Japan: a State Strategy for the Twenty-first Century*, London: Routledge.

Nathan, A.J. and E.P. Link (eds) (2001) *The Tiananmen Papers*, New York: Public Affairs.

Nathan, A.J. (1999) 'China and the international human rights regime', in E. Economy and M. Oksenberg (eds), *China Joins the World: Progress and Prospects*, New York: Council on Foreign Relations.

Nesshöver, C. (1999) 'Bonn et Paris face à Pékin (1989-1997): vers une stratégie commune?', *Politique Etrangère*, 1(99): 91–106.

Nuttall, S.J. (1996) 'Japan and the EU', *Survival*, 38(2) (Summer): 104–20.

Nuttall, S.J. (2000) *European Foreign Policy*, Oxford: Oxford University Press.

Øhrgaard, J.O. (1997) 'Less than supranational, more than intergovernmental: European political cooperation and the dynamics of intergovernmental integration', *Millennium,* 26(1): 1–29.

Patten, C. (2001) 'Commission statements in urgency debates, by External Relations Commissioner in the European Parliament, Plenary Session, Strasbourg, 5 July 2001, SPEECH/01/33', http://ec.europa.eu/external_relations/news/patten/sp01_331.htm#5, consulted 10 June 2007.

Piening, C. (1997) *Global Europe: the European Union in World Affairs*, Boulder, Colorado: Lynne Rienner.

Pompidou, G. (1973) 'Message du Président Pompidou au peuple japonais publié dans le journal "Yomiuri" 01.01.1973', http://www.doc.diplomatie.gouv.fr/BASIS/epic/www/doc/DDW?M=29059&K=1112227841&W, consulted 2 September 2003.

Regelsberger, E. et al. (eds) (1997) *Foreign Policy of the European Union: From EPC to CFSP and Beyond*, London: Lynne Rienner.

Rigaudis, M. (1998) *Japon mépris … passion: regards de la France sur le Japon de 1945 à 1995*, Paris: L'Harmattan.

Sautter, C. (1996) *La France au miroir du Japon: croissance ou declin*, Paris: Odile Jacob.

Seizelet, E. (2001) 'Japon: contraintes et défis de la puissance', in F. Charillon (ed.), *Les Politiques étrangères: ruptures et continuités*, Paris: La Documentation Française, pp. 179–96.

Shambaugh, D. (1996) *China and Europe 1949–1995*, London: Contemporary China Institute, SOAS.

Smith, H. (2002) *European Union Foreign Policy: What It Is and What It Does*, London: Pluto Press.

Stares, P. and Régaud, N. (1998) 'Europe's role in Asia-Pacific security', *Survival* 39(4) (Winter): 117–39.

Tonra, B. and T. Christiansen (eds) (2004) *Rethinking European Union Foreign Policy*, Manchester: Manchester University Press.

Tsardanidis, C. and S. Stavridis (2005) 'The Europeanisation of Greek foreign policy: a critical appraisal', *European Integration*, 27(2): 217–39.

Umezu, I. and Lord Howell of Guildford (2000) 'The Anglo-Japanese relationship: looking into the future', in Daiwa Anglo-Japanese Foundation (eds), *UK and Japan: Bridging the Millennium, Bridging the Countries*, London; Daiwa Anglo-Japanese Foundation.

Wellons, P. (1994) 'Sino-French relations: historical alliance vs. economic reality', *The Pacific Review*, 7(3): 341–8.

White, B. (2001) *Understanding European Foreign Policy*, Basingstoke: Palgrave.

Wilkinson, E. (1990) *Japan versus the West: Images and Reality*, Harmondsworth: Penguin Books.

Wong, R. (2005) 'The Europeanisation of foreign policy', in C. Hill and M. Smith (eds), *The International Relations of the European Union*, Oxford: Oxford University Press, pp. 134–53.

Wong, R. (2006) *The Europeanisation of French Foreign Policy: France and the EU in East Asia*, Basingstoke: Palgrave Macmillan.

Wong, R. (2007) 'Foreign policy', in P. Graziano and M. Vink (eds), *Europeanisation: New Research Agendas*, Basingstoke: Palgrave Macmillan, pp. 321–34.

5
The Burdensome Heritage of Prestige Politics

Albrecht Sonntag

Introduction

In the weeks preceding the French referendum of 30 April 2005 on the European Union Constitutional Treaty, former President Giscard d'Estaing put his weight behind a text over whose elaboration he had presided. In town halls and television studios, he tried to convince his compatriots that accepting the treaty was in their interest. He argued that a major reason to vote 'yes' was because the constitution would 'give back to France its rank in Europe and the world'.[1] This argument implied that France had lost its rank, that it was no longer a nation which 'is not a country like all the others', as claimed by President Chirac (2007), and that something had to be done to recover its former prominent rank. Such calls are frequently heard in French political debates. The recurrent use of the term 'rank' speaks volumes about how France is perceived by its political elite: the term implies notions of hierarchy, superiority and distinction.

Grosser (1992) contrasted the notion of *rank* with that of *role*. Whereas *role* was assigned by others according to one's proven capacities and potential, *rank* referred to the prestige derived from a seemingly inalterable hierarchical position that was self-proclaimed and deemed self-evident. His remarkable analysis ended with a rhetorical question about the essence of prestige: 'Is it what you drape yourself in or what the others grant you?' (Grosser, 1992: 365). In his famous West Point speech, Dean Acheson stated that Britain had lost an empire but had 'not yet found a role' – could it be that France, having lost its empire and great power status, has not cared to find a role? Why should it? After all, France has a rank.

In relation to this obsession with rank, the British and American media often comment on the supposed psychological difficulties of the French political elite in coping with the sense of national decline. Attempts to slow down the irreversible loss of national influence in a globalised world are often ridiculed as useless protectionism, aimed at preserving the relics of a bygone era instead of adapting to the geopolitical, cultural and linguistic constellations of the age of globalisation. A similar perspective has also been adopted by a large number of French intellectuals and editorialists, who have become experts in 'declinology'.[2] A point of agreement between foreign observers and French commentators lies in the accusation that France's political leaders of recent decades are responsible for the depressing current situation.

However, a diagnosis of nostalgia for *grandeur* (national greatness) falls short of explaining why the French political class behave as they do, especially on the world stage. How is it that the rhetoric of rank is so important to the political elite that they forget the role that France plays or could play? What factors cause them to uphold the old ambition of 'prestige politics', namely a strategy of stressing appearance and reputation over essence and efficiency? Arguably, the pursuit of 'prestige politics' does not allow for an honest, self-critical reassessment of a nation's resources and opportunities on a stage that must be shared with other actors, but rather creates a situation where a changing reality needs to be moulded to pre-existent and firmly held beliefs. In the terms of social psychology, this strategy leads to cognitive dissonance. The ensuing state of mental stress is relieved by a set of repetitive and self-persuasive invocations – heard in the media, on party platforms and during election campaigns – which imply that national rank has not withered. In the twenty-first century's global landscape of rising new powers, increasing interdependence and growing domination of Anglo-American communication strategies, French 'prestige politics' has become a burdensome heritage from the past that makes adaptation to changing geopolitical configurations more difficult.

To explain the causes of these problems, this chapter first analyses France's fascination with the politics of power and prestige in international relations. Its second section explores the consequences in terms of the scapegoating of Europe. The third section interprets French responses using an explanatory model which identifies behavioural patterns that are culturally induced and deeply rooted in French history, restricting the capacity of political leaders to make free choices. The conclusion reflects on the scope available for adaptation to current challenges.

The politics of power and prestige

In the French language, the term 'power' has two distinct translations and accompanying connotations: *le pouvoir* refers to authority over subordinates (subjects, citizens, employees and so on) whilst *la puissance* refers to the influence of an international actor (usually a nation state) in relation to others. This semantic distinction explains why it is difficult to translate the expression *l'Europe puissance*, a phrase assigning a strategic objective to the European Union (EU) and implying a vision of it as a self-conscious political actor providing a counterweight to American power. In French political rhetoric, '*l'Europe puissance*' is juxtaposed to '*l'Europe espace*', which refers to an Anglo-Nordic vision of Europe as a free-trade zone with no political dimension. The strategic objective of *l'Europe puissance* has long been a cornerstone of France's European policy. Thereby Europe is considered to add to French power.

How this occurs is best explained by the concept of 'soft power' as developed by Nye (1990a, 1990b) who argued that 'in an age of information-based economies and transnational interdependence, power is becoming less transferable, less tangible, and less coercive' (Nye, 1990b: 33). While traditional sources of 'hard power', such as military potential, demographic weight and raw materials remain essential, Nye (1990b: 9) identified the increasingly determining role of economic strength and technological know-how, internal cohesion and cultural attractiveness (including a nation's language and societal model whose notoriety and appeal depend on international communication channels), and – most of all – perceived credibility and legitimacy as an agenda-setting actor in international institutions.

France is not, of course, devoid of hard power resources. French military forces are deployed in various world 'hot spots', with over 14,000 troops posted abroad, especially in Africa but also in Afghanistan. Yet France's power is clearly decreasing in relative terms, in comparison not only with the USA but also with other global actors. French leaders realise that this trend will not be reversed (for economic, budgetary and other reasons), which explains their strong interest in soft power as a means to compensate for declining hard power resources and to strengthen French diplomacy. The concept of 'soft power' has also found strong resonance in intellectual circles. The three major French think-tanks for international relations – the Institut Français des Relations Internationales, the Centre d'Etudes et de Recherches Internationales, the Institut des Relations Internationales et Stratégiques – have discussed the topic widely during the last decade. The media have echoed the debate, with mainstream publications picking up on the emblematic question asked in the title of Pascal Boniface's book *Is France still a Great Power?* (Boniface, 1998). For anyone unsure about the official line, Hubert Védrine (the French Foreign Minister from 1997 to 2002) emphatically replied 'We are not a medium power!' (Védrine, 2002). Védrine made soft power the focal point of his doctrine of international relations, insisting that, despite a relative decline in its hard power resources, France was still a major player on the world stage provided that 'all aspects of power – whether they be modern or ancient, tangible and non-tangible, hard or soft' were taken into account when assessing national influence (Védrine, 2001: 5; see also Védrine, 1998). Some observers in the USA concluded that Védrine's obsession with soft power resources represented an attempt to position France as an alternative to the allegedly hegemonic American model. However, the ascription of the term 'Védrinism' to this French doctrine (Caldwell, 2000; Gordon, 2000) is misleading because this school of thought is independent of a single politician or party line.

Indeed, successive governments have consistently pursued the mobilisation and projection of France's soft power resources over the last fifteen years, a strategy which rests on both European and national pillars. According to Gaullist doctrine, European integration contributes to French prestige. Recognition as a founding member, as a main driver and leader of a successful, continuously enlarging EU can only be beneficial to France's standing in the world. To achieve these goals, a series of national initiatives was launched of which the most important can be categorised as 'public diplomacy'. This neologism describes interaction not only with governments (classic diplomacy) but also public opinion in target countries, by addressing non-governmental actors and mass media. The aim of 'public diplomacy' is to influence international public opinion in order to create an environment favourable to the pursuit of national economic and political objectives. For Leonard (2002: 9), this involved 'increasing people's familiarity with one's country (making them think about it, updating their images, turning around unfavourable opinions)' and 'increasing people's appreciation of one's country (creating positive perceptions, getting others to see issues of global importance from the same perspective)'. The need for improved coordination of 'public diplomacy' led in 1998 to the establishment of the Direction générale de la coopération internationale et du développement (DGCID). Within the DGCID, a unit named France Coopération Internationale was launched in 2002 in order 'to promote French thought' globally.[3]

Accompanying initiatives included the creation in 1998 of the Edufrance agency, whose mission is to attract high-flying students from abroad, strengthen France's positioning as a major producer of knowledge and compete successfully with destinations such as the USA, the UK, Germany and Australia. Edufrance operates 77 offices in 45 countries worldwide, participating in major higher education fairs and working in close cooperation with French embassies and the Alliance Française. Since study programmes are in French, Edufrance contributes strongly to the dissemination of the French language as a means of international communication. To federate the French-speaking world (*la Francophonie*), France promotes an intergovernmental organisation which brings together 50 states and 13 observing members. The strategic objective is to make the French voice and language more audible on the world stage. One of the most significant attempts to strengthen the impact of *la Francophonie* beyond the defence of linguistic and cultural diversity was the introduction of a mission statement in 1997 (updated in 2005) giving this relatively loose intergovernmental grouping a 'full political dimension', according to its founding charter.[4] Since December 2006, the France 24 satellite news channel and website – the French equivalent of CNN and BBC World – has been entrusted with a mission to 'reinforce the French presence in the global audio-visual landscape' and 'contribute to a strategy of durable influence of France in the world' (Amalou, 2003). (See also Chapter 12 by Raymond Kuhn.)

The organisation of global sports events constitutes a further category of 'public diplomacy' initiative. These provide a prestigious, if expensive, showcase for the host nation and possess a strong political dimension (Dauncey and Hare, 1998). The 1998 football World Cup, as well as the unsuccessful bids for the 2008 and 2012 Olympics are in line with a long-standing French self-perception as guardian of the universalist values of sport. The tradition of instigating global sports events goes back to Pierre de Coubertin and his Olympic movement at the end of the nineteenth century. It was therefore fitting that France should host the last world cup of the twentieth century, having presided over the creation of FIFA (*Fédération internationale de football association*) in 1904 and of the World Cup in 1930.[5] Having previously failed to win the World Cup, the 1998 triumph of the French team in the aptly named *Stade de France* was greeted with joy and relief. It also served as an occasion to celebrate the republican model of integration that the ethnically-mixed national team was said to represent. On the other hand, the bitter reactions to the failure of the French Olympic bids highlighted the extent to which this kind of global showcase is considered to be an essential means to increase soft power resources.

Because the outcomes of 'public diplomacy' are largely intangible, their evaluation must be tentative. What remains of the 1998 World Cup victory with its almost flawless organisation and the endearing pictures of French national cohesion and self-celebration when compared to the 2005 riots in suburban ghettoes, repeatedly dubbed a 'civil war in France' by CNN? It remains uncertain whether such events – despite their media echo – are capable of updating a nation's reputation around the planet (Sonntag, 2007). The same scepticism applies to the impact of campaigns by Edufrance to attract high-flyers. The agency justifies its existence by publishing impressive graphs that show a significant increase in the market share of foreign students in French higher education at masters and PhD levels. Yet a scrutiny of the figures reveals that, with the exception of some world-class *grandes écoles*, the French university system is not competitive. Most foreign students in France hail from francophone Africa and would probably have come anyway, if only for linguistic and cultural reasons. For high-flyers from Asia, Latin America or Central Europe, France is a second or third choice at best (Sonntag, 2006). As regards France 24, the viability of yet another news channel in a crowded international market place is questionable. Establishing the new brand is an ambitious endeavour requiring a large promotion budget which the French state has not been willing to consent. Whilst a global crisis such as another 9/11 or international war may yet build up the visibility and credibility of France 24, the question remains whether it will exert an influence on the way France is perceived in the world. It may be an almost impossible task to modify, yet alone rectify, the innumerable stereotypes and prejudices about France which have taken root over the years. Rather than concentrate on worldwide self-promotion through prestige-enhancing projects, French 'public diplomacy' might be well advised to direct efforts more towards the European stage, which is probably where the stakes for France are higher than anywhere else.

Scapegoating Europe

The growth and development of the EU has completely changed the power game in Europe. Its rules are no longer based on 'traditional' strategies of distinction and singularisation within a restricted group of players, but on strategies of mutual persuasion and intelligent compromise-building among 27 member states. The question is whether French diplomacy is willing and able to play according to the new rules.

Unfortunately, successive French governments have squandered many of France's remarkable soft power resources in Europe. A major case in point was their reluctant and inconsistent attitude towards the 2004 enlargement. An ingenious strategy between the 2004 Nice Treaty and the accession of the new Central and Eastern European member states would have positioned France as a 'generous leader' of the new EU, with open arms for newcomers, expressing firm views yet tolerant of diverging opinions and with constructive propositions to offer – a kind of *force tranquille*, to use François Mitterrand's campaign slogan. Instead, France is perceived more and more by old and new member states alike as a nervous has-been, unwilling to let go of old privileges (such as the benefits it draws from the Common Agricultural Policy), as a rather intolerant opinion-leader unable to recognise that its vision of Europe is no longer shared by a majority of members and as the defender of a socio-economic model that hardly anybody wants to copy. How has this happened?

Analysis of the results of the 2005 referendum on the EU Constitutional Treaty can provide some explanations. The causes of the 'no' vote were manifold and have been explored elsewhere.[6] One crucial motivation, however, was the disavowal of a political elite who – with the exception of the Socialist Laurent Fabius and of fringe parties of the Left and Right – had backed the treaty across party lines. Jacques Chirac, Jean-Pierre Raffarin, François Bayrou, François Hollande, Valéry Giscard d'Estaing, Simone Weil, Lionel Jospin, Jacques Delors had all thrown their weight behind the campaign – and were rejected along with the treaty itself. Yet this result should come as no surprise. For years, the elite had made 'Brussels' a scapegoat for domestic inadequacies and dissatisfactions. Their past discourse and behaviour had constantly reminded citizens that Brussels not only remains second in importance to Paris but constitutes an obstacle to the effectiveness of domestic policies. This revealing discourse was summed up by Christine Ockrent (2005) in the formula 'never explain, always complain'. In consequence, the sudden and enthusiastic defence of the European constitution was perceived to be unconvincing and non-credible – as suspicious inconsistency at best and at worst as sheer hypocrisy.

When successive French finance ministers presented the Growth and Stability Pact as damaging to France's economic prosperity; when Prime Minister Raffarin condescendingly alluded to the European Commission as 'this or that office in this or that country', insisting that his main task was to protect jobs and thus implying that 'Brussels' actually destroys them (Jakubyszyn, 2003); when President Chirac treated the 'poorly educated' new member states with open contempt because they 'missed a good opportunity to keep quiet' (Zecchini, 2003); when professional politicians from all sides have shown little interest in standing for European elections and, once elected, only reluctantly show up in Brussels and Strasbourg; when all political parties prefer to draw instant populist benefit by their indignation at the Bolkestein directive; when Europe is held in such little esteem – what can be expected in a referendum? The public could not have failed to notice the discrepancy between France's traditional self-perception as natural leader and driving force of the European integration process and the flagrant narrow-mindedness its leading politicians had shown for this process since the disastrous Nice Treaty presidency. In a society where opinion polls show overwhelming support for European political integration, citizens are perfectly capable of identifying their national leaders' European policy for what it is, namely lip-service.

Thus the European question is a significant illustration of the divorce between French citizens and their politicians. What the public wants from Europe is prosperity and limits on social inequality. What the political elite wants from Europe is a screen on which to project French prestige and an indirect multiplier of power.

Trapped within the prison walls of culture

A number of observers have concluded that the French elite's handling of European issues over the last decade reveals an inability to adapt to a changing world. Alain Minc (2004: 128–30) drew up a list of the skills required to succeed in an EU environment where subtle lobbying and efficient coalition-building have replaced posture and distinction as vectors of power. He argued that 'making Europe into our lever of Archimedes … would presume a radical change in method, a long-term wager based on diligent modesty, knitting networks of complicity and influence but no longer aping the behaviour of a great power – an all too frequent practice for the French', yet he concluded pessimistically that 'for those familiar with the culture of French diplomacy and the behaviour of our administration towards Brussels, this first step can seem impossible'. On the other hand, French corporate actors have proved to be very successful players in the global economy. Zaki Laïdi (2001: xvi–xvii) differentiated between France's economic agents, who 'have adapted remarkably well to globalisation', and political elites, who have developed a 'neurotic relationship with the process of globalisation' by continuing to give 'absolute priority to distinction' and maintaining a 'culture of singularisation'. Likewise Nicolas Baverez (2003: 47) blamed the state elite for bringing France 'to the verge of marginalisation in Europe and in the world' by persisting with a 'discourse of power which is disconnected from its real means of influence and action'.[7] Although this diagnosis has often been made, it has not led to significant changes in attitude. The apparent inability to adapt suggests that the causes for resistance are anchored deep within the national culture. Culturally-specific behaviour patterns do not change overnight, especially if there is no reform of the institutional framework which has rewarded them for generations and continues to reproduce them. Arguably, members of the French political elite can be considered prisoners of the very system which made their success possible in the past. Although the limits of this chapter do not allow for detailed exploration of their cultural prison, an outline description of its four highest walls will be offered.

The first prison wall is Gaullist dogma which forms a cultural legacy shared across party lines, producing a 'tenacious … continuity in obstinate and distinctive ambition' (Hoffmann, 2001: 137). It would be difficult to overestimate the evocative power of the oft-quoted opening sentences of de Gaulle's *Mémoires de Guerre* in which he sets out his mystical idea of France's identity, stating with all his authority that 'France cannot be France without greatness' and claiming that France 'must aim high and hold itself straight on pain of mortal danger' (de Gaulle, 1989: 9). These words have become a mandatory credo for all French politicians, making them – with the possible exception of François Bayrou – Gaullists at heart and Europeans by necessity. The problem is that the Gaullist credo is inseparable from a posture of *grandeur* and the rank-conscious discourse that goes with it. In the context of globalisation and today's European Union, this facet of Gaullism has become counter-productive (Mahoney, 1997).

The second prison wall is the concept of *la République*, which is nothing short of a dogma whose principles must never be called into question by anyone bent on a political career. For the sake of sacrosanct 'Republican values', a coherent process of decentralisation is systematically diluted and slowed down, a policy of integration of so-called 'visible minorities' through 'positive discrimination' is virtually impossible to put into place and attempts to soften the radical secularism of *laïcité* are systematically accused of putting into danger the very basis of French society.[8] The French Republican model is not, of course, without merit. A centralised state may in theory ensure equal access to public services, for instance. And French citizens may be more open to change in these matters than many of their political leaders suspect. But what converts 'Republican values' into a prison wall is the absoluteness with which they are defended in the political discourse. This aggressive stance often comes close to the paranoia characterising nationalist movements who perceive themselves to be beleaguered by ideological enemies. Indeed, the Republican discourse is often labelled 'national republican' and as such is nationalist. It promotes the thesis that the link between democracy and the Jacobin nation state is causal and structural, and not circumstantial and contingent, as the historical evidence indicates (Lacroix, 2004: 33–66; Ferry, 2002: 137–52). According to the dominant preconception, the French ideal-type Republic – even if only imperfectly realised so far – is intrinsically superior to more pragmatist models of democratically organised communities. As a result, it breeds a discourse which 'drips with condescension' (Judt, 2001: 18).

These prison walls are supported by a third, the educational pyramid which breeds – in the best Gaullist and Republican tradition – the elitist attitudes of 'distinction'. As French sociology in the wake of Pierre Bourdieu has shown, the French educational system not only fails to deliver on its egalitarian and meritocratic promises, but increasingly favours social reproduction on a grand scale (Bourdieu, 1979, 1989; Bauer and Bertin-Mourot, 1995, 1997). One of its most striking characteristics is the subtly graduated hierarchy within its constituent elements. It seems that the main purpose of the system is not to educate and award qualifications on the basis of competence or achievements, but to classify in terms of the prestige of the institution attended (Fauconnier, 2005). The elite produced by this system is homogeneous and incestuous to an extent unknown in other developed countries. To quote Tony Judt (2001: 19) again: 'what makes the French elite truly distinctive is a narcissistic fascination with its own uniqueness'. Its legitimacy is based on the intellectual brilliance which has allegedly been proven in a meritocratic competition, but is hardly ever put to the test. However, this legitimacy is limited to the national cultural environment. The French educational system does not provide the type of skills and know-how required to play a role on the international stage. Once the priority is not on establishing vertical hierarchies but excelling in horizontal networks, its limitations are exposed. Michel Crozier (1995: 32–3) wryly noted that 'the Frenchmen who have really marked the world since the Second World War … are Jean Monnet and Jacques Delors who do not belong to this elite'. Yet during a recent television vote on the 'Greatest Frenchman of all time', neither of them figured on the list of 100 candidates proposed to viewers.

The fourth prison wall is the least visible because it originates further back in time than the emergence of Gaullism, the design of the educational system or the definition of Republican principles. The incapacity to redefine prestige by giving priority to 'role' above 'rank' is firmly rooted in cultural codes, aesthetic norms, social rituals and behavioural patterns that were shaped under the *ancien régime* (Iribarne, 2006). The cultural legacy of the 'court society' as meticulously described by Norbert Elias (1983) accounts to a significant extent for the French obsession with distinction, hierarchy and rank. Its organising principle is 'refinement' – in arts and letters, of the senses, of taste in all meanings of the term, of elegance and *esprit* in interpersonal relations. Just how much of these cultural codes, norms and rituals survived the tempest of the Revolution is observable in contemporary French society. Much has been written about the monarchic features of the Fifth Republic: the regal status of its president, the courtesan atmosphere in Parisian circles of political and media power, the aristocratic heritage and aura of the places of power themselves, the pharaonic architecture of Mitterrand's *grands projets* (prestige projects). The same legacy is visible in the economic sphere, not only in the global leadership enjoyed by the French luxury goods industry (in fashion, jewellery, perfumes, wines and spirits) and which is based on the same refinement of taste that reached its zenith in eighteenth-century Versailles, but also in economic policy where the protectionist heritage of Colbertism is still alive. The discourse of 'economic patriotism', the insistence on 'national champions', the massive state support given to prestige projects such as Concorde and Airbus, the TGV (*train à grande vitesse* – high speed train) and the nuclear industry all bear witness to national ambitions of distinction. Even within the everyday business environment, the findings of intercultural management studies by Trompenaars (1993) and Iribarne (1989) have highlighted dominant behavioural patterns – such as deference to hierarchy – that can be traced to the codes of rank and prestige inherent in the court society. Thus the continuing influence of pre-revolutionary cultural norms and values is crucial to understanding the adaptation difficulties of contemporary French society.

The Dutch anthropologist Geert Hofstede (1991: 23–6) developed an 'onion model' of culture. Applied to the French case, the 'prison walls' formed by Gaullist dogma, Republican principles and an elitist education system form successive outside layers. But the legacy of the court society lies at very heart of French national culture. Because its values are absorbed and internalised very early in the socialisation process, they remain largely resistant to change both for the individual and society at large.

Conclusions

The 'prison wall' model provides a tentative explanation of the persistent French tendency to favour 'rank' and inefficient prestige politics over a more modest but perhaps more influential 'role'. This preference is not just some political strategy gone wrong, but a burdensome heritage for the twenty-first century. Values do change, but very slowly, and mostly through exposure to influences from the exterior – though not by grafting an Anglo-American model onto a culture that could only reject it for reasons of profound incompatibility. Ways out of the cultural prison exist. The Europeanisation of an increasing number of policy fields and the irreversible internationalisation of French higher education allow for prudent optimism. If pressures for European convergence continue to act on French policy-making, if the future French elite can no longer succeed within France without having acquired international experience, then attitudes and behaviour patterns are likely to evolve over time.

Even the proponents of the current 'declinology' agree that France has the capacity to rebound and reinvent itself. The key to recovering an appropriate role on the world stage – and even outside France one might agree that the world is better off when France plays a major role – is cultural change, rather than just an adjustment of social and economic policies. The Parisian circle of the political elite would do well to remember de Gaulle's own premonitions, noted by his loyal companion André Malraux: *'la grandeur* – that's over and done' (Malraux, 1971: 41). Only when freed from the obsession with greatness and rank may the second part of the same quotation also come true: 'Oh! France may again surprise the world; but at another time'.

Notes

1. Said on the 21 April 2005 during the television programme '100 minutes to convince', broadcast by France 2.
2. For example, see Baverez (2003), Duhamel (2003), Rouart (2003), Julliard (2005) and Lellouche (2006). The twentieth anniversary issue of the journal *Commentaire* (Spring 1998) included over forty pessimistic contributions on 'the situation of France'.
3. Details can be found at http://www.fci.gouv.fr.
4. The quotation is from the preamble to the *Charte de la francophonie* and can be found at http://www.francophonie.org/doc/txt-reference/charte_francophonie.pdf.
5. The trophy carried the name of its founder, Jules Rimet, for almost half a century.
6. See Fondation Jean Jaurès (2005), and Binet (Chapter 7) and Startin (Chapter 6) in this volume.
7. For similar criticisms, see Gauchet and Rémond (2006: 5) and Lanxade and Tenzer (2002: 113–19).

8. The principle of *'laïcité'* involves a strict separation of public life and the sphere of religion. Its most publicised effect is the ban on the wearing of highly visible religious insignia in state secondary schools. It has had a particular impact on Muslim girls wishing to wear a headscarf, but has also affected other religious groups.

References

Amalou, F. (2003) 'La création d'une CNN à la française accélérée', *Le Monde*, 22 April.

Bauer, M. and B. Bertin-Mourot (1995) *L'Accès au sommet des grandes entreprises françaises*, Paris: Boyden.

Bauer, M. and B. Bertin-Mourot (1997) 'La triple exception française. À propos de la formation des elites', *Esprit* (October): 47–59.

Baverez, N. (2003) *La France qui tombe*, Paris: Perrin.

Boniface, P. (1998) *La France est-elle encore une grande puissance?*, Paris: Presses de Sciences Po.

Bourdieu, P. (1979) *La Distinction*, Paris: Editions de Minuit.

Bourdieu, P. (1989) *La Noblesse d'Etat*, Paris: Editions de Minuit.

Caldwell, C. (2000) 'Védrinism: France's global ambition', *Foreign Policy*, 103 (October–November): 19–32.

Chirac, J. (2007) 'Déclaration télévisée, dimanche 11 mars 2007', http://www.elysee.fr/elysee/elysee.fr/francais_archives/actualites/a_1_elysee/2007/mars/declaration_televisee_du_president_de_la_republique.73970.html, consulted 20 May 2007.

Crozier, M. (1995) *La Crise de l'intelligence*, Paris: InterEditions.

Dauncey, H. and G. Hare (eds) (1998) *France and the 1998 World Cup*, London: Frank Cass.

De Gaulle, C. (1989) *Mémoires de guerre*, Paris: Plon.

Duhamel, O. (2003) *Le Désarroi français*, Paris: Plon.

Elias, N. (1983) *The Court Society*, Oxford: Blackwell.

Fauconnier, P. (2005) *La Fabrique des meilleurs*, Paris: Seuil.

Ferry, J.-M. (2002) 'La référence républicaine au défi de l'Europe', *Pouvoirs*, 100 (January): 137–52.

Fondation Jean Jaurès (eds) (2005) *Le Jour où la France a dit non*, Paris: Plon.

Gauchet, M. and R. Rémond (2006) 'Le temps du marasme', *Le Débat*, 131 (September–October): 4–22.

Gordon, P. (2000) 'The French position', *The National Interest* (Fall 2000): 57–65.

Grosser, A. (1992) 'Le rôle et le rang', *Commentaire*, 58 (Summer): 361–5.

Hoffmann, S. (2001) 'Classic diplomacy in the information age', *Foreign Affairs* (July–August): 137–42.

Hofstede, G. (1991) *Cultures and Organisations: Software of the Mind*, London: McGraw-Hill.

Iribarne, P. d' (1989) *La Logique de l'honneur*, Paris: Seuil.

Iribarne, P. d' (2006) *L'Etrangeté française*, Paris: Seuil.

Jakubyszyn, C. (2003) 'M. Raffarin prend le risque d'un affrontement avec L'Europe', *Le Monde*, 7 September.

Judt, T. (2001) 'The French Difference', *The New York Review of Books*, 12 April, 18–21.

Julliard, J. (2005) *Le Malheur français*, Paris: Flammarion.

Lacroix, J. (2004) *L'Europe en procès*, Paris: Les Editions du Cerf.

Laïdi, Z. (2001) *Un Monde privé de sens*, Paris: Hachette.

Lanxade, J. and N. Tenzer (2002) *Organiser la politique européenne et internationale de la France*, Paris: La documentation française.

Lellouche, P. (2006) *Illusions gauloises*, Paris: Grasset.

Leonard, M. (2002) *Public Diplomacy*, London: The Foreign Policy Centre.

Mahoney, D. (1997) 'De Gaulle and the death of Europe', *The National Interest* (Summer): 46–56.

Malraux, A. (1971) *Les Chênes qu'on abat*, Paris: Gallimard.

Minc, A. (2004) *Ce Monde qui vient*, Paris: Grasset.

Nye, J. (1990a) 'Soft power', *Foreign Policy* (Autumn): 153–69.

Nye, J. (1990b) *Bound to Lead*, New York: Basic Books.

Ockrent, C. (2005) 'The price of arrogance', *International Herald Tribune*, 23 April.

Rouart, J.-M. (2003) *Adieu à la France qui s'en va*, Paris: Grasset.

Sonntag, A. (2006) 'Grandes Ecoles und Classes Préparatoires unter Globalisierungsdruck', in Deutsch-französisches Institut (ed.), *Frankreich-Jahrbuch 2005*, Wiesbaden: Verlag für Sozialwissenschaften, pp. 121–38.

Sonntag, A. (2007) 'Sommernachtsträume', in Deutsch-französisches Institut (ed.), *Frankreich-Jahrbuch 2006*, Wiesbaden: Verlag für Sozialwissenschaften, pp. 257–78.

Trompenaars, F. (1993) *Riding the Waves of Culture*, London: Economist Books.

Védrine, H. (1998) 'L'autre grandeur', *Le Nouvel Observateur*, 28 May.

Védrine, H. (2001) *France in an Age of Globalization*, Washington: Brookings Institution.

Védrine, H. (2002) 'Nous ne sommes pas une puissance moyenne', *Le Figaro*, 6 February.

Zecchini, L. (2003) 'M. Chirac fustige les pays candidats "pas très bien élevés" trop prompts à soutenir Washington', *Le Monde*, 19 February.

6
The French Rejection of the 2005 EU Constitution in a Global Context: a Public Opinion Perspective

Nicholas Startin

Introduction

The French electorate's decision to reject the proposed constitution of the European Union (EU) on 29 May 2005 came as something of a shock to many commentators in France, despite the fact that the majority of opinion polls in the run up to the referendum appeared to indicate that the 'no' vote would be victorious. As one of the founding members of the EU, France has always been a country that has taken its European credentials seriously. From the outset, the country's political elites have been at the forefront of closer European cooperation; and in a country which has spawned Europhiles such as Jean Monnet, Robert Schuman, François Mitterrand and Jacques Delors, it seemed almost unthinkable that France would be the first of the EU's 25 nation states to say 'no' to the constitution. However, faced with the realities of the ballot box, the French electorate rejected the constitution with 54.87 per cent voting 'no'.

In reality, the result should not have come as any great surprise. The writing had been on the wall since the Maastricht referendum back in 1992, where the very narrow margin of the 'yes' victory (just over 51 per cent in favour) indicated that French citizens did not entirely share the pro-European enthusiasm of France's mainstream political elites and the bulk of its media. This, in spite of the fact that three past and future presidents from each of the three main parties (Giscard d'Estaing, François Mitterrand and Jacques Chirac) had endorsed Maastricht. With hindsight, the 1992 Maastricht referendum acted as something of a turning-point in France, a watershed in terms of raising the profile of a previously dormant issue (namely opposition to the EU) in the domestic political arena. This in turn led to the galvanisation of Eurosceptics on both the Left and the Right of the political spectrum, which only served to reinforce the perceived 'gap' between France's pro-EU political leaders and a less than, on the face of it, Eurocentric electorate. In this context, it is no surprise that neither the introduction of the euro nor the 2004 EU enlargement were put to a referendum of the French people by President Chirac. Nor was it really a shock that the 'no' vote was victorious in the 2005 referendum on the EU constitution.

The real significance of the 'no' vote in France in 2005, however, is that it reveals more about French voters' concerns and anxieties about what they perceive as the negative socio-economic and cultural consequences of globalisation than it does about public attitudes towards the European Union per se. Cambadélis (2005: 26) sums up the prevailing mood in France: 'Faced with globalisation which is giving nation states a real pounding, France wanted to go back home and hide ...' The outcome of the 2005 referendum marks the moment when the French electorate's perception of the EU became inextricably linked to the wider global economy, and with it the dominance of the neo-liberal model. Pascale Lamy (2005: 24), former French Socialist politician and the Director General of the World Trade Organisation (WTO), summed up this feeling of *malaise* or unease among France's citizens by stating that the referendum demonstrated 'anxiety about the transformation taking place in the global economy' and the 'existence of a growing demand for protectionist measures against the uncertainties caused by economic globalisation, which is often felt to be a threat rather than an opportunity'. Growing public hostility towards globalisation on the part of the French populace raises a fundamental ideological question for France's pro-EU political elites concerning the nature of this uneasy *ménage à trois* that is France, the EU and globalisation: how to convince the public that the EU can operate as a 'counterbalance' to some of globalisation's perceived negative socio-economic consequences rather than as a reinforcing 'agent' of global capitalism? A failure to persuade French voters that the EU can act as a positive force in a global context, a pragmatic 'go-between' capable of softening the impact of globalisation on the French social model, could have major consequences for the current French political class, the stability of the Fifth Republic and the future direction of the EU.

Focusing primarily on the 2005 referendum on the EU constitution, this chapter explores the nature of this uneasy *ménage à trois*, and demonstrates that this troubled triangular relationship is rapidly becoming a major line of political conflict in France, which divides the mainstream parties such as the Parti Socialiste (PS) and the Union pour un Mouvement Populaire (UMP), sets them apart from those on both the far-left and the far-right, and splits voters demographically along clear, class-based lines of socio-economic status. The chapter begins with an overview of the 2005 referendum campaign, and illustrates that the 'no' campaign was dominated by what we refer to as 'socio-economic issues linked to the wider global context' as opposed to traditional Eurosceptic or pro-sovereignty concerns.[1] Drawing on Eurobarometer and national data, the chapter then demonstrates that 'no' voters were largely influenced by issues relating to the socio-economic global context in their decision to reject the constitution, before leading into a socio-demographic and geographic analysis of the 2005 'no' voter, which reinforces the primacy of the socio-economic argument. Finally, we explore the debate surrounding France, the EU, the constitution and globalisation two years on, arguing that opposition to globalisation has, if anything, hardened since the May 2005 referendum, and that the French electorate is discontented with the EU's perceived lack of progress in facing up to some of its negative socio-economic consequences.

Dominant issues in the French referendum campaign on the EU constitution

Jacques Chirac informed the French public of his decision to hold a referendum on the EU constitution during his annual Bastille Day speech on 14 July 2004. With the referendum taking place on 29 May 2005, this ensured that the debate stayed salient within the French media for nigh on a year. Once the campaign proper commenced, the polls, which had initially predicted a victory for the 'yes' vote, quickly began to tell a different story, with the 'no' campaign soon in the ascendancy. In party political terms, supporters of the 'no' campaign were diverse and, in the main, on the fringes of the political spectrum. On the Left, the Communist party, the far-left Lutte Ouvrière (LO) and Ligue Communiste Révolutionnaire (LCR), a significant faction of the Socialist Party fronted by Laurent Fabius and a significant number of Greens were in the 'no' camp.[2] On the Right, a faction in favour of the 'no' vote emerged from within the ranks of the UMP, organised by the *souverainiste* 'Debout la République' think-tank, and fronted by the National Assembly member for *Essonne*, Nicolas Dupont-Aignan. The pro-sovereignty position was also represented by the former Presidential candidate Philippe de Villiers and his Mouvement pour la France (MPF) party, as well as by the remnants of Charles Pasqua's neo-Gaullist, pro-sovereignty Rassemblement pour la

France (RPF). Also, the rurally-dominated Chasse, Pêche, Nature et Traditions (CPNT) called for a 'no' vote, while on the far-right, Jean-Marie Le Pen's Front National (FN) was vehemently opposed to the constitution.

In essence, the theme which united those campaigning against the constitution across the French political spectrum was that of the uncertainties posed by the wider issue of France's changing role in a global context, and, more specifically, the negative socio-economic impact and cultural consequences of globalisation for France's economic and political future. Much debate centred on the perceived threat posed by the contents of the constitution to France's social model, with EU enlargement and its implications for future unemployment and immigration flows a key issue in the campaign. The constitution was vehemently portrayed as neo-liberal and Anglo-Saxon, and a threat to the very fabric of the French welfare state. As part of this threat, the Bolkenstein directive, permitting free movement of services within the EU (although not actually mentioned in the text of the constitution) was effectively deployed as a campaign tactic by supporters of the 'no' vote from across the political spectrum. This drew on voters' fears of the perceived risk of an influx of workers from the new EU member states, as symbolised by the fictitious 'Polish plumber' who would undercut the prices of a typical French plumber. As Cambadélis (2005) points out, this 'effectively placed the issues of deregulation, social dumping and the foreigner in the same bracket'. Related to this, *délocalisations*, where large companies transfer production to low-wage economies in search of cheap labour, were constantly cited as a threat to the French model, and a core reason to reject the constitution; the numerous examples of the relocation of French companies which emerged during the campaign struck a chord with the electorate. The slogan adopted by the LCR, 'our lives are worth more than our profits', captured the imagination of more than just voters on the far left. With unemployment persistently hovering around the 10 per cent mark in France under governments of both Left and Right, and as high as 25 per cent among voters under 25, the campaign was also portrayed in some circles as a retrospective judgement on respective governments' inabilities to reduce the nation's persistently high rate of joblessness. From a global context, this issue was symbolised by the debate about the cheap importing of Chinese textiles within the EU. Allied to this, the debate surrounding the '35 hour week' and its reform by the UMP government played an important role, with advocates of reduced working time, such as France's major trade union, the Confédération Générale du travail (CGT), arguing that the EU constitution would threaten this fundamental right, successfully fought for by the union on behalf of French workers.

Underpinning all of the above issues from a global context was the question of EU enlargement, both retrospectively and in terms of potential future developments. France had been alone among the EU-15 countries with a majority of respondents opposed to the 2004 enlargement, according to a Eurobarometer 2003 poll (see Table 6.1), and the feeling seemed to develop during the campaign that the 2004 'big bang' enlargement had taken place without proper consultation of the French public.

Allied to the economic consequences, enlargement raised questions in France about security, asylum and borders, issues which opponents of EU enlargement had been quick to exploit from the moment the 10 new states were given the green light for 2004, and which remained constant themes in the campaign, particularly for the far-right FN. The referendum debate was made more controversial by the prospect of Turkish accession to the EU (see Chapter 7 by Laurent Binet). This remained an emotive issue throughout the campaign (particularly on the Right of the political spectrum), and was persistently opposed by the Christian Democrat centre-right UDF, leading Gaullists such as Alain Juppé, as well

Table 6.1   Respondents in favour of EU enlargement by country (EU-15) (%)

Country	For EU enlargement	Against EU enlargement
Greece	71	19
Denmark	63	25
Spain	60	17
Republic of Ireland	60	19
Portugal	60	22
Italy	59	22
Sweden	56	34
Luxembourg	53	40
Finland	50	40
Holland	48	38
EU-15	46	35
Austria	43	44
Germany	42	39
Belgium	38	44
UK	36	36
France	31	54

Source: Eurobarometer EB 59 (2003).

as by the leadership of the FN. Objections ranged from concern about a non-Christian country joining the EU to the cultural consequences of Turkish membership.

Scrutiny of the referendum campaign reveals that the core arguments espoused by those campaigning against the constitution were based around a broad unease with, and uncertainty towards, France's role in the global economy, rather than traditional Eurosceptic arguments based on hostility towards the EU. True, general pro-sovereignty arguments relating to a loss of French identity were put forward as a justification for rejecting the constitution by right-wing populists such as Phillipe de Villiers, but on the whole such issues were secondary features of the campaign. As with all referenda, 'domestic protest' factors also played their part, and did affect the campaign to some extent. A decade ago, Schneider and Weitsman (1996) described referenda on European integration as possible 'punishment traps', where governments and leaders expose themselves to punishment by voters for poor economic performance or general unpopularity, and just as in 1992 when some voters wanted to give Mitterrand a bloody nose, in 2005 the anti-Chirac factor a decade into his presidency, combined with a general anti-government and anti-political corruption sentiment, served to harden the electorate's hostility towards the constitution. Added to this, there was the length and inaccessibility of the text itself. As Marthaler (2005: 10) points out: 'it was an over-long, highly complex and ambiguous text, associated in the minds of many left-wing voters with former right-wing president Giscard d'Estaing, a factor which certainly played a part during the campaign'. Overall though, in campaign terms, it is worth reiterating that the domestic protest factor and traditional Eurosceptic concerns were secondary to the issues identified relating to the socio-economic global context; this is borne out by an analysis of the motivations of 'no' voters in the 2005 referendum.

The motivations of 'no' voters at the referendum on the EU constitution

The findings of the Eurobarometer Flash survey (EB171) conducted shortly after the referendum reveal the primacy of socio-economic concerns, clearly linkable to France's role in a global context, as the predominant motivation among 'no' voters. Faced with the question, 'What were the reasons you voted "no" at the referendum on the European constitution?', 31 per cent indicated the option that 'the constitution would have negative effects on the unemployment situation', 26 per cent that 'the economic situation in France was too weak', 19 per cent that 'economically speaking the draft was too liberal', and 16 per cent mentioned 'the absence of enough social Europe' (see Table 6.2).

Traditional Eurosceptic concerns elicited low levels of response, with just 5 per cent identifying 'a loss of national sovereignty', and only 4 per cent citing 'anti-Europe/European integration sentiment' as a reason for rejecting the constitution; the low percentage of respondents identifying with these two latter responses suggests that opposition to the EU per se was not a major motivation for 'no' voters. Away from socio-economic issues linked to the wider global context, the domestic protest context of the referendum was identified by 18 per cent of respondents, perhaps a surprisingly low figure given the unpopularity of Chirac and de Villepin and the centre-right government. The complexity of the treaty and a lack of information were cited by 12 per cent and 5 per cent respectively, which, given the constant coverage in the media throughout the campaign surrounding the length and inaccessibility of the text, were not significant percentages. The findings of the Eurobarometer post-referendum survey in France, which clearly suggest that socio-economic issues relating to the global context were the chief motivation among 'no' voters, is in contrast to the findings of the post-electoral survey (EB172) conducted in the Netherlands, where the major reason cited by Dutch voters for rejecting the treaty in their referendum of June 2005 was a 'lack of information on the constitution' (32 per cent), followed by more traditionally Eurosceptic concerns such as

Table 6.2   What are the reasons why you voted 'no' at the French referendum on the European constitution? (Responses of 5% or more)

It will have negative effects on the employment situation in France/relocation of French enterprises/loss of jobs	31
The economic situation in France is too weak/there is too much unemployment in France	26
Economically speaking, the draft is too liberal	19
Oppose the president of the Republic/the national government/certain political parties	18
Not enough social Europe	16
Treaty too complex	12
Opposed to Turkey in the European Union	6
A loss of national sovereignty	5
A lack of information	5

Source: Eurobarometer (EB171) (2005).

a 'loss of national sovereignty' (19 per cent), 'Europe being too expensive' (13 per cent) and 'opposition to European integration' (8 per cent). 'Socio-economic issues related to the global context' were much less predominant in the Netherlands, with only 7 per cent of Dutch voters stating that the constitution would have 'negative effects on unemployment', and 5 per cent mentioning both that the 'economic situation in the Netherlands was too weak' and that the 'draft was too liberal economically'.

The predominance of 'socio-economic issues related to the global context' also emerges among French 'no' voters from an analysis of the IPSOS exit poll (see Table 6.3).

Faced with eight different answers, and given the liberty to choose as many responses as possible, the two which elicited the greatest response confirm similar findings to the Eurobarometer EB171 poll. 'Discontent with France's economic situation' was cited by over half of the 'no' voters (52 per cent), while 'the constitution being too liberal economically' was mentioned by two-fifths. Furthermore, the third most popular response (it would allow a 'better constitution to be negotiated') was mentioned by 39 per cent, which, given the context of the referendum campaign, would appear to imply a text that was not a neo-liberal Anglo-Saxon one. As many as 35 per cent of respondents identified opposition to Turkish entry, a significantly higher percentage than in the Eurobarometer poll. Similarly to the Eurobarometer survey, traditional Eurosceptic concerns and 'domestic protest grievances' did not feature as predominantly. As many as 32 per cent answered that they were motivated to vote 'no' because 'the constitution represents a threat to French identity', while just over a quarter (27 per cent) cited 'the process of European cooperation as being negative for France', which, given the liberty to choose all responses, was not an overwhelming score. Furthermore, a cross-tabulation of these two responses reveals that of the 32 per cent who identified 'the constitution as a threat to French identity', 81 per cent also cited 'the process of European integration as being negative for France'. With regard to domestic protest grievances, these were mentioned by 31 per cent and 24 per cent of 'no' voters respectively; again, a cross-tabulation reveals that 76 per cent of voters who mentioned that they wanted 'to manifest discontent towards the whole political class' also mentioned that 'it was the right moment to show opposition to the government and to Jacques Chirac'. Overall, the IPSOS data backs up the findings of the Eurobarometer poll, and confirms that socio-economic issues relating to the global context acted as the major motivating force for rejecting the Constitutional Treaty.

Table 6.3   The motivations of 'no' voters at the 2005 referendum on the EU constitution by party (%)

What were the main reasons, from the following list, why you decided to vote 'no' to the EU constitution?	Total	PCF	PS	Verts	UDF	UMP	FN	No party preference
You are discontented with the current socio-economic situation in France	52	57	54	59	63	40	54	40
The constitution is too liberal in economic terms	40	57	49	50	30	35	18	45
It will allow a better constitution to be renegotiated	39	44	47	55	38	48	17	36
It's the right moment to oppose Turkish entry of the EU	35	23	26	16	44	56	56	37
The constitution represents a threat to France's national identity	32	20	22	22	40	38	44	36
You wanted to manifest your discontent towards the whole political class	31	29	31	31	31	26	26	40
The process of closer European cooperation has been negative for France	27	26	25	27	32	27	29	24
It is the right moment to show opposition to the government and to Jacques Chirac	24	22	26	15	23	11	38	19
No response	2	2	2	2	–	2	3	3

Source: http://www.ipsos.fr/CanalIpsos/poll/8074.asp#04.

A demographic and geographic breakdown of 2005 'no' voters and the link to socio-economic status

A socio-demographic breakdown of two national French exit polls allows us to strengthen the argument further. Analysis reveals that the 'no' vote was particularly prominent statistically among those from socio-economically disadvantaged backgrounds, those on low incomes, the unemployed and those with low levels of education. This is significant on two levels: first, it is the electorate potentially most at risk from the negative economic consequences of globalisation; and second, according to polls, it is the electorate most concerned by globalisation and its impact on France (see EB251).

At the time of the 1992 Maastricht referendum in France, Duhamel and Grunberg (1993: 79) observed the beginning of a similar demographic trend, and noted the existence of '*deux France sociologiques*', concluding that the 'no' vote predominated among those from socio-economic disadvantaged backgrounds often with low levels of educational qualifications. Analyses of the SOFRES exit polls from the 1992 and 2005 referenda indicate that the correlation between the 'no' vote and class status has widened in France (see Figure 6.1).

According to the 1992 SOFRES exit poll, 57 per cent of those without any qualifications voted 'no'. Data from the same polling company reveal that 79 per cent of those without formal qualifications rejected the Constitutional Treaty, a 22 per cent swing in this socio-demographic category, compared to an overall swing of roughly 7 per cent to the 'no' vote.

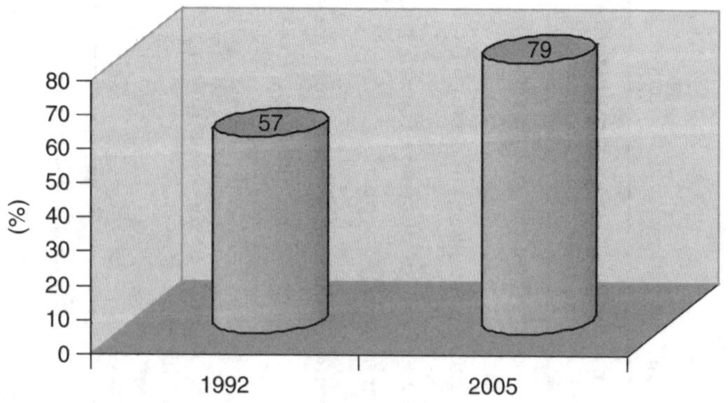

Figure 6.1   Percentage of 'no' votes among respondents without formal qualifications at 1992 Maastricht and 2005 EU constitution referenda
Sources: SOFRES (1992) and TNS/SOFRES (2005).

The polarisation of the 'no' vote around socio-economic status is further demonstrated by the data with regard to manual workers. Back in 1992, according to the SOFRES exit poll, 58 per cent of French manual workers had rejected the Maastricht Treaty. By 2005 this figure had leapt to 81 per cent, a 23 per cent swing (see Figure 6.2).

Similar percentages with regard to manual workers are to be found in both the 2005 IPSOS exit poll and the Eurobarometer post-referendum survey, with 79 per cent and 78 per cent of workers rejecting the Constitutional Treaty according to the respective data. The three polls all confirm a similar story with regard to the strength of the 'no' vote among manual workers at the 2005 referendum. Further evidence of the link between the 'no' vote and socio-economic status is also evident from an analysis of the unemployed vote in France. A very significant percentage of unemployed voters rejected the constitution (71 per cent and 79 per cent according to the respective IPSOS and SOFRES exit polls). Analysis of the farming vote in France also confirms the polarisation of the 'no' vote in traditional socio-economic class terms. According to the 2005 IPSOS exit poll, 70 per cent of French farmers voted against the constitution, well above the national average, whereas 57 per cent of rural voters as a whole rejected the constitution, only 2 per cent higher than the overall national result.

This link between the 'no' vote and socio-economic status in France is further underlined by a geographical analysis of the 2005 referendum result. Evidence from the referendum statistics published by the

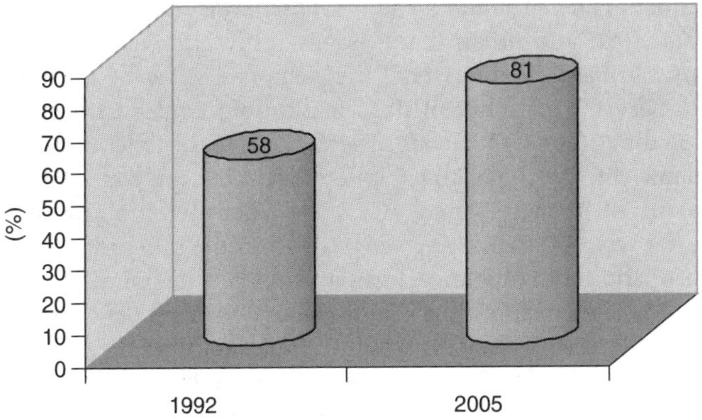

Figure 6.2   Percentage of 'no' votes among manual workers at 1992 Maastricht and 2005 EU constitution referenda
Sources: SOFRES (1992) and TNS/SOFRES (2005).

French Ministry for the Interior clearly demonstrates that the 'no' vote was more pronounced in France's socio-economically deprived suburbs (the *banlieues déshéritées*), while the 'yes' vote was more prominent in France's more affluent urban areas (the *communes bourgeoises*). A brief survey of the 25 communes where the 'no' vote in France was higher than 70 per cent shows how, in nearly all cases, it reaches its uppermost proportions in urban communes experiencing socio-economic deprivation and high levels of unemployment, such as the former mining areas of the North (Liévin, Hénin Beaumont and Lens), northern French ports (Calais, Dunkerque and Grande Synthe), the three most disadvantaged *arrondissements* of Marseilles, and Parisian suburbs like Bobigny and Goussainville.

Boy and Chiche (2005) point out that, with the exception of Grand and Petit Quevilly (Rouen's industrial centre close to the Seine), where former Socialist Prime Minister and prominent 'no campaigner' Laurent Fabius is deputy mayor, the majority of these communes are either former Communist and/or current FN urban strongholds. No real surprises there, as the Eurobarometer post-election survey reveals that the 'no' vote in France was particularly prominent on the political margins in terms of party affiliation, with 94 per cent of Communist and 95 per cent of FN voters rejecting the treaty, in line with their parties' recommendations. The IPSOS exit poll reveals similar findings, with 98 per cent rejection of the constitution from Communist voters and 93 per cent from FN voters.

In contrast, the 20 *communes* in France where the 'no' vote was less than 30 per cent reads like an estate agent's paradise, a roll-call of exclusive affluent Parisian suburbs and *arrondissements* where property prices have spiralled, and urban living is now only affordable by the most wealthy.[3] In Paris, where overall the electorate voted by 66.5 per cent to 33.6 per cent in favour of the constitution, contrast the difference between the affluent 7th *arrondissement* (home to the Eiffel Tower), where less than a fifth (19.5 per cent) of voters rejected the constitution, and the suburb of Bobigny, where 72.17 per cent voted 'no'. Examination of the 'no' vote in contrasting *cantons* within the same region, in both the north and south of France, further illustrates the point. In the Nord-Pas-de-Calais, for example, nearly three-quarters (74.4 per cent) of those who voted in the working-class port of Calais rejected the constitution, while in the nearby, well-to-do holiday resort of Le Touquet less than a third (32.5 per cent) did so. In the south, in the Provence-Cote-d'Azur region, the percentage of 'no' votes in Marseille's socio-economically disadvantaged 15th *arrondissement* was 78.6 per cent, compared to 45.1 per cent in nearby affluent Aix-en-Provence. Both the socio-economic and geographical data clearly indicate a polarisation of the 'no' vote along socio-economic lines. As Tiberj (2005: 49) sums up: 'the lower down the social ladder the voter, the more likely his or her chances of voting no'.

France, the EU and globalisation

An analysis of the 2005 referendum on the Constitutional Treaty in France indicates that the issues that both dominated the campaign and influenced electors in their rejection of the constitution were first and foremost socio-economic concerns linked to France's role in a wider global context. The electorate made the link between a macroeconomic threat to the French social model and a microeconomic threat to their own job security in an enlarged EU, and these central issues became increasingly salient as the 'no' campaign (on both sides of the political spectrum) was able to provide examples (real or perceived) of the dangers ahead for the French: the threat of *délocalisations*, social dumping, the arrival of Polish plumbers, the importation of Chinese textiles and the Bolkenstein directive all served to add to the saliency of the 'no' campaign's message by relating these threats to the wider global economic context. Tiberj (2005: 49–50) argues that in essence the 'no' vote on the Left was largely socio-economic and on the Right that it was largely *souverainiste* driven. In reality, the 'no' vote does not compartmentalise that easily around the traditional Left/Right axis (see Table 6.3). According to the IPSOS exit poll, a higher percentage of centre-right UDF 'no' voters (63 per cent) identified dissatisfaction with the current economic situation in France than Communists (57 per cent) or Socialists (54 per cent). Admittedly, the second most popular response from 'no' voters in this survey ('the constitution is too liberal in economic terms') did fall more neatly in line with the expectations of party politics, gaining a greater response from 'no' voters supporting parties on the Left than on the Right. Similarly, the Eurosceptic response, 'the process of closer European integration has been negative for France', did in percentage terms invite a greater response from 'no' voters supporting parties on the Right. However, if we take the three main parties of the Right (the UDF, the UMP and the FN) as a whole, a higher percentage of respondents from these three parties cited economic discontent as a motivation for rejecting the Constitutional Treaty than either a threat to French identity or a perception of European integration in negative terms. In reality 'no' voters in general from across the political spectrum were primarily motivated by socio-economic issues relating to France's global context rather than by opposition to the European Union per se. This is reflected by public opinion data following the 2005 referendum.

Continuing opposition to globalisation in France is clear from various polls, which demonstrate first that a majority of French people are uneasy with or hostile towards globalisation; second, that this opposition is continuing to rise; and third, that France is the country within the EU which is the most concerned about the effects of economic globalisation. An IPSOS poll from April 2005, conducted a month before the referendum on the Constitutional Treaty, revealed that 54 per cent of respondents had a negative view of globalisation (a rise of 3 per cent compared with 2004), while only 39 per cent had a positive view (a decline of 4 per cent compared with 2004). In the same 2005 poll more respondents agreed that globalisation was 'mainly a bad thing for France' (47 per cent) than 'a good thing' (45 per cent). Six months on from the referendum, according to a December 2005 BVA poll, attitudes showed no signs of shifting amongst the French electorate, with only 38 per cent of respondents citing globalisation as 'a source of hope' compared to 52 per cent who see it as 'a source of concern'.

Clear evidence that opposition to globalisation continues to rise in France is evident from the CSA tracker poll, *Les Français et la mondialisation*. Here the percentage of respondents answering either that globalisation inspires 'uncertainty' or 'hostility' has risen across five data sets from 66 per cent in July 2001 to 74 per cent in December 2005 (see Figure 6.3).

The proportion of those expressing 'enthusiasm' or 'confidence' in globalisation has declined to a mere 12 per cent. With regard to French

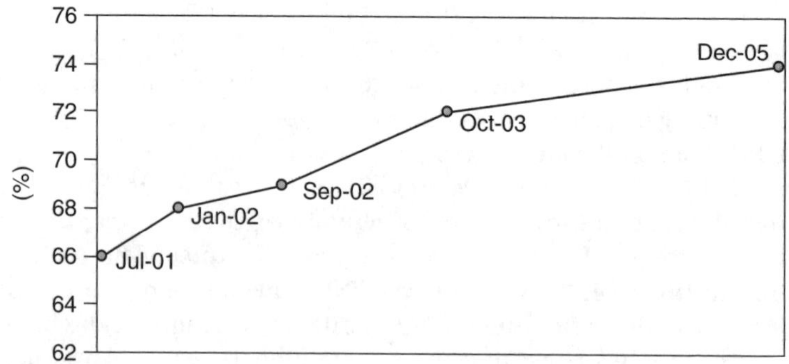

Figure 6.3 Percentage of respondents either 'uncertain' or 'hostile' to globalisation
Source: CSA (2005).

attitudes compared to other countries, an international survey conducted by Globalscan confirms that only 36 per cent of French respondents agreed with the statement 'opening the free market to globalisation is the best way forward for the future'. This compares with 74 per cent of American, 71 per cent of Italian, 67 per cent of British, 65 per cent of German and 63 per cent of Spanish respondents, placing France clearly at odds with its main EU partners and the USA in its attitudes towards the global economy. This unease with globalisation compared to other EU countries is borne out by the findings of the Eurobarometer survey (EB251) published in April 2006, where 72 per cent of French respondents agreed that 'globalisation represents a threat to employment and companies in our country', the most opposed of all the EU-25 countries at the time, and 25 per cent above the EU average. Conversely, only 21 per cent responded that 'globalisation represents a good opportunity for national companies thanks to the opening up of markets', the least in favour of the EU-25 countries and 16 per cent behind the EU average. This growing hostility towards globalisation in France (which is across the political spectrum), and this marked opposition towards it among the French public compared to other EU countries, is largely based around a desire to protect the French social model and to reject the neo-liberal global economic model. It is reinforced from a cultural perspective by the fact that many French voters see anti-Americanism and anti-globalisation as one and the same, which has served to harden anti-globalisation sentiment in France. Growing feelings of anxiety (*insécurité*) on three levels (the personal-physical dimension, the international terror dimension, and the socio-economic dimension identified in this study) have also contributed to this increasingly anti-global sense of unease pervading France. Set in this context, the riots in the Parisian suburbs in autumn 2005 (see Chapter 13 by Gino Raymond), and the demonstrations against the *contrat première embauche* (the youth job contract), designed to reduce youth unemployment, in spring 2006, are products of a growing sense of alienation within the French public, particularly among those from socio-economically disadvantaged backgrounds.

Significantly, the 2005 referendum on the EU constitution in France marks the moment when a majority of the French public was no longer prepared to support the argument of mainstream political elites, namely that France's political and economic destiny in the global economy are necessarily linked to a positive approach towards the EU. The French electorate are clearly divided about the EU's ability to act as a 'go-between' or a 'counterbalance' to some of the perceived negative economic consequences of globalisation. An IPSOS poll conducted in April 2005 (just prior to the referendum) found that 47 per cent felt that European co-operation only served to reinforce the effects of globalisation, while 42 per cent saw it as a means of protecting against its effects. Significantly the findings of the Eurobarometer (EB251) survey of April 2006, reveal that 'only 9 per cent of those who see France's membership of the EU as a bad thing perceive globalisation as an opportunity for national companies, while 86 per cent of the same group think it represents a threat to national employment and companies', which indicates that a vast majority of Eurosceptic electors in France are also sceptical about globalisation. However, hostility in France towards the EU is not as pronounced as it is towards globalisation. Although, one year after the referendum, a Eurobarometer survey (EB65) revealed that less than half of French respondents (49 per cent) agreed that membership of the EU was 'a good thing for France' (down from 56 per cent in October 2004), while only 17 per cent were prepared to answer that it was 'a bad thing' (a rise of 3 per cent on October 2004). Added to this, 62 per cent of French respondents still supported the idea of an EU constitution. France's pro-EU elites should, however, not take too much comfort from the findings of this poll, as it also gives clear indicators that a majority of the French electorate is not satisfied with the direction in which the EU is proceeding, and that they are dissatisfied with the EU's role as a bridge between the French model and the global economy.

Eurobarometer EB65 from 2006 clearly shows that socio-economic concerns related to the wider global context continue to predominate above all issues for the French electorate. From a list of fifteen problems (and given the chance to select two), 65 per cent of respondents identified unemployment as the major problem facing France today, with security (28 per cent) and the economic situation (27 per cent) some way behind but clearly second and third. Significantly, only 13 per cent of French respondents believed that the 'EU has played a positive role with regard to the fight against unemployment in France', and less than a quarter (21 per cent) believed the same with regard to immigration. Negative perceptions of the EU's role with regard to the impact of globalisation were also evident from the fact that only 30 per cent of French respondents believed that the EU has played a positive role with regard to the economic situation in France. Perhaps significantly, there has also been a drop in support for the euro in France, down to 70 per cent (compared to 78 per cent just prior to the referendum), and interestingly, only 21 per cent of respondents believed that the EU has had a positive effect on inflation in France. Neither did the EU score highly with regard to the 'fight against *l'insécurité*' with again only 30 per cent seeing the

EU's role here in positive terms. Moreover, a clear majority of the French public remained opposed to the principle of EU enlargement (31 per cent) according to the poll, a drop of 8 per cent since October 2004 (the twenty-second least enthusiastic state in the EU-25). This Eurobarometer poll appears to confirm that the French public seem to want something different from the EU with regard to its future direction. The two leading responses, from a choice of 15 answers, to the question 'what should be the three main future priorities of the EU?', were the 'struggle against unemployment' and the 'struggle against poverty and exclusion', both of which were identified by 58 per cent of respondents, clearly ahead of two massive EU/global issues, 'preserving peace in Europe' (25 per cent) and 'protecting the environment' (24 per cent).

Conclusion

It is clear where the French electorate's priorities lie: more emphasis on a social Europe and one which does more to stem the advance of economic globalisation. The Constitutional Treaty was rejected by voters in France precisely because it was perceived as a neo-liberal, 'Anglo-Saxon' text, which would not protect the French social model. The outcome represented the failure of France's political elites to persuade the French public that the EU can provide a positive response to some of the negative socio-economic and cultural consequences of globalisation. Failure to act on this message could lead to the French electorate turning their backs on the European project and causing it irreparable damage, threatening to derail the EU from the rickety track on which it currently finds itself. Furthermore, in the domestic context, France runs the risk of more unrest like that experienced in autumn 2005 and spring 2006, as the French public becomes increasingly hostile to the threat of economic globalisation. This, in turn, may open the door wider to those parties opposed to European integration and globalisation, such as the Front National in a post-Jean-Marie Le Pen era. France is currently at a crossroads with regard to its role in the global economy. It needs to follow a path which can restore the public's confidence with regard to the impact of economic and cultural globalisation. This will be the major challenge facing Nicolas Sarkozy as French President. His task will be easier if the EU can be successfully portrayed as a pragmatic 'go-between' capable of softening the blow. A failure to persuade French voters that the EU, which enlarged further in 2007, incorporating two additional member states from Eastern Europe, can act as a positive force in a global context will not only damage the credibility of the EU, but will also put great strain on the future of France's Fifth Republic.

Notes

1. The term 'socio-economic issues linked to the wider global context' refers to traditional domestic socio-economic issues such as the state of the economy, unemployment, security and immigration, which have increasingly taken on a global context and which have become increasingly perceived as such in the eyes of the electorate, often from a negative standpoint.
2. The PS chose to conduct a referendum of party members in December 2004 to ascertain the party line on the constitution. Fifty-nine per cent of members voted in favour, indicating a significant split within the party. The Greens had also opted to conduct a referendum of its membership back in February 2004, which resulted in 53 per cent voting in favour, also demonstrating a clear divide within the movement.
3. This includes twelve Parisian *arrondissements* (the 1st, 2nd, 3rd, 4th, 5th, 6th, 7th, 8th, 9th, 15th, 16th and 17th), the wealthy Parisian suburbs of Neuilly-Sur-Seine, St Cloud, Le Chesnay, Gif-sur-Yvette, Boulogne Billancourt, Saint-Germain-en-Laye and Maisons-Laffitte. The affluent 6th *arrondissment* in Lyon is the only non-Île-de-France address. Ironically, Neuilly-sur-Seine is the former fiefdom of the champion of *souverainiste* politics from the Maastricht era, Charles Pasqua, and St Cloud is the home to the Front National's headquarters.

Bibliography

Boy, D. and J. Chiche (2005) 'Les structures politiques et sociales du vote "non"', in A. Laurent and N. Sauger (eds), *Le Referendum de ratification du traité constitutionnel européen: comprendre le "non" français*, Paris: Les Cahiers du CEVIPOF, 42, pp. 92–109.

Cambadélis, J.-C. (2005) 'Pourquoi le non a été irrésistible', in Fondation Jean Jaurès (eds), *Le Jour où la France a dit non*, Paris: Plon, pp. 26–36.

Cautres, B. (2005) 'Une fracture générationnelle', in Fondation Jean Jaurès (eds), *Le Jour où la France a dit non*, Paris: Plon, pp. 78–99.

Cornick, M. and R. Elgie (1993) 'Dossier on the French referendum concerning the Maastricht Treaty', *Modern and Contemporary France*, 1(1): 111–26.

Duhamel, O. and G. Grunberg (1993) 'Référendum: les dix France', in O. Duhamel and J. Jaffré (eds), *L'Etat de l'opinion 1993*, Paris: Seuil, pp. 79–85.

Hug, S. (2002) *Voices of Europe: Citizens, Referendums and European Integration*, Lanham: Rowman and Littlefield.

Lamy, P. (2005) 'L'enjeu européen du non français', *France Forum*, 19 (September): 23–6.

Mallet, J. (2005) 'La crise européenne ne fait que commencer', *France Forum*, 19 (September): 60–6.

Marthaler, S. (2005) 'The French referendum on ratification of the Constitutional Treaty 29 May 2005', Sussex European Institute; European Parties, Elections and Referendums Network, Referendum Briefing Paper 12, http://www.sussex.ac.uk/sei/documents/epern_rb_france_2005.pdf, consulted 24 October 2006.

Neocleous, M. and N. Startin (2003) 'Protest and fail to survive: Le Pen and the great moving right show', *Politics*, 23(3): 145–55.

Schneider, G. and P. Weitsman (1996) 'The punishment trap: European integration referendums as popularity contests', *Comparative Political Studies*, 28: 528–607.

Startin, N. (2005) 'Maastricht, Amsterdam and beyond: the troubled evolution of the French Right', in H. Drake (ed.), *French Relations with the EU*, London: Routledge, pp. 64–85.

Tiberj, V. (2005) 'Les clivages sociologiques', in Fondation Jean Jaurès (eds), *Le Jour où la France a dit non*, Paris: Plon, pp. 42–55.

Opinion polls

All websites cited below were consulted on 21 September 2006.

BVA (2005) 'Les Français, la mondialisation et l'OMC', Survey in collaboration with Europe 1 and *Libération* (December), www.ccfd.asso.fr/e_upload/pdf/sondageOMCdec2005.pdf.

BVA (2006) 'Les Français et l'insécurité', Survey for *Le Figaro* (June), www.bva.fr/pdf/insécurité060607.pdf.

CSA (2005) 'Les Français et la mondialisation', Exclusive survey for *Le Parisien* (November), http://www.csa-tmo.fr/dataset/data2006/opi20060111b.htm.

Eurobarometer (2003) (EB59) 'Standard biannual survey' (conducted March–April), http://ec.europa.eu/public_opinion/archives/eb/eb59/eb59_en.htm.

Eurobarometer (2003) (EB151) 'Globalisation', Flash survey (conducted October), http:ec.europa.eu/public_opinion/flash/FL151b/globalisationREPORT.pdf.

Eurobarometer (2005) (EB171) 'The European constitution: post referendum survey in France' (conducted 30–31 May), http://europa.eu.int/comm/public_opinion/flash/fl171_en.pdf.

Eurobarometer (2005) (EB172) 'The European Constitution: post referendum survey in the Netherlands' (conducted 2–4 June), http://europa.eu.int/comm/public_opinion/flash/fl172_en.pdf.

Eurobarometer (2005) (EB178) 'Quelle Europe: la construction européenne vue par les Français' (conducted March), http://ec.europa.eu/public_opinion/flash/fl178_fr.pdf.

Eurobarometer (2006) (EB251) 'The Future of Europe' (conducted February–March), http://www.eurobarometerconference.eu/pdf/future/ReportEBComm FutureofEuropeEN20060428_v7.pdf.

Eurobarometer (2006) (EB65) 'Standard biannual survey' (conducted May–July) http://ec.europa.eu/public_opinion/archives/eb/eb65/eb65_en.htm.

IPSOS (2005) 'La perception de la mondialisation', Survey by l'Institut Ipsos for la Fondation Gabriel Péri (conducted April 2005), http://www.gabrielperi.fr/article. php3?id_article=88.

IPSOS (2005) 'Referendum 29 mai 2005', Comparative exit poll (conducted 29 May 2005 and 20 September 1992), http://www.ipsos.fr/referendum/soiree/referendum.htm#01.

SOFRES (1992) 'Le référendum de Maastricht', Exit poll survey (conducted 22 September (communication to author).
TNS/SOFRES (2005): 'Le référendum du 29 mai 2005', Survey for TF1, RTL et *Le Monde* (Conducted 29 May), http://www.tns-sofres.com/etudes/pol/290505_referendum_r.htm.

Election data

French Ministry for the Interior (2005) 'The 2005 referendum result on the EU constitution', http://www.interieur.gouv.fr/avotreservice/elections/rf2005/.

7
Supporting Europe and Voting No?

Laurent Binet

'Je ne comprends pas' ('I don't understand'). This sentence, repeated by the French Commissioner for the European Union (EU), Jacques Barrot, on the evening of the clear victory of the 'no' camp, and broadcast the following day on French television, shows how difficult it has been for some to understand the motives of the opponents of the Constitutional Treaty. It echoed President Chirac's clear bewilderment during the first debate with young voters on 14 April 2005, when he openly admitted that he did not understand the audience's concerns in relation to the treaty.

The fact that a founding member, traditionally considered to be the driving force behind European integration, was to stop the ratification of the Constitutional Treaty, already adopted by nine other member states, certainly merits further analysis, particularly of the reasons put forward for voting against the ratification of 'the Treaty establishing a Constitution for Europe'.

The aim of this chapter, therefore, is to examine the discourses and arguments of the 'no' supporters, subjecting these to close scrutiny. The reasons for this are threefold. First, polls indicated a clear shift in French public opinion from the early stages of the debate, when an overwhelming majority supported the Constitutional Treaty (consistently above 60 per cent between September 2004 and March 2005, according to CSA polls), to a majority against, which appeared as the debate gained currency, and which was confirmed by the final results, which gave the 'no' camp a clear victory with 54.68 per cent of the votes. The high turnout (close to 70 per cent) confirmed the significance of the result; it is therefore worth analysing more closely the arguments which may have prompted such a shift in public opinion. Second, the referendum campaign sparked an intense public debate, which was characterised by the involvement of numerous public figures. Political organisations traditionally categorised as Eurosceptic took part in the debate: on the Right, the Front National (FN), the sovereignists from the Mouvement pour la France (MPF) and the Rassemblement pour la France (RPF) and to some extent the hunters of Chasse, Pêche, Nature et Traditions (CPNT); on the Left, Chevènement's Mouvement Républicain et Citoyen (MRC), the Parti Communiste Français (PCF), the Ligue Communiste Révolutionnaire (LCR) and Lutte Ouvrière (LO). However, dissidents from traditionally pro-European parties also played an important role in the debate, such as sovereignist MP Nicolas Dupont-Aignan of the Union pour un Mouvement Populaire (UMP),[1] and key figures from the Parti Socialiste, such as former Prime Minister Laurent Fabius and Henri Emmanuelli, and a minority of the ecologist party Les Verts. Also of note was the role of intellectuals and members of *la société civile*, who took an active role in the discussions preceding the vote, both through the publication of books and articles and through participation in public and televised debates.

Third, studies of the discourses opposing the EU, as far as France is concerned, have been relatively limited since the 1992 Maastricht referendum. Most academic studies have concentrated on electoral results and commentaries on the rise of Euroscepticism in France (Todd, 1995; Perrineau, 1996; Cautrès and Denni, 1996). But few have attempted to present the discourse underlying opposition to the EU, and any such attempts have generally taken place within broader analyses (Benoit, 1998; Milner, 2004).

With regard to the 'no' discourses on the Constitutional Treaty, four types of argument can be identified. First, traditional Eurosceptic arguments based on the defence of French sovereignty and identity characterised the early 'no' campaign on the Right. However, they were progressively eclipsed by a discourse dominated by social and economic concerns. This anti-liberal discourse, massively used on the Left and the far-left, and in many ways echoed by the Right, represented the second main and decisive theme of the 'no' discourse. Third, Right and far-right opponents of the treaty managed successfully to introduce the issue of Turkish membership into the debate. Lastly, all opponents of the treaty relied on an 'anti-establishment' discourse. Criticism of the political, economic, cultural and media elites in France and of the European 'system' was an underlying feature of most of the 'no' supporters' discourses, underlining both France's unease and how out of touch her leaders were.

This chapter will conclude with a paradox. The opponents of the treaty consistently claimed they were pro-European. Both on the Right (Nicolas

Dupont-Aignan) and the Left (the PCF), 'no' campaigners used a *'J'aime l'Europe, je vote non'* slogan ('I love Europe, I vote no'), and never has pro-Europeanism in principle been so widely proclaimed in France as it was during this referendum. This ultimately raises questions about the Eurosceptic discourses in France. (See also Chapter 6 by Nicholas Startin.)

Economic and social issues

The 'no' discourse was characterised above all by economic and social issues. Reservations about the European liberal economic model – *'l'eurolibéralisme'* (Husson, 2005) – which the Constitutional Treaty, particularly Part III,[2] allegedly promoted, and criticisms of attempts to constitutionalise liberal policies indeed dominated the discourses of the 'no' camp. The text was described as a 'liberal straitjacket' (*'une camisole libérale'*) by Communist leader Marie-George Buffet, which allegedly would undermine social rights and threaten public services (Husson, 2005). It was said to 'set in stone' (*'graver dans le marbre'*) competition and the Anglo-Saxon vision of a liberal free-market, arguably at odds with France's values and her social model.

Whereas sovereignists from the Right started their campaign on more traditional Eurosceptic themes, the Left succeeded in imposing the economic and social agenda as the key theme of the campaign, as Claude Askolovitch (2005) observed: 'The referendum campaign got underway with an attack on Turkey and then veered to the Left, with a denunciation of neo-liberalism … And sovereignty became peripheral.'[3] This happened to such an extent that the Right either adopted a rather silent stance on this issue, or, on the contrary, added their voices to criticism levelled at the treaty for being too economically liberal. In the case of the Front National, there was a clear shift in the far-right party from the Thatcherite economic approach it had adopted in the early 1980s to an anti-free-market position demonstrated by its recurrent criticisms of *'l'euromondialisme'*.

The episode of the proposed Bolkenstein directive on services was another key element that contributed to the denunciation of *'la dérive libérale de l'Europe'* ('the shift to a liberal free-market Europe'). Whereas the plan to introduce the free movement of services had initially been denounced by Henri Emmanuelli, it became a major argument, with all opponents of the treaty denouncing the threat of the 'Polish plumber', and Philippe de Villiers, for example, referring to *'Bolkenstein-Frankenstein'*.

Economic and social concerns in the 'no' discourses were also fuelled by the fear of *délocalisations* (relocations) due to social and fiscal dumping. Several events which occurred during the campaign gave ammunition to the 'no' supporters. On 4 April 2005, the Alsatian company Sem Suhner/Schirmeck offered nine employees that it had made redundant a contract to work in Romania. On offer was a salary of €110 per month (approximately £80). A few days later, a similar offer was made by a Breton company, Max Sauer, to its employees: work in Mauritius for €118. Both episodes were fiercely denounced by the PCF, the LCR and groups such as the Association pour la taxation des transactions financières et pour l'aide aux citoyens (ATTAC), which joined the 'no' camp. As for Henri Emmanuelli's *'collectifs du "non" socialiste'*, they made a direct link to the draft constitution: 'This underlines, once more, that the unchecked neo-liberalism that prevails nowadays, which, regrettably, is the driving force behind the draft European Constitution, puts employees at considerable risk' (*L'Humanité*, 30 April 2005).

Lastly, and more surprisingly, the euro and its economic consequences were also challenged. Whereas the general assumption was that French public opinion had been reasonably happy with the new currency, claims that the euro had had an inflationary impact and reduced spending power resurfaced during the campaign. Such comments were particularly salient in de Villiers' speeches, but they also featured prominently in media accounts of the 'no' voters' preoccupations. A passer-by interviewed for a France 2 news bulletin a few days before the vote declared, for example: *'Depuis l'euro, on n'a plus de sous* ('Since [the introduction of] the euro, we have no money'). The newspaper *Le Figaro* (30 May 2005) recalled grievances against the euro amongst the 'no' voters: 'It's a real con! Everything has gone up and we are earning less and less'; the paper also reported the statement that 'anyone can tell that you can buy less with a 20 euro note than a 100 franc note. Everything is more expensive and growth remains on hold.' This echoed numerous claims made by politicians and economists that the changes linked to European integration had had a negative effect overall: 'Our lives have not improved in Europe, and especially in France, since they have been controlled by the European Central Bank, the Stability and Growth Pact, and the decisions of the Court of Justice of the European Communities aiming to enforce competition laws' (Raveaud et al., 2005).

The debate, therefore, on the Constitutional Treaty provided many people with an opportunity to express dissatisfaction with the economic situation in France, for which the EU was also seen to be responsible. It was alleged that adoption of the treaty, particularly Part III, would make the situation worse, especially with regards to social protection, public services and employment.

A traditional but fading sovereignist discourse

Alongside the economic and social arguments, a second category of arguments linked to the *souverainiste* vision can be analysed. Whilst these arguments dominated the 'no' camp's campaign during the Maastricht referendum, in particular the rhetoric of Philippe Séguin, they faded slightly and were partly eclipsed by the economic and social arguments presented above. Nonetheless, these arguments have regularly featured highly on the 'no' camp's agenda, in particular on the Right of the political spectrum and in the discourse of de Villiers, Dupont-Aignant and Pasqua. For the latter, there was no need to read beyond Article 1 of the Constitutional Treaty, since it proposed a federal state: 'There is no need to read beyond Article 1. We learn in the very first article that the Constitution creates a new state equipped with full state powers. As of that point, it is quite clear that this is a new step towards the creation of a federal state' (France 2, 2005). For Marie-France Garaud, the former *éminence grise* of Georges Pompidou, federalism was the main reason for opposing the treaty. It was its original sin, linked to globalisation, and the reason for flawed European integration:

> The initial error lies in the idea that Europe could be set up as a super-state annexing nations, just as nations once assimilated towns and provinces. The idea is akin to globalisation, which wants to believe in a universal international order conceived, too, as a super-state. The error of these two visions of history stems from the same simplistic view. It consists in regarding all communities as similar, irrespective of their size, and in believing that they could all be slotted together using an identical federalist strategy.
>
> (Garaud, 2005: 13–14)

Another key argument was the irreversible nature of the constitution and the fact that unanimity was required to revise it. This was presented as another threat to French sovereignty. On the Left, Jean-Pierre Chevènement noted that the Constitutional Treaty would be superior to French law, and even the French Constitution, irrespective of the opinion of the *Conseil Constitutionnel* (the French Constitutional Council), given the principle of non-unilateral interpretation of treaties (France 2, 2005).

Alongside the defence of French sovereignty and the rejection of a federal model, French identity has been a traditional theme of right-wing French Eurosceptics. Since Maastricht, French Eurosceptics have tried to establish a link between the French economic and social model (*'le modèle français'*) and the notion of French identity, as Bertrand Benoit (1998) has shown. The repeated claims during the campaign that the text of the constitution promoted an Anglo-Saxon vision of Europe shaped much of the 'no' discourse in relation to the economy, and also to identity. Denis Tillinac, for example, believed that many of the issues connected to the 'no' vote were identity related, as he commented in the *Guardian* (Henley, 2005): 'Today one is European and only residually French. That was fine in a Europe with 6 or 12 members: we know the Italians, the Germans. But a Europe of 25? We don't know who and where we are.'

France's secular republican model was also said to be at risk. Article II-70 of the Constitutional Treaty would undermine the French principle of *laïcité* (secularism), since, according to Jean-Pierre Chevènement and other Eurosceptics, it would give supporters of the headscarf, worn by Muslim women, the right to challenge French law in order to end the ban on wearing the headscarf in state schools. Overall, comments on sovereignty and identity featured less prominently than in past electoral campaigns, and right-wing opponents of the treaty discovered the issue of Turkey to be another powerful argument.

'Non à la constitution turque!'

France is one of the European countries in which opposition to Turkish accession to the EU is consistently strong (Eurobarometer, 2005). Exit polls on the day of the vote on the European constitution in France showed that opposition to Turkey was one of the key reasons for voting 'no' (IPSOS, 2005). Before the vote, another poll even indicated that the issue of Turkey was the primary stated motivation for a 'no' vote (CSA, 2005).

It is difficult accurately to establish when the theme of Turkey became important in the debate on Europe in France, but it is clear that the start of negotiations on the accession of Turkey in December 2004 – supported by President Chirac – sparked an intense debate. Demesmay and Fougier (2005) noted that nowhere in Europe had the theme of Turkish accession caused such reverberations. Several books specifically devoted to this issue were published in the wake of the referendum (de Villiers, 2005;

Maillard, 2005). Numerous other publications calling for a 'no' vote also gave a prominent place to the issue (Garaud, 2005; Dupont-Aignan, 2005).

Between December 2004 and May 2005, most of the discussions on European integration revolved around the implications of Turkey's future accession and the enlargement process. The referendum debate focused heavily on the issue of Turkey, after some politicians on the Right managed to link the issue of Turkey to the Constitutional Treaty, such as de Villiers, who repeatedly denounced *'la constitution turque'* ('the Turkish constitution'). The lack of debate on European enlargement in 2004 was crucial in this respect; however, opponents of Turkish accession developed a discourse which went far beyond mere criticism of enlargement. Concerns over Turkey's EU membership were based on a range of arguments, which can be grouped into six key themes.

The first of the reasons for some people's refusal to accept Turkey's accession to the EU is religion. The prospect of the future largest country in the EU being Muslim is deemed unacceptable, particularly on the Right of the political spectrum. Yet, however important the religious objection might be, it was, paradoxically, not the first to be raised systematically. Although opposition to Turkey was readily advocated, the religious aspect seemed, in many ways, taboo, particularly as far as voters were concerned. MP Pierre Lequilier (UMP), for instance, noticed in the debates preceding the referendum of 2005 that: 'Nobody ever stands up and says that they won't accept this country because it is Muslim, but you deduce as much' (Dupont, 2005).

Current unease in France with respect to Islam has been noted in academic research, and polls indicate that Islam has the poorest image of all the religions in France. The principle of *laïcité*, the debate over the headscarf in schools – one of the most publicised episodes featuring two Turkish girls in a college of Flers in 1999 – and the difficulty in integrating the Muslim community, are amongst the examples that account for this. In this context, French Eurosceptics were keen to stress that 99 per cent of the Turkish population is Muslim (Maillard, 2005), while de Villiers (2005) emphasised that whereas 12 per cent of the Turkish population was Christian in 1900, in 2004 Christians only constituted 0.1 per cent of the total. Clearly, the secular nature of the Turkish regime since Ataturk has been acknowledged. However, it was argued that Ataturk's achievement, as far as secularism is concerned, is incomplete, and the concept clearly does not have the same meaning as in France (Graeff, 2005: 150–2). The recent victory of Islamists in key elections, starting with the success of the Adalet ve Kalkinma Partisi (AKP) in

November 2002 and in the 2004 local elections, offered an additional reason to be cautious about the place of religion in Turkey.

The second criticism of Turkey's application is linked to geography: to put it bluntly, Turkey is not in Europe. The stance taken is that since only 3–5 per cent of Turkish territory belongs to the European continent (del Valle, 2004; Graeff, 2005), and the remaining 95 per cent is in Asia, mainly in Anatolia, Turkey is simply not a European country. The geographical location of Turkey leads to another criticism: geopolitics. Turkey is located in an area where conflicts and tensions are numerous. Turkish accession would bring the borders of the EU into direct contact with Iraq, Syria, Iran, Armenia and Georgia. Moreover, it would bring Europe into the vicinity of other geopolitical hot spots, such as Chechnya. Political objections to Turkey's accession were also raised. The political compatibility of the regime in Ankara with the EU was questioned. Although the evolution of Turkey towards a pluralistic democratic system was acknowledged, Ankara's record on human and minority rights was still not considered satisfactory (Maillard, 2005). The role of the army also provoked ambivalent comments. On the one hand, it was acknowledged to be the guardian of secularism, but on the other, there was awareness that it could act as a anti-democratic force, as the so-called 'postmodern coup' demonstrated in 1997. The concomitant doubts about Turkish secularism and the place of the army were well captured in the words of Dupont-Aignan, who criticised 'jackbooted and ambiguous secularism' (*'une laïcité bottée et ambiguë'*) (Dupont-Aignan, 2005: 25). In addition, Turkey's refusal to recognise the Armenian genocide raised further doubts about the precise nature of the Turkish regime.

Other political criticisms of Turkish accession concentrated on the direction of the EU, which, with Turkey as a member state, would diminish France's position and influence, which – or so it is alleged – has already been constantly eroded by successive enlargements. French Eurosceptics presented impressive figures: Dupont-Aignan estimated that there would be 100 million Turks by 2030. According to Maillard (2005: 47), Turkey could have '20 per cent of the votes', and he queried: 'Might we be destined to be governed by Turkey one day?' (*'Serions-nous destinés à être un jour gouvernés par la Turquie?'*). Meanwhile, Pierre Avril (2004) predicted 'a European Council and Parliament in which Turkey has the largest representation' (*'un Conseil et un Parlement européen où la représentation turque sera majoritaire'*).

The demographic size of Turkey was not only a political issue; it also represented a major concern with regards to immigration. Turkey's application was criticised on the basis that it would lead to a massive influx of immigrants. Predictably, competition for local workers and employees was stressed. Other arguments, of a more xenophobic complexion, highlighted the problems that allegedly some countries and people have had with immigrants from Turkey: 'In Austria, the Benelux countries, Denmark and the United Kingdom, Turkish immigrants have settled in large minorities. Proximity to these minorities has often made the man-in-the-street "Turkosceptic"' (Graeff, 2005: 155). Immigration fears were, furthermore, not limited to Turkish citizens, as Turkey could become an entry point into Europe for Muslims, wherever they might come from, as de Villiers (2005) warned in unequivocal terms: 'given the length of the Turkish border and the fact that police and customs officers can be easily bribed, Muslims will be able to enter Turkey easily, and from there flood into Europe'.

In relation to the economy, the gap between Turkey and the EU was denounced. According to Graeff (2005: 155), Turkey's annual gross domestic product (GDP) represented 27 per cent of the average EU GDP. Given this, Turkey would receive between €5–6 billion, putting considerable strain on EU finances. Agriculture would be another problem for France. As a predominantly agricultural country, Turkey would become the second largest beneficiary of the Common Agricultural Policy (CAP) behind...France. In total, Turkish membership would cost the EU an estimated €10–11 billion. This represented the amount spent on the ten new member states between 2004 and 2006 (Graeff, 2005: 157).

Labelled as a poor country (*'un pays pauvre'*) (Graeff, 2005), Turkey also raised fears about relocations and social dumping – issues that were particularly prominent in France during the debate, as explained. For the PCF, Turkey represented a genuine risk in that respect:

> Are we to let the successive enlargements of the EU – Turkey following those towards the East – serve as base camps for the big multinationals to operate their social dumping strategies? This is not in the interests of Turkish workers any more than it is of those in existing member states.
>
> (PCF, 2004)

In conclusion, the discourse against Turkish accession relied on a wide range of themes and arguments. Many of these themes correspond to problems France was and is currently struggling with: the Islam-secularism debate, the question of immigration, the place and role of France within the new EU, fears linked to globalisation and relocations ... All issues which French Eurosceptics were keen to associate with

Turkish accession during the 2005 debate. This prompted Demesmay and Fougier (2005) to suggest that French opposition to Turkish EU membership was a sign of French unease, explaining that it demonstrated France's current difficulties with its identity.

Interestingly, the issue of Turkey was one of the few themes which broke the conspiracy of silence amongst opponents of the treaty. Besancenot insisted that the popular 'no' vote from the far-left was at odds with '*le non raciste de de Villiers et Le Pen à la Turquie*' ('De Villiers' and Le Pen's racist "no" to Turkey'), and he reiterated his party's position with regard to the EU's stance on Turkey: 'We are opposed to any refusal by the European Union to allow a country to join that has democratically chosen to do so. Especially when the refusal, under the "common civilisation" pretext, rests on racist or religious criteria, as is the case with Turkey' (Ligue Communiste Révolutionnaire, 2004).

As was the case with Turkey, the issue of immigration was hotly contended amongst the so-called 'nonistes': the far-left denounced the EU for being '*une Europe forteresse*' ('Fortress Europe'), whereas the Right denounced the risk of '*une Europe passoire*' ('a sieve-like Europe', that is, an open Europe), linked to Article III-257, unable not only to control the migration flows from new member states, but also from the rest of the world. Although the issues of Turkey and immigration revealed marked differences between the different groups opposing the treaty, it can however be argued that they all relied on an anti-establishment or 'anti-system' discourse.

An 'anti-system' discourse

The fourth key aspect of the 'no' discourse during the campaign was its 'anti-system' dimension. 'Anti-system' here signifies more than mere opposition to the Raffarin government and President Chirac: it indicates a rejection of all those in power and *modes de gouvernement*, whether at national or European level.

The 'no' discourse was indeed first and foremost a multi-layered criticism of the way in which the EU had been operating. European integration was not challenged per se, but its objectives, modes of operation and results were. The sentence '*ça ne marche pas*' ('it is not working') was repeated on numerous occasions, alongside traditional attacks on technocracy, bureaucracy and lack of democracy. The very issue of the lack of democracy within the EU decision-making process, which was highlighted in 1992 by the 'no' camp, resurfaced in 2005 when key EU developments were retrospectively challenged, starting with the 2004 enlargement and the absence of public debate on the issue. Bernard Spitz highlighted 'the anger felt by French society at the conjuring act that consists in making it vote in the wrong referendum, namely on the treaty, whilst the outcome of the proper referendum that never took place – on enlargement – was presented as a fait accompli' (Spitz, 2005). Jacques Rupnik, a researcher from the Centre d'études et de recherches internationales (CERI), confirmed this point, when he noted 'the referendum on the constitution is turning into a retrospective referendum on enlargement' (*'le referendum sur la constitution se transforme en referendum rétrospectif sur l'élargissement'*) (*Libération*, 27 May 2005).

The criticism of the EU as a system was also linked to the European Convention in charge of the drafting of the Constitutional Treaty, and to the personality of former President Valéry Giscard d'Estaing. According to many, including Marie-France Garaud, the European Convention which prepared the text was not representative. For Jacques Calvet, former head of Peugeot, it was not a surprise that the text of the treaty was considered a clumsy 'compromise'. Usherwood (2005) points out that several anti-EU groups, including the French Alliance pour la Souveraineté de la France, criticised the European Convention for its lack of democracy.

In addition, some observers have interpreted the results of the referendum on 29 May 2005 as an anti-government protest vote. This claim should be considered with caution. First, several polls published before and after the vote showed that the desire to sanction the government only rated fourth or fifth when 'no' voters were asked to explain why they had voted as they had. Second, when the discourse of the 'no' leaders is analysed, Jacques Chirac and the Raffarin government were not their prime targets, other than for Laurent Fabius, who clearly pointed out that voting 'no' to the treaty was voting 'no' to Chirac. Nonetheless, few people during the campaign directly linked the results of the referendum to the fate of the then president and prime minister. Clearly, there were criticisms of the government during the campaign, but it must be remembered that the 'yes' campaigners from the Left were also heavily criticised. One of the key moments at the start of the campaign was a demonstration in defence of *services publics* in Guéret on 5 March 2005, where Socialist leader François Hollande (the long-term partner of Socialist presidential candidate, Ségolène Royal, until their separation in June 2007), was booed and pelted with eggs and snowballs by demonstrators.

More than an anti-governmental discourse, the 'no' discourse represented in many ways a neo-Poujadist, anti-system, anti-elitist discourse.

Not only were French and European political elites targeted: economic, media and even artistic pro-yes figures were stigmatised as unrepresentative of the real people. This anti-elite discourse was presented by the 'no' camp as a legitimate reaction to the arrogance of the 'yes' camp and the way it caricatured the *nonistes*. Jack Lang's criticisms of the '*non tripal*' ('gut-reaction no') prompted Max Gallo to sarcastically admit '*Je vote non, donc je suis une bête*' ('I'm voting no, that makes me a donkey'). The gross charges made against the 'no' camp, in fact, were to its advantage. The 'no' campaigners recognised the benefits to be derived from being portrayed as ignorant, grass-roots, down-to-earth people in a country where anti-elitist feelings were running high. The 'yes' camp certainly managed to rally the economic, media, military, religious and artistic opinion leaders, as Lang's 'Comité du oui' showed. But it was soon ridiculed as an indication of the gap between a privileged 'yes' camp oblivious to the situation faced by ordinary French people, and a 'no' camp that was much more in touch with them. Henri Emmanuelli's comments on Lang's 'Comité du oui', referring to the film '*La vie est un long fleuve tranquille*', were: 'That is the Le Quesnoy committee. We are going to endeavour, with the French people, to form the Groseille committee' ('*C'est le comité Le Quesnoy. On va tâcher avec les Français de former le comité Groseille*'). The plot of this popular film is based on the contrast between two very different French families: the Le Quesnoy family – affluent and traditional – and the Groseille family – poor and rumbustious. Emmanuelli's choice of words, '*avec les Français*', was a clear indication of the attempt to contrast the ordinary, genuine French with a distant, non-representative, elitist 'yes' camp.

Lastly, the anti-establishment tone of the 'no' camp's discourse reached a new peak following declarations made by Jean-Claude Juncker, Prime Minister of Luxembourg, and Giscard d'Estaing – on La Chaîne Info (LCI), two days before the vote – that the French people might have to vote again if the 'no' vote were to win. These declarations, which can be compared with the absence of reactions following the major electoral defeats suffered by the French government in 2004, opened the way for further criticism of aloof, out-of-touch elites, whether French or European.

The French Eurosceptic discourse: heterogeneous, inward-looking, evolving and ambivalent?

This presentation of the discourses of the opponents of the treaty demonstrates that a variety of themes and messages, sometimes contradictory, were used by a variety of – often antagonistic – groups and individuals. The heterogeneous and fragmented nature of the Eurosceptic – or, more accurately, the EU-sceptic – discourses previously noted (Binet, 2004) seems to have been confirmed.

Some common patterns, however, appear. Whatever themes were chosen, the discourses of opponents of the treaty were largely inward-looking. Concerned with issues linked to the domestic economy, social and political problems, these discourses did not seem to embrace purely European preoccupations.

Besides, the nuances between right- and left-wing versions of Euroscepticism previously noted by commentators paradoxically have both been confirmed and blurred. Cautrès and Denni argued in the 1990s that there were few shared opinions, as far as values were concerned, between Eurosceptic voters on the Left and those on the Right, and that the discourse of political parties reflected this difference. Whereas the Right opposed European integration on the grounds of nationalism and inward-looking perceptions, opposition on the Left, by contrast, was based more on policies and social and economic considerations than the rejection of the principle of European integration (Cautrès and Denni, 1996: 350–4).

It can be argued that much of this remains true, with two additional observations. In two key areas of discussion during the 2005 debate, the distinction between right- and left-wing Euroscepticism became slightly blurred. Thus, on economic and social questions, numerous 'no' campaigners from the Right and the far-right adopted much of the Left's anti-liberal rhetoric, and displayed a common rejection of globalisation. The issue of enlargement, particularly in relation to Turkey, highlighted a similar ambiguity. If, on the one hand, the Left was quick to denounce the 'racist no' of the far-right, it did, however, show concern with *the others*, in particular with regard to competition faced by French workers.

The second finding of our analysis has to do with the ever-evolving nature of Eurosceptic discourses. Whereas, in 1992 and subsequent years, sovereignty and identity were the dominant anti-EU themes, in 2005 they were eclipsed by economic and particularly social issues. Enlargement, although previously favoured, was increasingly viewed as a political, economic and social threat, while criticism of a Europe that was remote and out-of-touch broadened to embrace France's elite and ruling classes.

Lastly, what is most surprising was the insistence throughout the campaign by most leaders of the 'no' camp that they were not against Europe; on the contrary, some even adopted the slogan *'J'aime l'Europe, je vote non'*. This was, for instance, the title of Dupont-Aignan's book published in the wake of the campaign, and the slogan used by the PCF. The dissident Socialist leader from *Nouveau Monde* (New World), Henri Emmanuelli, even insisted he was a federalist. There is, therefore, a genuine ambivalence, if not a paradox, for political organisations and leaders, some of whom have consistently fought the EU, in the fact that they seem to feel the need to proclaim their attachment to the European ideal. Extreme versions of Euroscepticism, as defined by Szczerbiak and Taggart (2001), seem to be therefore no longer politically acceptable in France.

The slogan *'J'aime l'Europe'* was also accompanied by the claim that another Europe (*'une autre Europe'*) was possible,[4] Europe being presented as an ideal, a *'projet'* worth realising, but through different means than the ones currently chosen by the EU. The hypothesis of another Europe accounted for the confused claims during the debate that a 'Plan B' was ready, supporting the assumption that an alternative Europe was possible, although its contours were yet to be defined. This idea, however, remained very vague, and the alternative, when described, chiefly referred to French concerns and had a Hexagonal perspective. In many ways, the slogan *'Je n'aime pas cette Europe, je vote non'* would have been more accurate.

Both from a domestic and from a European perspective, it is difficult to assess the medium- and long-term implications of France's rejection of the Constitutional Treaty. One of the main reasons for this is that the forces behind the 'no' vote represented different messages. On the one hand, they expressed a desire to regain control of public affairs, a *réappropriation de la chose publique*, deemed to be abandoned to aloof elites, and called for citizens to be more systematically involved in key decisions at both a national and a European level. On the other hand, since it did not present a clear alternative project and was largely inward-looking and synonymous with French fears and unease, the 'no' discourse may be interpreted as an indication of the erosion, desired or otherwise, and the weakening of France's position on the world stage. The future of France as a driving-force in Europe may ultimately depend on its ability to present, sooner rather than later, an alternative to the Constitutional Treaty. The story of European integration is comprised of cycles. In May 2005, together with the Dutch, the French contrived to bring one of those cycles to an end. Today, in a Europe of 27 member states, France's future, not only as a European but also as an international power, may ultimately rest on its ability to take or contribute to an initiative that will launch a new cycle.

Notes

1. Nicolas Dupont-Aigan is also the leader of the neo-Gaullist Debout la République movement.
2. Part III of the Constitutional Treaty entitled 'The Policies and Functioning of the Union', included most of the controversial articles relating to public services (or Services of General Economic Interest) and the social dimension of the EU.
3. All translations in this chapter are by Laurent Binet.
4. One of the placards used during demonstrations by the 'no' camp featured the message *'Pour moi c'est non, une autre Europe est possible!'* ('I'm voting no, another Europe is possible!').

References

Askolovitch, C. (2005) 'Les paradoxes du non de droite', *Le Nouvel Observateur*, 2 June.

Avril, P. (2004) 'Le risque d'un choc économique pour l'Union', *Le Figaro*, 24 September.

Benoit, B. (1998) *Social-Nationalism: an Anatomy of French Euroscepticism*, Aldershot: Ashgate.

Binet, L. (2004) 'Disparate themes and fragmented messages? The Eurosceptic discourse in France', *Discourse, Persuasion and Public Perception in France*, ASMCF Conference, University of Surrey, 2 July.

Cautrès, B. and B. Denni (1996) 'Les attitudes des Français à l'égard de l'Union Européenne: les logiques de refus', in F. d'Arcy (ed.), *De la Vième République à l'Europe*, Paris: Presses de la FNSP, pp. 323–54.

CSA/Marianne (2005) 'Sondage CSA/Marianne: ce non qui porte plusieurs rejets', *Marianne*, 23 March, 21.

Del Valle, A. (2004) *La Turquie en Europe: un cheval de Troie islamiste?* Paris: Editions des Syrtes.

Demesmay, C. and E. Fougier (2005) 'La France qui fronde: l'adhésion de la Turquie en débat', *Le Débat*, 133 (January–February): 126–37.

Dupont, G. (2005) 'La question de l'adhésion de la Turquie continue à peser sur la campagne du referendum', *Le Monde*, 20 March.

Dupont-Aignan, N. (2005) *J'aime l'Europe je vote non*, Paris: François-Xavier de Guibert.

Eurobarometer (2005) Eurobarometer 63.4 (Spring).

France 2 (2005) *100 minutes pour comprendre l'Europe*, 21 April.

Garaud, M.-F. (ed.) (2005) *Oser dire non à la politique du mensonge*, Monaco: Editions du Rocher.

Graeff, C. (2005) 'Intégration de la Turquie, désintégration de l'Europe', in M.-F. Garaud (ed.), *Oser dire non à la politique du mensonge*, Monaco: Editions du Rocher, pp. 145–60.

Henley, J. (2005) 'EU referendum prompts French identity crisis', *Guardian*, 24 May.

Husson, M. (2005) 'Les services publics au risque de l'euro-libéralisme', in G. Raveaud, A. Saïdi and D. Sauze (eds), *Douze Economistes contre le projet de constitution européenne*, Paris: L'Harmattan, pp. 69–80.

IPSOS (2005) *Référendum 29 mai 2005: le sondage sorti des urnes,* 29 May.

L'Humanité (2005) 'Pour 110 euros par mois en Roumanie', 30 April.

Le Figaro (2005) 'Voyage dans la France du non', 30 May.

Libération (2005) 'Jacques Rupnik, chercheur, explique l'incompréhension à l'Est du non de gauche français', 27 May.

Ligue Communiste Révolutionnaire (2004) 'Une autre Europe est possible', *Programme pour les élections européennes de 2004.*

Maillard, P. (2005) *La constitution et la Turquie: L'Europe et de Gaulle trahis,* Paris: François-Xavier de Guibert.

Milner, S. (2004) 'For an alternative Europe: Euroscepticism and the French Left since the Maastricht Treaty', in R. Harmsen and M. Spiering (eds), *Euroscepticism: Party Politics, National Identity and European Integration,* Amsterdam: Rodopi, pp. 59–81.

PCF (2004) *Turquie/Europe: la droite joue la peur,* Dossier hebdomadaire d'aide à la communication de proximité, 6–12 October.

Perrineau, P. (1996) 'L'enjeu européen, révélateur de la mutation des clivages politiques dans les années 1990', in F. d'Arcy (ed.), *De la Vième République à l'Europe,* Paris: Presses de la FNSP, pp. 45–59.

Raveaud, G., A. Saïdi and D. Sauze (eds) (2005) *Douze Economistes contre le projet de constitution européenne,* Paris: L'Harmattan.

Spitz, B. (2005) 'Les deux référendum', *L'Express,* 2 May.

Szczerbiak, A. and P. Taggart (2001) 'Parties, positions and Europe: Euroscepticism in the EU candidate states of Central and Eastern Europe', Sussex European Institute Working Paper, 46.

Todd, E. (1995) 'Aux origines du malaise politique français, les classes sociales et leur représentation', *Le Débat,* 83: 98–120.

Usherwood, S. (2005) 'Realists, sceptics and opponents: opposition to the EU's Constitutional Treaty', *Journal of Contemporary European Research,* 2: 4–12.

Villiers, P. de (2005) *Les Turqueries du grand Mamamouchi,* Paris: Albin Michel.

8
Using Europe to Keep the World at Bay: French Policy on EU Economic Governance

David J. Howarth

Introduction

French governments have, since the start of discussions on the shape of Economic and Monetary Union (EMU) in 1988, been the principal proponents of the establishment of some form of *'gouvernement économique'*, economic governance (EG) at European Union (EU) level. This French preoccupation reflects concerns linked to the traditionally widespread reluctance to accept central bank independence, opposition to the 'sound money' bias of the EMU project, and the French tradition of state intervention in the economy. EG has been seen as a means of counterbalancing the monetary policy-making power of the European Central Bank (ECB) in EMU, qualifying the 'sound money' bias of the bank and EMU fiscal policy rules, and encouraging coordinated reflation to ensure economic growth in the Eurozone.

EG and the EMU project more broadly can be seen as mechanisms through which French governments have sought to manage both European and international constraints, in this way using Europe to keep the world at bay. In the 1980s and early 1990s, key French policy-makers turned to EMU as an option when German governments refused to reform the European Monetary System (EMS). The EMS was centred around the German mark, and created what the French saw as asymmetric adjustment pressures imposed principally upon weak (more inflationary) currency countries (Howarth, 2001). If French governments wanted to keep the franc in the Exchange Rate Mechanism (ERM) of the EMS, they were required to lower French inflation and control public expenditure. They were also required to maintain interest rates above those in Germany – given the anchor role of the German mark – whether or not these rates were appropriate for the French economy. In the early

1990s, the operation of the ERM resulted in record high real interest rate levels, contributing to sluggish economic growth. While French governments wanted exchange rate stability in Western Europe, they did not fully accept the economic constraint imposed upon them to achieve that stability.

International developments stimulated initial French interest in European monetary integration. In the 1960s and 1970s, President de Gaulle and his successors criticised what they saw as US monetary policy irresponsibility (Maclean, 2002: 77). With the collapse of Bretton Woods in the early 1970s and the rise in speculative capital flows, the French turned to European monetary cooperation for exchange rate stability. In the 1980s and 1990s, EMU was seen by some French policy-makers (Howarth, 2001) as a mechanism to eliminate speculative pressures against the franc once and for all, significantly reducing international financial pressures for adjustment. For many in France, a single European currency was also seen as a potential rival to the US dollar as the most used international currency, a status which would provide European economies with similar advantages enjoyed by the US (Howarth, 2001).

EMU has represented a paradox for French policy-makers. The loss of monetary policy, the creation of an ECB hawkish on inflation, and the fiscal policy rules of the Maastricht convergence criteria and the Stability and Growth Pact (SGP) have suggested constraint. Many have concluded that EMU would reinforce the liberalising pressures created by European and international market integration, and thus the need to push through domestic structural reforms. At the same time, EMU involves a form of protection for the French economy (and, indeed, for most West European economies), sheltering it from the speculative attacks that previously reinforced adjustment pressures.

French policy on EU-level economic governance has, since the late 1980s, reflected an effort to manipulate the constraint-shelter paradox of EMU with the aim of loosening the constraint. EMU is to be a shelter in the flux of international capital flows. EMU is not to be inconveniently constraining. The term 'economic governance' can signify several different things. In general terms, EG is an institutional set-up at the European level designed to establish some form of macroeconomic policy, be it only 'soft', non-binding economic policy coordination, that has direct impact upon the member states. This is a form of collective governance (Wallace, 2000: 541ff.) 'among core actors from several institutions and bodies in a multi-faceted network which is constituted by mutual participation patterns' (Wessels and Linsenmann, 2002). In the academic literature – describing what *has been* created or recommending what *should be* created – this includes different modes of governance: the 'hard' coordination in the realm of monetary and fiscal policies, and the 'soft' coordination in the area of economic and employment policies.

What various French proponents mean exactly when they espouse EG has been unclear, even though there has been a limited attempt by French academics and government economic advisers to explore possible EG scenarios (Boyer, 1999; Boyer and Dehove, 2001). Different governments – indeed different policy-makers – place different emphasis on different kinds of coordination and the appropriate role to be fulfilled by the Eurogroup (for more detail on the evolution of the Eurogroup, see below). There are four roles and objectives of 'economic governance' – some overlapping, some contradictory – that can be discerned from French policy statements over the past two decades.

(1) As economic policy coordinator with other member state governments and with the ECB to achieve an 'appropriate' policy mix;
(2) As a more energetic EU-level interventionism to stimulate economic growth and create jobs;
(3) As a political interlocutor of the ECB to contribute to the legitimisation of ECB monetary policy-making and as an exercise in political communication to reinforce the credibility of Eurozone monetary policy; and
(4) As an explicit limiter of the ECB's independence.

The inconsistent, and often incoherent, presentation of the concept of EG by leading members of the French political class reflects the inherent contradiction between two well-established French policy-making preferences. On the one hand, the consequences of an interventionist approach in the context of EMU encourages French governments to match the single monetary policy with some form of supranational economic governance that can bring about a tight coordination of national macroeconomic policies, but also serve as a potentially useful device to empower French governments in the domestic political and economic context. On the other hand, the Gaullist reflex to retain a national policy-making margin of manoeuvre ('sovereignty') as far as possible is manifested in the preference that EU-level policy-making is conducted in an intergovernmental manner. The difficulty elaborating a clear French policy on EG has thus paralleled the incoherence in French policy on European integration more broadly, and the failure of successive French governments to move beyond the divisive questions of principle ('should we transfer sovereignty?') to the more consensual challenge of managing such change: not 'why' but 'how' to transfer sovereignty (Arnaud, 2000; Drake, 2001). French governments have sought to construct EG in order to increase the national margin of manoeuvre in the context of European (EMU and Single Market) and international (principally financial) constraints. However, paradoxically, French governments have been prevented by their insistence upon the national margin of manoeuvre in relation to EU-level policy-making from developing forms of EG that could potentially be more effective in terms of reducing these European and international constraints.

The four versions of EG noted above can be juxtaposed with the objective of EG that was explicitly established by the Maastricht Treaty and the SGP: EG as coordination of macroeconomic policies to achieve greater price stability to support fiscal policy coordination (which is supposed to involve binding rules and even fines). Thus, EG was expected to reinforce the primary – low inflation – objective of the ECB (with economic growth and employment as a secondary objective), promote a positive coordination role between the Economic and Financial Affairs Council (Ecofin) and the ECB, and prevent individual member states 'free-riding' off the low inflation achieved by the central bank and other Eurozone member states. EG as the achievement of price stability has involved the supposedly 'hard' coordination of the convergence criteria rules (with rules for the imposition of fines established in the Stability Pact) and 'soft' coordination consisting of the mutual surveillance of national macroeconomic policies begun in Stage One of EMU in 1990 with the establishment of the Broad Economic Policy Guidelines (BEPG) and the requirement that member states prepare and submit medium-term reports, which was reinforced by Regulation 1466/97 of the SGP that established the Stability and Convergence Programmes. For economists, the price stability elements of the treaty and the SGP are designed to prevent the dangers of a 'chicken game' between fiscal and monetary authorities, and of certain participating states 'free-riding' off the stability achieved by other member states. At an international level, the SGP was to reinforce the credibility of EMU in financial markets and help bolster the strength of the euro in relation to other major world currencies.

The 'price stability' function has consistently been marginalised in French government (right-wing and left-wing) discourse and policy on EU economic governance, precisely because of the ostensibly binding nature of this function. The emphasis placed on the other three forms of economic governance reflect more the domestic political and economic tradition – still crucial to government legitimisation in France – of state intervention in the economy (Schmidt, 1997: 229; Hall, 1986; Shonfield,

1969). While the treaty-based price stability dimension of European economic governance has conformed to the preferences of French governments seeking to push through significant structural reforms to lower the French public spending deficit and contain the rising debt burden, the rigid design of the SGP rules has contradicted French preferences in favour of intergovernmentalism and margin of manoeuvre in macroeconomic policy-making. The SGP was accepted by the Juppé government (1995–97) only after lengthy and bitter debate (Heipertz and Verdun, 2004; Milesi, 1998) to meet intransigent German demands and ensure the start of Stage Three of EMU.

French visions of EU-level *'gouvernement économique'*

Economic governance as 'effective policy mix'

No French politician would claim that EG exists only to achieve price stability. Thus, this understanding of EG associated with the application of the Maastricht Treaty and SGP rules is always presented in the context of EG as achieving an 'effective policy mix', which aims to promote a more active coordination of member state policies to increase economic growth and employment creation in the context of the 'sound money' goals of the EMU project. This is about qualifying/counterbalancing – but not directly challenging – the drive for monetary stability. This form of EG would involve a positive coordination between the Council and the ECB, which also has for secondary goals the promotion of employment and investment in the Eurozone. Such emphasis on effective policy mix can either involve an acceptance of an ECB (monetary policy) leadership role (thus the Council places clear limits on its pursuit of improved economic growth, and this does not become inflationary), or a direct challenge to this role, emphasising instead the need for a tighter co-ordination of national macroeconomic policies (although not necessarily via precise binding rules) to achieve stronger economic growth and employment creation. French government rhetoric and policy has presented both these forms of 'policy mix', while tending to favour the latter.

Initial French interest in EU-level economic governance – in the context of the discussions and negotiations on EMU in the late 1980s to the final agreement on the design of EMU at the December 1991 Maastricht Summit – stemmed, in large part, from widespread French concern for the need for an effective policy mix which involved containing ECB monetary policy in a broader macroeconomic policy established by governments. Pierre Bérégovoy, Minister of Finance from 1988 to 1992, sought to counter what he saw as the excessive influence of the national central bank governors in the design of EMU (Howarth, 2001). During the period following the first meetings of the Delors Committee, Bérégovoy and Treasury officials introduced the idea of '*gouvernement économique*'. In the French draft treaty of January 1991 they insisted:

> Everywhere in the world, central banks in charge of monetary policy are in dialogue with the governments in charge of the rest of economic policy. Ignore the parallelism between economic and monetary matters ... and this could lead to failure.
>
> (*Agence Europe*, 28–29 January 1991: 5419)

Moreover, the Treasury proposed that the European Council, on the basis of Ecofin Council reports, define the broad orientations for EMU and the economic policy of the Community. Within these orientations, Ecofin would coordinate the policies of member states and make recommendations to individual governments, and the ECB would manage European monetary policy. Bérégovoy and Treasury officials also argued in favour of giving the ministers of economics and finance control over exchange rate policy (*Agence Europe*, 28–29 January 1991: 5419). The French draft treaty sought to limit the European Bank's margin of manoeuvre as much as possible. It also very much reflects Treasury attitudes regarding the goal of price stability and French monetary policy tradition. It keeps a foot in both camps, maintaining the primacy of monetary stability (article 2-3.1) while giving the European Council and Ecofin the means to challenge this primacy. The Germans opposed any powers to the Council beyond ensuring that member states respect the specific convergence criteria they sought to place in the EMU treaty. Ironically, given subsequent French government difficulties in keeping the budget deficit below 3 per cent of annual gross domestic product (GDP), French negotiators were flexible on the inclusion of the convergence criteria, and even proposed the precise 3 per cent figure which proved so economically and politically constraining in subsequent years. In 1991, France was one of the few EC member states to respect all five criteria, having avoided a public spending deficit greater than 3 per cent (with the exception of 1983) since the Second World War.

Since 1992, French governments have translated 'effective policy mix' into increased national margin of manoeuvre in macroeconomic – and notably fiscal – policy. All French governments since 1996 publicly opposed the constraining features of the original Stability and Growth Pact, and none undertook the kinds of structural reforms needed to ensure that France would meet the medium-term goal of a budget 'close to balance or in surplus'. The Jospin government in its latter years (especially from 1999) and the Raffarin Union pour un Mouvement Populaire (UMP) government both prioritised tax cuts over deficit cuts. Major reductions in tax were one of the principal campaign pledges of President Chirac and the UMP in the 2002 presidential and legislative elections. Chirac spoke with a forked tongue for domestic public and European political elite audiences. While emphasising tax cuts in the domestic debate, he and the UMP also regularly confirmed France's commitment to meeting the medium-term SGP goals. The newly-elected President Sarkozy has also called for significant cuts to income taxes – to create a fiscal boost to the economy – which some have estimated as costing the French state around €15 billion, and thus jeopardising deficit-cutting commitments under the SGP (*Financial Times*, 5 June 2007). Sarkozy has, however, continued to insist upon his commitment to the reformed pact.

Repeated German failure to meet the 3 per cent deficit figure from 2002 gave the French greater political margin of manoeuvre on the SGP rules. The Raffarin government formed a pro-reform alliance with the Schröder government. The French government then accepted the Schröder government's demands that the application of the SGP's Excessive Deficit Procedure (EDP) be suspended, and joined with the Germans to force through the suspension at the 25 November 2003 Ecofin meeting. Official French policy on the SGP insisted that the non-application of the EDP did not amount to an abandonment of France's commitment to the pact (*Le Monde*, 26 November 2004). However, the Raffarin government insisted upon a more flexible application that would, officially, take into consideration the economic situation facing a participating member state, and, in practice, allow more scope for political bargaining and thus margin of manoeuvre for French (and other) governments.

Both the Jospin and Raffarin governments let it be known that a re-formulated pact should take into consideration deficit spending on public investment (notably physical infrastructural and research spending) – eliminating this from total public deficit considerations – which would allow for greater margin of manoeuvre. This was defended through a report published on 18 November 2004 by economists in the Economic Analysis Council (*Conseil d'analyse économique*) attached to the prime minister's office. Allied to the Schröder government, the Raffarin government insisted on discounting public spending on research, especially given the EU's official (Lisbon) research spending objective of 3 per cent of total GDP by 2010. The Raffarin government also accepted (*Le Monde*, 3 December 2004) the Schröder government's insistence that all national spending on EU engagements be taken into consideration when judging national deficits: thus allowing net contributors to the EU budget, such as Germany, but also France, more leeway in comparison to net recipients. With the largest total defence budget in the EU, President Chirac and the Raffarin government also demanded that defence spending be excluded from deficit calculations. French governments, of both Left and Right, supported a more flexible, medium-term target that did not insist upon balanced budgets, as in the original pact, yet was still designed to reduce debt in the long term. The French wanted each country to have its own medium-term objective that, in effect, would increase governments' margin of manoeuvre by submitting the determination of this target exclusively to ministerial judgement, and thus abandoning completely the automaticity enshrined as a central tenet in the pact, which arguably impeded the development of an appropriate policy mix for each Eurozone member state. Both the Jospin and Raffarin governments were officially hostile (Treasury officials, interviews April and May 2005) to proposals to render the pact more 'symmetric' by increasing the constraint on fiscal policy – forcing the further reduction of deficits – during periods of economic growth. This constraint was considered politically unacceptable to governments wanting to ensure maximum margin of manoeuvre in fiscal policy.

The Raffarin government also expressed some reservations with regard to proposals by the Commission and leading European economists (for example, Charles Wyplosz) that increased focus should be placed on debts rather than deficits. It has been suggested that member states with debt levels below the 60 per cent threshold be allowed the possibility of higher deficit levels, thus effectively rendering more complex and subject to political judgement the application of the EDP, emphasising the 'soft' law elements of the pact, rather than the 'hard' law dimension of the current rules. French debt load had risen rapidly above the 60 per cent mark. While the Raffarin government accepted the consideration of debt in the more flexible determination of country-specific, medium-term objectives, the government opposed (*Le Monde*, 3 December 2004) the use of the debt figure to determine the application of pact deficit procedures.

After lengthy and rather acrimonious debate in the Eurogroup, Ecofin and the European Council, on 20 March 2005, the EU member state governments reached an agreement on SGP reform which increased national margins of manoeuvre in two crucial ways. First, it allowed a member state to exceed temporarily the 3 per cent figure to a limited extent – in the event of slow economic growth (no precise figures being provided). Second, it allowed consideration of several 'other relevant factors' to permit deficits above the 3 per cent threshold: (1) investment;

(2) research and development; (3) structural reforms (only those which have a long-term impact on the solidity of public finances will be taken into account); (4) EU policy goals; (5) European unification; and (6) international 'solidarity' (which the French insisted would include spending on both aid and defence). Other commitments under the original SGP were restated, notably the expectation that governments are to avoid pro-cyclical budgets in good times (when real growth is superior to potential growth) and target balanced budgets in the medium term. However, no new obligation was created for member states to achieve these goals.

The new spirit of the SGP presented by French Finance Minister Thierry Breton – designed 'to help rather than to punish' (*Le Monde*, 22 March 2005) – together with the elimination of the elements of automaticity in the original pact, and the introduction of considerable room for interpretation, conform well to French interventionist and intergovernmental preferences. They also reflect the 'effective policy mix' dimension in the French approach to economic governance. There is an obvious tension between greater flexibility allowed in the application of the SGP and the potential effectiveness of its sanction mechanisms. There is also the potential for tension between this more flexible version of economic governance and EG as macroeconomic policy coordination. Under the new pact, there is considerably greater scope for counterclaim in the event of non-compliance with existing rules, given that member states can justify their borrowing with reference to numerous factors.

Economic governance as interventionism

The second version of EG that can be discerned in French government rhetoric and policy is more interventionist, involving EU job creation strategies and infrastructure programmes. This could involve varying degrees of intervention in the context of the EU's employment and social chapters, or in terms of EU sponsored investment. To the extent that intervention involves reflation, and thus a direct challenge to the price stability goals of the ECB, this understanding of EG is likely to overlap to some extent with the final objective of economic governance explored below.

The French Socialists made this more interventionist version of economic governance a central element of their policy on EMU during the campaign prior to the June 1997 National Assembly elections (Howarth, 2002a, 2002b; Pochet, 1998). Together with their Plural Left coalition partners, they supported European economic governance as a means to promote growth and employment, goals which were ostensibly given equal weight to the 'growth and stability' goals in the Amsterdam Treaty due to Prime Minister Jospin's insistence on parallel resolutions. Rhetorically, the construction of EG was linked to the establishment of an EU-level economic and monetary policy mix described as *'euro-social'*, designed to counterbalance aggressively, or even directly challenge, the 'sound money' policies pursued by the ECB. The Plural Left government called for collective EU-level interventionism to include both joint spending on major infrastructural projects and a high-profile EU employment strategy, forced through by Jospin at the June 1997 Amsterdam European Council, to involve regular 'Jobs Summits'. However, the Plural Left government's preferences in this area were not met: the Employment Chapter of the Amsterdam Treaty, the Luxembourg and Cardiff Jobs Summits of November 1997 and March 1998, and the Cologne and Lisbon Summits of June 1999 and March 2000 established a non-binding 'soft' or 'open' form of coordination that fell far short of the kind of intervention sought by the French. Nonetheless, EU employment policy served its legitimising purpose at the domestic political level, and French Socialist ministers consistently stressed – if not exaggerated – the significance of developments in this area (Howarth, 2002a, 2002b). The Jospin government also made a deliberately symbolic gesture, playing down the stability element of economic governance, and emphasising the government's margin of manoeuvre. France was the only aspiring participant of EMU to fail officially to respect the 3 per cent deficit figure for its 1997 budget: the 3.1 per cent figure announced demonstrated French pique at German insistence that the deficit criterion be respected for participation in EMU. However, the overriding objective of starting EMU by 1999 – the design of which the Germans would not allow to be altered – demonstrated the hollowness of the Jospin government's rhetoric. Socialist-led governments have not been alone in advocating this more interventionist form of economic governance. In September 2003, the Raffarin UMP government joined with Chancellor Schröder to launch a Franco-German growth initiative, and attacked the Commission for being 'anti-industry' and excessive in its drive for budget cutting, pledging further tax cuts in both countries and 10 major jointly funded infrastructural projects (*Le Monde*, 19 September 2003). President Chirac has regularly called for EU-level and Franco-German projects which involve deficit spending to stimulate the economy and develop particular industrial sectors (see Chapter 10 by Trouille and Uterwedde).

Economic governance as credibility and legitimacy building

EG has also been perceived and advocated as a means to improve the credibility of ECB monetary policy. This form of EG can link in with the price stability version of EG embodied by the Maastricht Treaty and SGP rules by reinforcing the credibility of the ECB's efforts to manage Eurozone monetary policy. Crucially, this form of EG concerns communication – the coordination of different national government voices regarding ECB monetary policy and desirable economic policy. There has been a problem of many voices making different pronouncements on ECB policy-making. This version of EG has involved the creation of a single political interlocutor of the ECB, which focuses on maintaining good relations with the central bank, and contributes to the improved coordination of the international representation of the Eurozone. Thus, the emphasis is on the effective operation of the inter-governmental/political dimension of the Eurozone. This version of EG has also involved embedding the independent ECB in a political framework to reinforce its democratic legitimacy and public accountability. Despite the rhetorical and real emphasis placed upon reinforced co-ordination, in their search for margin of manoeuvre French governments have done much to undermine this form of economic governance.

The former Socialist finance minister Dominique Strauss-Kahn succeeded in achieving a formal agreement on the creation of what he labelled the 'Euro-Council' (*conseil de l'euro*) in December 1997, which the Jospin government widely presented as a manifestation of economic governance. This body was subsequently relabelled the Euro-X (prior to the 1998 decision on euro participants, 'X' meaning 'unknown', later becoming the Euro-XI when the decision was taken that 11 member states would join). This was due to German opposition that the label 'Council' incorrectly suggested that the new body had legal status. It was then given its present name of 'Eurogroup' at the time of the French Council presidency during the second half of 2000. Leading French officials also made the exaggerated claim that the creation of the new Economics and Financial Committee, the rebaptised Monetary Committee, helped to reinforce the control of the Euro-XI over the economic framework in which monetary policy was made, thus promoting the construction of EU economic governance (*Libération*, 13 January 1999; Puetter, 2004). Emphasising the role of the Economic and Financial Committee was – as with the Eurogroup – important to the Jospin government, which sought to demonstrate and enhance the importance of intergovernmental decision-making in EMU as a counterbalance to supranational rules.

The French Council Presidency of the second half of 2000 had two specific goals with regard to the political dimension of the Eurozone: to improve the visibility of the Eurogroup, and improve economic policy coordination. Progress in both goals was limited, but potentially significant. Regarding the first goal, the French scored a minor victory in convincing the Eurozone governments to adopt the 'Eurogroup' title. The French also succeeded in effecting an agreement to produce a clearer, published agenda for Eurogroup meetings, to have longer meetings, to discuss more current matters at them, and to improve their communication output (notably through the organisation of a press conference immediately after the Eurogroup meeting, which allowed the Eurozone Finance Ministers to make announcements prior to their confirmation by Ecofin the following day). However, the French failed in their aim to give the Eurogroup a legal personality of its own. Thus, all Eurogroup agreements still had to be ratified by Ecofin. Also, Ecofin remained very much the most important body for coordination (including discussion of the Stability/Convergence Programmes and the BEPG, which were also prepared by EU member states not participating in the Eurozone, and thus not attending Eurogroup meetings). With regard to Eurogroup-ECB relations, the French government sought, unsuccessfully, the organisation of more frequent bilateral meetings between the presidents of the two bodies. The aim here was to improve the coordination of member state positions on ECB policy-making, and channel this through the Eurogroup to the ECB president. The then French Finance Minister, Laurent Fabius, also blamed the weakness of the euro at the time on the lack of strong political leadership in the Eurozone, the absence of an EU equivalent to the American Secretary of the Treasury (*Le Monde*, 4 July 2001). He raised the idea of a 'Mr Euro' (previously introduced by the French), a position to be held by an individual over a period of several years who would be responsible, in conjunction with the Council presidency, for the international representation of the Eurozone – an economic policy equivalent to 'Mr CFSP' (Common Foreign and Security Policy), the EU's foreign policy representative. With regard to the second goal of the French Council Presidency, there were no great strides towards tightened policy coordination. Moreover, the development of a common communications strategy appeared to stall, with different publicly expressed views on a range of Eurozone related matters, including the decline of the euro and attacks on Duisenberg's competence as ECB president (Howarth and Loedel, 2005).

While breaking the pact's rules and agreeing to suspend the EDP, the Raffarin government nonetheless continued its efforts to reinforce the Eurogroup as the principal intergovernmental forum for Eurozone coordination. With EU enlargement, the French saw the Eurogroup as assuming even greater importance as an informal forum for discussion to counterbalance the potential dilution of French influence in the context of Ecofin meetings. The Franco-German proposal on the reinforcement of the Eurogroup to the EU Convention met with the objection of the 'euro-outsiders', member states which had remained outside the Eurozone, such as the UK. The French sought to enable Ecofin to meet in a forum consisting of only the Ministers of Finance of Eurozone member states, thus enabling them to make legally binding decisions without the approval of the euro-outsiders. These proposals were not included in the Draft Treaty (2003), and the French have had to content themselves with the limited reinforcement of the Eurogroup, including the creation of a Mr Euro, who would chair meetings for two years and provide a political face to the Eurozone (Convention Working Group on Economic Government, 2002; Draft Treaty Establishing a Constitution for Europe, 2003). Prior to treaty ratification, at the start of 2004, the Luxembourg Prime Minister and Finance Minister, Jean-Claude Juncker, was appointed as the first two-year head of the Eurogroup.

Economic governance as an explicit challenge to the ECB's goals and goal-setting and operational independence

French politicians have challenged explicitly both the goals and independence of the ECB. There are four roots to French opposition to central bank independence required by the German-imposed design for EMU (Howarth, 2001): first, French republican tradition; second, the belief that control over economic and monetary policy should not be separated; third, the perception, rooted in the history of French political economy, that low inflationary economic policies can be maintained by democratically elected officials, guided by enlightened bureaucrats and advisers (notably those from the French Treasury and, in particular, the elite corps of Financial Inspectors); and finally, power considerations within the French administration. None of the leading French political parties supported the concept of central bank independence until 1991, either at the national or European level (Balleix-Banerjee, 1997). The neo-Gaullist Rassemblement pour la République (RPR) was opposed for nationalistic reasons, and sought the maintenance of Council control over a future European monetary policy. The Socialist Party placed stress on social goals and the appropriate policy mix. Moreover, surprisingly, the Union pour la Démocratie Française (UDF) confederation supported only a more cautious, evolutionary approach, although one of its more pro-European components came out strongly in favour of central bank independence.

Despite this tradition of opposition, following the ratification of the Maastricht Treaty the large majority of mainstream political leaders either defended central bank independence and the ECB's goals, or abstained from comment. However, since the start of EMU's Stage Three in 1999, and, in particular, since the start of the economic slowdown in 2001, the antagonistic opinions of influential advisers and leading politicians alike have been heard. On 23 January 2002, Pascal Lamy, the French Socialist commissioner for trade and Jean Pisani-Ferry, then head of Prime Minister Jospin's Economic Analysis Council, published (in a 'personal capacity') a pamphlet calling for the Eurogroup to be assigned the responsibility for setting the inflation target that the ECB is expected to meet (Lamy and Pisani-Ferry, 2002). The authors argued that the ECB's pursuit of low inflation was too restrictive, hindering economic growth in the Eurozone. The European monetary policy model, they maintained, should be re-established along the lines of fiscal-monetary authority relations in Britain, Denmark, Sweden and New Zealand, where the government sets the inflation target that the central bank is expected to follow (Lamy and Pisani-Ferry, 2002). The authors also argued that the British target of 2–3 per cent, set by the government, had proved its merit in comparison to the more restrictive 2 per cent set by the Governing Council of the European Central Bank, with its unique objective of price stability.

Several leading French politicians have also called for the transformation of the ECB's goals. The sound money core of the EMU project and the independence of the ECB were objects of attack by the Socialist-led Jospin government in its early months. Leaders in the Raffarin and de Villepin UMP governments have been similarly critical, especially given their criticism of insufficient interest rate cuts and a strong euro, which they claimed slowed French economic growth in the new millennium, resulting in a major commercial deficit from 2004 onwards, after a decade of large commercial surpluses. On 14 July 2004, in his annual televised Bastille Day speech, President Chirac chose to focus on the need to reform the mission of the ECB in order to qualify the pursuit of low inflation – implying that ECB policy contributed to sluggish economic growth in the largest Eurozone economies. Nicolas Sarkozy, then finance minister, called for the ECB to adopt a Federal Reserve-style target that included economic growth (*Financial Times*, 11 June 2004). Later, as the UMP's 2007 presidential candidate, he attacked the ECB's focus on low inflation. The ambition of all Europeans, he argued, 'should be to re-define the principles and the rules of economic and monetary union by carving in them a humanist and social dimension that is so dearly lacking in Europe' (Euroactiv.com, 23 February 2007). Proposal 89 of Ségolène Royal's 2007 presidential electoral programme called for the inclusion of an employment creation objective in the ECB's statute. Several leading politicians and 2007 presidential candidates – including Sarkozy, de Villepin and Royal – also made thinly veiled attacks on the ECB's goal-setting independence (*Le Monde*, 9, 19 and 22 December 2006). In December 2006, when criticising the ECB's decision to raise its interest rate, Royal insisted that the bank be 'submitted to political decisions' because it was not its job 'to control [*commander*] the future of our economies' (*Le Monde*, 22 December 2006).

Conclusion

French policy positions on EU-level economic governance over the past two decades have reflected the strong interventionist state tradition in France that is crucial for government legitimisation. These positions also reflect French efforts to maximise national margins of manoeuvre in relation to both EU-level fiscal and monetary policy, and the pressures of European and international market integration, in an effort to keep the world at bay. The clearest examples of French government success in bending the rules were the non-application of the EDP and the reform of the SGP. The elaborate nature of the potential flexibility in the application of the reformed SGP's rules embodies the French paradox of wanting EG, yet insisting on intergovernmental policy-making and margin of manoeuvre. Politically, the design and rules of the EMU project have been most explicitly challenged in the context of electoral contests: hence the positioning of the Plural Left coalition in the 1997 legislative elections and the Chiracian Right in the 2002 presidential and legislative elections. For both the mainstream political Left and Right, the rules have been criticised as having contributed to a perceived liberalisation bias of European integration and the pressures of globalisation. EG as macroeconomic policy coordination has been presented as a desirable goal, as long as most of this coordination remains 'soft' and retains a broadly – if not actively – interventionist character emphasising growth and job-creation. EG is thus presented as a device to qualify liberalisation pressures.

EG, as the explicit elimination of the European Central Bank's goal-setting independence, has only occasionally been a stated goal of successive French governments since the signing of the Maastricht Treaty. A more regular feature of French government policy announcements has been the extension of some kind of political control through economic governance that effectively qualifies the bank's 'sound money' emphasis. However, French governments have never spelled out the institutional arrangements and decision-making procedures whereby this political control would be achieved.

The reinforcement of the role of the Eurogroup in Eurozone coordination remains a French objective. Notably, French governments have advocated giving the body a treaty-recognised status and power to make decisions. This reform objective stems in part from the French ambition to improve the communication and legitimisation dimension of economic governance. However, beyond the reinforced status of this intergovernmental body, French governments have never succeeded in clarifying precisely how macroeconomic policy coordination would be reinforced. Indeed, the most common feature of French discourse on EG has been the absence of any concrete proposal of transferring real economic policy competencies from the national to the European level. French efforts with regard to the reinforced status and role of the Eurogroup stem principally from the restrained and secretive nature of this body, which ensures a flexible application of the rules and a politically sensitive margin of manoeuvre, thus reflecting the paradox – indeed inherent confusion – of French policy on economic governance that is both intergovernmental and interventionist in nature.

References

Arnaud, J.-L. (2000) 'France and Europe: the European debate in France at the start of the French presidency', Notre Europe Research and Policy Papers, 10 (July).

Balleix-Banerjee, C. (1997) 'La France et la Banque Centrale Européenne: débats politiques et élaboration de la décision, janvier 1988–septembre 1992', Paris: University Panthéon-Assas (Paris II), doctoral thesis.

Boyer, R. (1999) *Le Gouvernement économique de la zone euro*, Paris: La Documentation française.

Boyer, R. and M. Dehove (2001) 'Du "gouvernement économique" au gouvernement tout court: vers un fédéralisme à l'européenne', *Critique Internationale*, 11 (April): 179–95.

Conseil d'Analyse Economique (1998) *Coordination européenne des politiques économiques*, Paris: La Documentation française.

Drake, H. (2001) 'France on trial? The challenge of change posed by the French Council Presidency of the European Union, July-December 2000', *Modern and Contemporary France*, 9(4): 453–66.

Euroactiv.com (2007) 'Sarkozy wants "protective EU" to offset globalisation', 23 February, updated 28 February, http://www.euractiv.com/en/elections/sarkozy-wants-protective-eu-offset- globalisation/article-161948), consulted 10 March 2007.

Hall, P. (1986) *Governing the Economy*, Cambridge: Polity Press.

Heipertz, M. and A. Verdun, (2004) 'The dog that would never bite? The past and future of the Stability and Growth Pact', *Journal of European Public Policy*, 10(5): 765–80.

Howarth, D. (2001) *The French Road to European Monetary Union*, Basingstoke: Palgrave Macmillan.

Howarth, D. (2002a) 'The French state in the Euro-zone: "modernisation" and legitimizing dirigisme', in K. Dyson (ed.), *European States and the Euro: Europeanization, Variation, and Convergence*, Oxford: Oxford University Press, pp. 145–72.

Howarth, D. (2002b) 'The European policy of the Jospin government: a new twist to old French games', *Modern and Contemporary France*, 10(3): 353–70.

Howarth, D. and P. Loedel (2005) *The European Central Bank: the New European Leviathan*, Basingstoke: Palgrave Macmillan.

Lamy, P. and J. Pisani-Ferry (2002) *L'Europe de nos volontés*, Paris: Plon.

Maclean, M. (2002) *Economic Management and French Business from De Gaulle to Chirac*, Basingstoke: Palgrave Macmillan.

Milesi, G. (1998) *Le Roman de l'Euro*, Paris: Hachette.

Pochet, P. (1998) 'The social consequences of EMU: an overview of national debates', in. P. Pochet and B. Vanhercke (eds), *Social Challenges of Economic and Monetary Union*, Brussels: European Interuniversity Press, pp. 67–102.

Puetter, U. (2004) 'The Eurogroup and informal governance in the European Union', doctoral thesis, Queen's University, Belfast.

Schmidt, V. (1997) 'Running on empty: the end of *dirigisme* in French economic leadership', *Modern and Contemporary France*, 5(2): 229–41.

Shonfield, A. (1969) *Modern Capitalism: the Changing Balance of Public and Private Power*, London: Oxford University Press.

Wallace, W. (2000) 'Collective governance', in H. Wallace and W. Wallace (eds), *Policy-Making in the European Union*, Oxford: Oxford University Press, pp. 523–42.

Wessels, W. and I. Linsenmann (2002) 'EMU's impact on national institutions – a *gouvernement économique* in the making: towards vertical and horizontal fusion?' in K. Dyson (ed.), *European States and the Euro: Europeanization, Variation, and Convergence*, Oxford: Oxford University Press, pp. 53–77.

9
French Corporate Governance in a Globalised World: a Changing Business Model?

Mairi Maclean

Introduction

This chapter examines French corporate governance in the context of a new, globalising world. It considers the extraordinary reach of globalisation – *la mondialisation* as it is known in France – and the continuing internationalisation of French business made possible by extensive inward and outward foreign direct investment (FDI). The motivation behind FDI, according to Dunning (1993), is fourfold, being to seek out new markets, natural resources, low costs and strategic assets. Added to this, leading French companies have been driven by the logic of 'critical mass', of having sufficient power to enable them to play comfortably on the world stage, and this has led in turn to extensive corporate restructuring across national boundaries. Fresh corporate governance challenges have emerged as rival stakeholder groups – shareholders, directors, managers, employees and governments – compete for position and local advantage. To what degree is the French national business system now changing, and to what extent is it likely to converge on what is often termed the 'Anglo-American model', as international standards of corporate governance begin to emerge? Despite some degree of convergence due to globalisation, the chapter nevertheless concludes that national distinctiveness remains, albeit in a context of significant progress in corporate governance reform.

France and globalisation

In few countries has the phenomenon of globalisation been as widely debated – or as deprecated – as in France (Cohen, 1996, 1997; Pasqua, 1999; Rocard, 2000). In the 1990s, globalisation became synonymous with danger, primarily in the form of relocation (*délocalisations*), where multinational companies transfer production sites to low-wage economies in search of lower costs and greater flexibility in hiring and firing (Le Billon and Bouvais, 1999). In 1993, Senator Jean Arthuis warned of the inevitability of firms chasing hourly labour rates of one franc in China as against fifty francs at home (Arthuis, 1993). When Hoover moved production sites from Lyon to the Scottish city of Dundee in 1994 – one of the earliest cases of Arthuis's prophecy seemingly coming true – a predictable public outcry ensued. Burdensome legislation in employment or environmental law has contributed, it is argued, to 'evasion investment' on the part of large firms, as they seek a less restrictive and regulated environment in which to do business (Lallement, 2001), the burden of social welfare on employment being a long-standing cause for complaint among French employers (Weber, 1986). The registration of a company outside its host environment, for tax reasons, is commonplace; hence the large numbers of French restaurants which have registered in the UK. The bestseller written by Viviane Forrester (1996) spoke of a new and 'strange dictatorship' of economics over politics; while a 1997 survey found that 73 per cent of French people feared the potential impact of globalisation on jobs, pensions, social security and the health service. Increasingly, globalisation was also perceived as a threat to national identity, a view championed by sheep farmer José Bové, whose attack on a McDonalds under construction in 1999 brought him international fame, and a prison sentence (Maclean and Milner, 2001). The anti-Americanism characteristic of Bové's stance grew in France after 9/11, when President Chirac chose not to support George W. Bush in the war in Iraq, leading to a boycott of French goods in the USA, and the renaming of French fries as 'freedom fries' (see also Chapter 2 by Guillaume Parmentier).

A spate of mega-mergers involving French firms around the turn of the millennium seemed to confirm the threat to national identity. Since the de Gaulle era, the belief has prevailed in France that the country could not be great without great companies (Servan-Schreiber, 1967; Stoléru, 1969) and that the route to international competitiveness lay in the acquisition of critical mass (Cohen, 1995; Maclean, 2002). In the late 1960s and early 1970s, and again in the lead-up to the Single European Market in 1993, takeovers were openly encouraged by government policy, which sought to restructure French manufacturing industry through concentration in both the public and private sectors, so as to create 'national champions'. The logic of critical mass continues to drive top French companies, leading to extensive corporate restructuring across national borders. A number of the mergers and acquisitions which took place at the turn of the millennium were strategic deals in oligopolistic markets often characterised by high entry barriers, as exemplified by Renault's purchase of a sizeable stake in Nissan. Several were hostile takeovers launched by French firms on fellow rivals, such as TotalFina-Elf, or Banque Nationale de Paris (BNP)-Paribas. A number, too, were Franco-German mergers, illustrating the growing industrial and technological cooperation which marks the Franco-German alliance (Trouille, 2001; Trouille and Uterwedde, 2001), explored by Trouille and Uterwedde in Chapter 10. A notable example of this was the merger of Aérospatiale-Matra and Dasa in 1999, leading to the creation of EADS (European Aeronautics, Defence and Space Company), a global leader in aerospace, defence and related services, which owns the aircraft manufacturer Airbus. Also in 1999, the merger of Rhône-Poulenc and Hoechst in the pharmaceutical sector gave rise to Aventis, taken over in turn five years later by Sanofi-Synthélabo, to form Sanofi-Aventis, the world's third largest company in pharmaceuticals.

Despite widespread hostility to globalisation among the population at large, there is a consensus amongst the French ruling elite that it will bring extensive benefits, and that corporate sector participation is to be actively encouraged. However, there is not the same level of commitment to labour and capital market freedoms that prevails in the UK. In France, the approach taken is to combine selected market freedoms with instrumentalism. The political and business elites are willing to sacrifice certain (lesser) markets and certain (smaller) companies in the name of global competition; but they are unwilling, as yet, to expose what are perceived as core markets and core companies to the full force of global competition. This said, the government does not always set out to prevent the takeover of key companies by foreign players. A $3.8 billion hostile bid for Péchiney, the aluminium and packaging company, by Alcan of Canada in 2003, for example, was approved by Finance Minister Francis Mer, partly because Alcan agreed to move its packaging and aerospace headquarters to Paris as part of the deal.

Nevertheless, domestic companies have colluded with the state whenever possible to manipulate the rules of the game in their favour, with the broad intention of creating opportunities to expand abroad while excluding foreign competitors from domestic markets (Maclean, 2002). Following the liberalisation of EU energy markets in 1996, for example, France dragged its feet, the largely state-owned Electricité de France (EdF) being shielded by regulation of its domestic market while being encouraged to pursue a bold internationalisation strategy, effectively underwritten by the state. Soon afterwards, it began to invest in the fully liberalised UK energy market, buying up London Electricity in 1999. By 2005, more than 40 per cent of EdF's turnover of approximately €50 billion originated outside the Hexagon. It is now Europe's largest electricity utilities company, and the twentieth largest non-financial company (by foreign assets) in the world (UNCTAD, 2006). As Vernholes points out (2001), French interpretation of EU legislation on the liberalisation of energy markets was deliberately protracted and minimalist. The partial privatisation of EdF in October/November 2005 did little to rectify this, with a small stake of 15 per cent sold off. Moreover, the motivation behind the sell-off was, ironically, the need to raise an additional €7 billion to pay for EdF's continuing expansion in Europe (Gow, 2005; Maclean et al., 2007). In a similar vein, the government has actively intervened in the pharmaceuticals sector to promote its own 'national champion'. In spring 2004, when the French company Sanofi-Synthélabo launched a hostile bid for Aventis, Nicolas Sarkozy, then Finance Minister, stepped in to back the bid, while opposing a counter-bid by the Swiss firm Novartis. An increased offer by Sanofi-Synthélabo met with success in April 2004, much to the consternation of the then German Chancellor, Gerhard Schröder, who accused Sarkozy of conducting himself in a 'nationalistic' manner.

The French government remains happy to intervene to help struggling firms, such as Alstom in 2003–04, often in the teeth of EU opposition; or to prevent takeovers or mergers that it sees as being against the national interest – the abortive takeover, for example, of the food company Danone by the soft drink giant, PepsiCo, in July 2005. As President Chirac put it, 'today's priority for France is to defend its industrial competitiveness and the strength of its companies'. Nicolas Sarkozy agreed, stating, 'it is important that one knows the state has not renounced and will not renounce the use of all the powerful means at its disposal to protect the economic and social interests of France'.[1]

This combination of pursuing bold internationalisation strategies abroad, together with a determination to repel foreign competitors at home, continues to serve France well. As can be seen from Table 9.1, France has emerged in recent years as a major international investor, though not quite on the scale of the UK. By the end of 2003, the accumulated stock of French FDI totalled $643 billion, 7.8 per cent of the world total, just ahead of Germany with 7.6 per cent (UN, 2005).

The greater part of France's FDI stock is concentrated in the hands of companies deemed by the state and the business elite as central to the national interest. In recent years, some of these have emerged as top-tier

Table 9.1   Inward and outward FDI flows for France and the UK, 1998–2003 ($ billion)

Year	France		UK	
	Inward	Outward	Inward	Outward
1998	31.0	48.6	74.3	122.8
1999	46.5	126.9	88.0	201.6
2000	43.3	177.4	118.8	233.4
2001	50.5	86.8	52.6	58.9
2002	48.9	49.4	27.8	35.2
2003	47.0	57.3	14.5	55.1

Sources: United Nations (2005); Maclean et al. (2006: Tables B1 and B2).

multinationals, ranked within the world's top 100 by the absolute value of their overseas holdings. Carrefour, for example, which took over Promodès in 1999, has become a world leader in retailing, while Renault acquired a 44.4 per cent stake in the Japanese car giant Nissan. French FDI is relatively concentrated, the top non-financial multinationals accounting for 62.1 per cent of the nation's outward FDI stock in 2003. France is strongly represented in construction, having three global top 15 companies, including Bouygues and Eiffage. In the post-war era, France moved headlong from being primarily an industrially and agriculturally based economy to one increasingly dominated by the service sector (Maclean, 2002). This is in keeping with world FDI trends, which reveal a move away from manufacturing (down from 44 per cent of world stock in 1990 to 29 per cent in 2002) towards services (up from 47 to 67 per cent over the same period) (UN, 2005). In advertising, France was home to five of the world's 15 largest multinationals in 2003 (led by Publicis), while in hotels France boasted the largest group of all, Accor. France has two of the top 15 global catering businesses, including Sodhexo. Meanwhile, Lagardère features amongst the world top media multinationals. In telecommunications, France Télécom ranked number one in 2002 by scope of international operations, while AXA was positioned second in the world by foreign income in insurance. That year, as many as six of the world's top 20 retailers, ranked by foreign sales, were French, headed by Carrefour and Pinault-Printemps-Redoute (PPR). Finally, also in 2002, two French banks featured amongst the world's top 20 most internationalised banks, namely the French market leaders BNP-Paribas and Société Générale.

Table 9.2 Mergers and acquisition deals worth $1 billion or more led by France's top 100 companies, 1998–2003

Location of merged or acquired Company	Number of deals	Total value ($ billion)
Domestic	9	122.7
European Union	30	169.7
North America[a]	21	115.0
Other international	3	11.4
Totals	63	418.8

Note: [a]US, Canada and Mexico.
Sources: United Nations (1999, 2000, 2001, 2002, 2003, 2004, 2005); Maclean et al. (2006); Datamonitor Reports.

Whilst in the European Union (EU) France is often perceived to be championing a social model at variance with the free-market liberalism advocated by the UK (Albert, 1991; Hall and Soskice, 2001; Hancké, 2001; Schmidt, 2003), this impressive catalogue of French companies with extensive global reach signals just how committed is its ruling elite to exploiting the potentialities of the new global economy. Between 1998 and 2003, as many as 23 of France's leading 100 companies made one or more acquisitions in excess of $1 billion (Maclean et al., 2006). There can be little more elegant tribute to the ambitions of already dominant firms within the new global economy. Table 9.2 charts the number, size and geographical spread of these deals. It demonstrates that the quest for critical mass normally begins in the domestic market. Thereafter, the approach taken by French companies, most typically but not always, is to internationalise within the EU before expanding further afield. Notably, despite the common perception of France as a country nurturing a natural antipathy to the US, in fact 21 deals worth more than $1 billion were led by French companies in North America between 1998 and 2003.

Corporate governance reform in an interdependent world

The above examples shed light on a national business system potentially undergoing far-reaching change. They demonstrate that despite the anti-globalisation rhetoric, leading French firms have been to the fore in dynamically engaging in strategies of international expansion and alliance building. In this they clearly recognise the need to reap economies of scale and scope, which is the logic underpinning the growth of large-scale enterprises and mega-mergers.

Yet the rapid internationalisation of French business in recent years cannot be explained merely in terms of the orthodox reasoning of mainstream business strategy theories. There is no doubt that members of the French business elite have grown increasingly sophisticated as strategic leaders, embracing in particular the principles of positioning, capability building and value chain configuration across national boundaries. But what is equally true is that business leaders have remained alive to the fact that markets are never completely free; rather, they are socially constructed institutions bound and conditioned by rules and regulations.

Pressure for corporate governance reform and the international harmonisation of standards has stemmed from two principal sources: institutional investors concerned that dysfunctional boards might destroy shareholder value, and national and supra-national authorities troubled that further corporate scandals, such as that which brought Vivendi Universal to its knees in 2002, might discredit and ultimately destabilise the institutional foundations of the global economic order, portending a new age of economic nationalism. The sense of urgency driving both groups of reformers is indicative of the extent to which corporate ownership rights are distributed increasingly across national boundaries. In the US, for example, CalPERS, the California Public Employees' Retirement System, the largest US pension fund, which had funds under management of $177 billion in December 2004, has championed the cause of investor rights and corporate governance reform around the world (Palmeri and Lacy, 2004). One tactic widely used by CalPERS has been to vote against the re-election of directors of companies which have violated its principles of good governance, such as employing an auditor to provide consultancy services (as Enron had done prior to its collapse in 2001). Since 1997, moreover, CalPERS has had significant holdings in France's top 40 listed companies, the *Cotation assistée en continu* (CAC-40) index, together with other international institutional investors, such as US mutual funds Templeton and Fidelity. By the year 2000, foreign ownership of the share capital of France's top 40 companies had reached an average of more than 40 per cent, a record among the world's leading industrial nations (Morin, 2000). By 2003, this had risen to 43 per cent (Clift, 2007; Mauduit, 2003). In the US, in the wake of the financial reporting debacles at Enron and WorldCom, the federal government has taken a more directive approach since the passing in 2002 of the Sarbanes-Oxley Act (SOX), also known as the Public Company Accounting Reform and Investor Protection Act, granting the Security and Exchange Commission (SEC) extensive powers to deal with non-compliant companies. Notably, this includes foreign firms with 300 or more individual shareholders based in the US, prompting significant share buybacks by non-US companies (Andrews, 2005).

The story of the collapse of Vivendi Universal is a salutary one, warning of the dangers of overspending and believing in one's own hype. Under the leadership of Jean-Marie Messier, Vivendi embarked in 1999 on a spate of acquisitions lasting three years and involving numerous multi-billion dollar deals. Messier had made his name in the privatisation programme implemented by Balladur in 1986–88 when, as a young civil servant, he quickly got used to handling large numbers and figures (without, of course, assuming any personal risk). His intention on becoming head of Vivendi was to transform it from a nationally-based utility company into a multinational media, services and communications empire, deriving synergies from its capabilities in managing media and distribution networks. Significant acquisitions were made in the US, including US Filter in 1999 for $6.3 billion, Cendant Software in 1999 for $1 billion, the publisher Houghton Mifflin in 2001 for $2.3 billion, and USA Networks in 2002 for $10.7 billion. The largest acquisition of all, however, in 2000, and at a cost of $40.4 billion, was the drinks and media conglomerate Seagram, the Canadian owner of Universal Studios, thus giving rise to Vivendi Universal.

In the event, the fall of Vivendi Universal was just as rapid as its rise. The company's debts mounted to €37 billion, and in March 2002 a loss of €13.6 billion was reported for 2001. By popular consensus, Messier was seen to have 'paid too much for too many acquisitions', leaving him with 'a pile of debt, a battered stock, and an iffy strategy' (Guyon, 2002). He resigned in 2002, when the eight French directors on the board, who had supported him in the face of opposition from the five US directors, withdrew their backing, one by one. In doing so, they acted in concert to safeguard the reputation of the French business model, which Messier was presumed guilty of bringing into disrepute.[2] By then, Messier had also lost the support of the French political class, whom he had offended in 2001 when, at a press conference, he had tactlessly announced the death of the French 'cultural exception'. This concerns the enduring tradition of state support for the French film industry, perceived to be struggling against the hegemony of Hollywood. The gaffe seems to have signalled the beginning of the end for Messier. As Péan and Cohen (2003: 425) wrote: 'Taken out of context, that sentence "killed" J2M [Jean-Marie Messier]. Repeated by film professionals and relayed by numerous intellectuals and politicians, the polemic [surrounding Messier] became rapidly inflated.'[3]

Corporate disasters on the scale of those suffered by Vivendi have raised the tempo of the debate on corporate governance and globalisation. Even before the fall of Messier, Vivendi had come under attack from shareholder activists, who, in June 2001, petitioned the Paris Commercial Court to appoint an auditor to investigate the failure of the company to alert shareholders to the financial consequences of its strategy of growth through acquisitions (Garrity, 2002). At the same time, the fund management company Hermes wrote to the board criticising the company for its 'archaic voting structure' and lack of accountability to shareholders (Gilbert, 2002). Messier had promised whilst promoting the merger with Seagram that Vivendi Universal would be a model of good governance. However, he went on to restrict shareholders' voting rights, such that shareholders with 2 per cent of company shares or more had to forgo their voting rights if the turnout at the annual general meeting was significantly less than 100 per cent (*The Economist*, 2000). This measure effectively removed the voting rights of major investors, turnout at annual meetings tending to be low. As Vivendi's share price plummeted, the disastrous consequences of the unbridled power wielded by Messier as Président Directeur-Général (PDG) focused attention on the relative lack of checks and balances in the French system of corporate governance. In January 2003, now under the leadership of Jean-René Fourtou, former head of Aventis, the company responded by introducing new governance rules and structures, embodied in an 'Internal Charter' and conforming to recommendations and regulations contained in the French Bouton Report of 2002 and the US Sarbanes-Oxley Act. Exhausted from so many acquisitions, and facing serious cash-flow problems, Vivendi had valuable assets that could be sold to reduce its debts. Its publishing business was the first to be sold, together with an impressive array of art works by Picasso, Rodin and Rothko, inherited from Seagram at the time of the takeover. Incidents of this kind, though relatively few in number, have helped to sustain the momentum for reform and the introduction of more robust international standards of corporate governance that might better protect investors from the dangers of reckless globalisation. The Sarbanes-Oxley Act sets an exacting metric against which corporate standards may be judged (Romano, 2004) (despite having been criticised for benefiting auditors and accountants, seen as responsible for the collapse of Enron and WorldCom in the first place). It is no small matter, therefore, for a company like Vivendi to assert compliance with its provisions. The message to investors is one of reassurance, of adherence to the highest international standards of corporate governance, signalling a change for the better since the cavalier days when Jean-Marie

Messier seemingly lost sight of shareholder value in the quest for global expansion. (Also see Chapter 12 by Raymond Kuhn.)

Key governance reports in France have included the Viénot Reports of 1995 and 1999, the Marini Report of 1996 and the Bouton Report of 2002 (AFEP/CNPF, 1995; AFEP/MEDEF, 1999; Marini, 1996; MEDEF/AFEP, 2002). With the *nouvelles régulations économiques* (NRE) of 2001 and the 2003 *loi de sécurité financière* on financial market regulation – which led to the establishment of the new Autorité des Marchés Financiers (AMF) – governance principles became enshrined in civil law. The early reports constituted preliminary responses to domestic corporate scandals and governance reforms elsewhere, particularly the Cadbury Report (Committee on the Financial Aspects of Corporate Governance, 1992), and its various successors, which originated in the UK. They were led by private-sector employers' associations, with the exception of the Marini Report, which was sponsored by the Juppé government (Maclean, 1999). The NRE, *loi de sécurité financière* and Bouton Report, on the other hand, may be seen as more significant attempts to respond to the far more serious corporate scandals and consequent governance reforms (the Sarbanes-Oxley Act in particular) of recent years.

The NRE legislation had a major impact on the corporate governance environment in France. It encourages the separation of chairman and CEO functions, giving companies with a unitary structure the choice of separating these or keeping them joint. It restricts the number of memberships on boards of directors which may be held concurrently to five. It strengthens the representation of top management on the board of directors but also facilitates the participation of minority shareholders through, *inter alia*, the introduction of new technologies (such as electronic voting and video-conferencing). Finally, it reinforces transparency by bolstering disclosure requirements, greatly expanding the scale and scope of the information that firms are required to provide in annual reports, which must henceforth include social and environmental performance (Egan et al., 2003). At the same time, the stock options of the ten most highly paid executives are to be disclosed (collectively) in the annual report, five in companies with fewer than 200 employees. The AMF, which combined the existing prudential institutions, the COB (Commission des Opérations de Bourse) and CMF (Conseil des Marchés Financiers), was likewise designed to improve the efficiency of the French system, and to make it more comparable to those of other countries (Bloch and Kremp, 2001; Clift, 2007).

Meanwhile, the Bouton Report recommended incremental improvement rather than radical reform. Of key concern was the internal control of boards of directors, which was to be tightened up to deal with key strategic issues, such as the company's financial position. Directors were to be individuals of integrity, selected for their competence, and given additional training if necessary; they were also to have regard for the interests of all shareholders, including minority shareholders. Information for company directors was to be timely, and directors' access to information was to be improved (including information of a negative nature). Directors were to be allowed to meet key executives without corporate officers present, provided the latter were informed. The definition of independence was modified – though, given the ties of friendship that bind members of the French business elite (Kadushin, 1995; Yeo et al., 2003), they rarely achieve real 'independence' in the sense in which Derek Higgs (2003) or Sir Adrian Cadbury (2002) might understand the term (see below). The proportion of independent directors was to be increased to half in companies where capital was dispersed, and two-thirds in the remainder. The performance of the board should be evaluated annually. Audit committees were to consist of two-thirds independent directors, and to be given the necessary time to study accounts. They should also be entitled to interview external auditors, and report annually on their work. The transparency of remuneration and bonuses was also stressed, in keeping with the NRE. The remuneration committee should consist of a majority of independent directors, and should devise a clear policy with regard to stock options, with bonuses linked to performance. Finally, both remuneration and audit committees were henceforth to report on their work in the annual report, commenting on how each committee had functioned, while the nominations committee should include the chairman, and should search pro-actively for future independent directors.

A changing business model?

These comprise a wide-ranging set of corporate governance measures, whose primary objectives, to all intents and purposes, would seem to be informed by the shareholder value paradigm, thus bringing France more in line with the Anglo-Saxon model.

Traditionally, however, the philosophy that has underpinned the French business model lies firmly in the *intérêt social* ('social interest') of the firm, as enshrined in the *arrêt Freuhauf-France* of May 1965. This may be defined as a belief in the common weal uniting the interests of workers and employers; a belief that economic and social affairs cannot be separated; and an expectation that employers should pay attention to their responsibilities as well as to their rights (Maclean, 2002; Weber, 1986). Interestingly, the NRE – as Clift (2007) emphasises – originated in the cause of *intérêt social*, having been initiated by former prime minister Lionel Jospin who sought, following the 'Affaire Michelin' of 1999 (when 7500 employees were made redundant, despite a 17 per cent increase in company profits for the first six months of the year), to redress the balance in favour of other stakeholders. Specifically, Jospin sought to reduce the likelihood of what were termed 'abusive lay-offs' in pursuit of higher corporate profits. Moreover, political resistance to the 'Anglo-American' shareholder value model had intensified in September 1999,[4] when it became known that Philippe Jaffré, former head of oil conglomerate Elf Aquitaine, had cashed in stock options worth an estimated $35 million on leaving Elf at the time of its takeover by Total. As President Chirac protested at the time, why should French workers suffer to protect 'Scottish widows and California pensioners?'[5]

Corporate governance regimes, in their reality and essential dynamics, are more the product of history, embraced in systems and mindsets, than conformance to a set of universally espoused principles (Roe, 1994). Key features continue to differentiate the governance regimes of France and the UK, which are fundamental to what is generally regarded as 'best practice' in corporate governance. These include the extent of separation in the roles of CEO and chairman, and the independence of non-executive directors from top management – the extent to which board members are willing, and able, to challenge the head of the company when necessary. While the option exists under French company law to separate the roles of chairman and CEO, in many quarters the belief persists that effective decision-making requires that power be concentrated in the hands of the PDG. In 1998, less than a quarter of the top 100 French companies (23) had separated the roles of chairman and CEO. By 2003, two years after the NRE, this had risen to just over one-third (37), highlighting the importance of cultural reproduction as a mechanism for moderating pressures for change (Bourdieu, 1994; Maclean et al., 2006). Some companies that had split the roles subsequently chose to reunite them, as transpired in the cases of Suez and Alstom.

The independence of non-executive directors is also a case in point. In the UK, there is a clear divide between the owners and managers of leading firms, shareholdings are dispersed, and institutional investors control over 70 per cent of equity. In France, however, there is enduring diversity in relations between owners and managers. Some companies conform to the Anglo-American norm, yet many others differ in remaining family-owned or state-owned (though state ownership has declined dramatically in recent years), or in having close relationships with other companies. In this situation, directors are often appointed to boards specifically to represent a family, institution or interest group, and for this reason alone cannot be classified as 'independent'. Senator Philippe Marini, author of the 1996 Marini Report, expressed doubts as to whether non-executive directors in France would ever be fully independent, given the quintessential importance of the ties that bind them to one another, which are such as to widen the role:

> The notion of the independent director is an empirical notion. I often prefer to speak of 'professional' directors rather than 'independent' directors. In French practice, to be a director is a complement of activities. It is linked to the ties with capital, it is linked to the ties of friendship; it is linked to all kinds of things.[6]

Similarly, a director at the employers' association MEDEF (Mouvement des Entreprises de France) stressed in a personal interview the importance of competency over independence: 'a board of directors must be competent, irrespective of whether it is independent'.[7]

Despite the substantial transfers of ownership that have taken place in recent years, coupled with significant reform in matters of corporate governance, national institutional arrangements and business systems are tenacious. Whitley (1999) argues that regardless of the degree of international influence to which an economy is subjected, where national business systems are cohesive and supported by integrated institutions in a close-knit system of economic coordination and control, so the domestic economy will be less susceptible to change due to internationalisation. He concludes that there is no reason to presume that increasing international competition, such as France has experienced in recent years, will in itself bring about far-reaching systemic change, let alone that it will do so in one, Anglo-American, direction. An example of change happening in the *opposite* direction, of a British company learning from the French or European business model, is provided by Airbus UK, whose General Manager, Iain Gray, made the following observation in a personal interview:

> A prime example of our learning from our French and German partners is post September 11th, when a lot of UK aerospace companies made very instant reactions to reduce and downsize the workforce. In Airbus in the UK, we followed the lead of what was happening in France and Germany, and worked together with the trade unions to develop a jointly agreed plan in terms of what we called

flexibility measures that we could introduce to try and preserve long-term employment. So, you could see a French and German influence on us, which was in stark contrast to the way other UK plcs were making their decisions, and I think, from my perspective, that actually has proved to have been the right thing to have done. And I think there is a lot of merit in the French and German system that we need to take cognisance of in our own decision-making process.[8]

Ultimately, Iain Gray sees Airbus as operating in an integrated, transnational way which, he argues, is rare despite the fact that there are many international companies with facilities around the world. At the same time, however, he points out that the company respects individual national cultures: 'Culturally, Airbus is trying to create a company culture, but one that doesn't actually break down the national cultures. So it respects the national cultures and it respects the different ways of working.'[9] Delays in the production of the new superjumbo, the A380 aeroplane, resulted in further downsizing at Airbus in spring 2007, with Airbus UK destined to lose as many as 1600 jobs. Whilst these job losses are clearly regrettable, nevertheless the redundancies were again to be managed consensually, in conjunction with the unions, being voluntary rather than compulsory, and staged over four years.

Despite some clear signs of convergence in matters of corporate governance, French business elites are not seeking to embrace the market-based Anglo-American model in its entirety. On the contrary, many of the features traditionally associated with the French system continue to play a key role. These include state intervention, coupled with continuing protectionism, especially in markets associated with public service, and a belief that ownership matters. Long-term interpersonal and inter-corporate relationships between different corporate constituencies still dominate business life. Effective networking continues to serve France well, and is arguably more suited to the ways of continental Europe. Elites are understandably reluctant to undermine their own power base by renouncing the perceived competitive advantages of long-standing institutional arrangements (Rhodes and van Apeldoorn, 1998).

Conclusion

The strength of global competition has forced French companies to provide value for shareholders, to become more transparent, and to focus more resolutely on financial issues and return on capital. The boards of directors of leading French companies are increasingly international, reflecting the changing composition of the shareholding body. Top companies are taking the issue of corporate governance much more seriously than previously, backed up by the legal muscle of the NRE and the *loi sur la sécurité financière*. They also recognise the importance of investor relations, as Jean-François Théodore, CEO of Euronext, confirms:

> Two years ago we didn't have any investor relations. We were speaking to institutional investors, but in an institutional way. We were speaking about the market or trading, but not speaking about us. Now we have a small investors' initiative, with four or five people, and we listen very, very carefully to what our shareholders are saying.[10]

However, the cultural substrata that underlie societies go deep, often acting as powerful impediments to change – though at times, paradoxically, deep-seated cultural features may also be harnessed to facilitate change. Some aspects of what is apparently new in French business may be, in fact, recast elements of continuity (Maclean, 2002). What is certainly true is that slow, incremental change at this sedimentary level is much harder to observe. The internal structures of leading French companies remain, essentially, remarkably similar to hitherto. There is, for example, little prospect of the French abandoning the close-knit corporate networks, bound together by multiple director interlocks which, viewed from an Anglo-American perspective, may compromise the independence of non-executive directors (Kadushin, 1995). Likewise, the strategy of overt expansion pursued by many large French companies in recent years is also, paradoxically, one of continuity, control and maintaining 'Frenchness' in the world. Increasingly, French business leaders regard themselves as international, while remaining fundamentally French. As Daniel Bernard, PDG of Carrefour, expressed it: 'I consider myself, really, as international, but of French culture' (*Fortune*, 2000: 79).

In the longer term, further convergence may well be likely. Yet national business systems are, to a significant degree, self-referring, that is to say they are supported and informed by pre-existing social structures, norms and practices; and differences in the modus operandi of governance in French and British or American companies, for example, cannot be erased merely by insisting on compliance with a universal code of best practice (Maclean et al., 2006; Nayak et al., 2007). Ultimately, the present study points not to the convergence of the French business system with the Anglo-American model, but rather to the persistence of French national distinctiveness, to continuing heterogeneity or patterned variation, and the continuing strength of cultural reproduction, despite increasing internationalisation and more than twelve years of corporate governance reform.

Notes

The author wishes to thank the Leverhulme Trust and Reed Charity for funding the research which has informed the present chapter, and also the business leaders concerned for kindly agreeing to be interviewed.

1. www.expatica.com/actual/article, accessed 25 April 2007.
2. Interview with M. Pierre Bilger, former PDG of Alstom, Paris, 3 January 2003.
3. Translated by M. Maclean.
4. Interview with Mme Agnès Lépinay, Director of Economic Affairs, MEDEF, Paris, 26 May 2003.
5. www.brookings.edu, accessed 25 April 2007.
6. Interview with Senator Philippe Marini, French Senate, Paris, 14 January 2004.
7. Interview with Mme Agnès Lépinay.
8. Interview with Iain Gray, Managing Director and General Manager, Airbus UK, Bristol, 4 February 2003.
9. Ibid.
10. Interview with Jean-François Théodore, CEO, Euronext, London, 7 November 2003.

References

AFEP (Association Française des Entreprises Privées)/CNPF (Conseil National du Patronat Français) (1995) *Le Conseil d'administration des sociétés cotées* Paris: IEP (Viénot I).

AFEP/MEDEF (Mouvement des Entreprises de France) (1999) *Rapport du Comité sur le gouvernement d'entreprise présidé par M. Marc Viénot,* Paris: IEP (Viénot II).

Albert, M. (1991) *Capitalisme contre capitalisme*, Paris: Seuil.

Andrews, D. (2005) 'Non-US corporations take buyback action over Sarbanes-Oxley', *International Law Review*, 24(2) (February): 12.

Arthuis, J. (1993) *L'Incidence économique et fiscale des délocalisations hors du territoire national des activités industrielles et de services*, Paris: Commission des Finances au Sénat, 337 (4 June).

Bloch, L. and E. Kremp (2001) 'Ownership and voting power in France', in F. Barca and M. Becht (eds), *The Control of Corporate Europe*, Oxford: Oxford University Press, pp. 106–27.

Bourdieu, P. (1994) *The State Nobility: Elite Schools in the Field of Power*, trans. L.C. Clough, Cambridge: Polity Press.

Cadbury, Sir A. (2002) *Corporate Governance and Chairmanship: a Personal View*, Oxford: Oxford University Press.

Clift, B. (2007) 'French corporate governance in the new global economy: mechanisms of change within models of capitalism', *Political Studies*, 55(3): 546–67.

Cohen, E. (1995) 'France: national champions in search of a mission', in J. Hayward (ed.), *Industrial Enterprise and European Integration: from National* to *International Champions in Western Europe*, Oxford: Oxford University Press, pp. 23–46.

Cohen, E. (1996) *La Tentation hexagonale: la souveraineté à l'épreuve de la mondialisation*, Paris: Fayard.

Cohen, E. (1997) 'On met n'importe quoi sur le dos de la mondialisation', *La Croix*, 4 January.

Committee on the Financial Aspects of Corporate Governance (1992) *The Financial Aspects of Corporate Governance*, London: Gee (Cadbury Report).

Dunning, J.H. (1993) *The Globalization of Business*, London: Thomson.

The Economist (2000) 'French corporate governance – ambivalent', *The Economist*, 7 October, 73.

Egan, M.L. et al. (2003) 'France's *Nouvelles Régulations Economiques*: using government mandates for corporate reporting to promote environmentally sustainable economic development', paper presented at 25th Annual Conference of Association for Public Policy and Management, Washington DC, November.

Forrester, V. (1996) *L'Horreur économique*, Paris: Fayard.

Fortune (Europe) (2000) 142(1) 26 June: 79.

Garrity, W. (2002) 'Vivendi governance under fire', *Billboard*, 29 June.

Gilbert, N. (2002) 'Hermes criticises governance at Vivendi', *Financial News*, 4 June.

Gow, D. (2005) 'French take a gamble on part-privatization of EDF', *Guardian*, 29 October.

Guyon, J. (2002) 'Getting Messier', *Fortune*, 10 June.

Hall, P.A. and D. Soskice (2001) 'An introduction to varieties of capitalism', in D. Soskice and P.A. Hall (eds), *Varieties of Capitalism: the Institutional Foundations of Comparative Advantage*, Oxford: Oxford University Press.

Hancké, B. (2001) 'Revisiting the French model: coordination and restructuring in French industry', in D. Soskice and P.A. Hall (eds), *Varieties of Capitalism: the Institutional Foundations of Comparative Advantage*, Oxford: Oxford University Press, pp. 307–34.

Higgs, D. (2003) *Review of the Role and Effectiveness of Non-Executive Directors*, London: Department of Trade and Industry (Higgs Review).

Kadushin, C. (1995) 'Friendship among the French financial elite', *American Sociological Review*, 60 (April): 202–21.

Lallement, R. (2001) 'Foreign direct investment and the diversity of socio-economic systems in Europe: France, Germany and Britain compared', in M. Maclean and J.-M. Trouille (eds), *France, Germany and Britain: Partners in a Changing World*, Basingstoke: Palgrave Macmillan, pp. 85–99.

Le Billon, V. and W. Bouvais (1999) 'Mondialisation: cette France qui dit non', *L'Expansion*, 7–20 October: 648.

Maclean, M. (1999) 'Corporate governance in France and the UK: long-term perspectives on contemporary institutional arrangements', *Business History*, 41(1): 88–116.

Maclean, M. (2002) *Economic Management and French Business from de Gaulle to Chirac*, Basingstoke: Palgrave Macmillan.

Maclean, M. and S. Milner (2001) 'Introduction: France and globalisation', *Modern and Contemporary France*, 9(3) (August): 285–7.

Maclean, M., C.E. Harvey and J. Press (2006) *Business Elites and Corporate Governance in France and the UK*, Basingstoke: Palgrave Macmillan.

Maclean, M., C.E. Harvey and J. Press (2007) 'Managerialism and the post-war evolution of the French national business system', *Business History*, 49(4) (July): 531–51.

Marini, P. (1996) *La Modernisation du droit des sociétés*, Paris: La Documentation française (Marini Report).

Mauduit, L. (2003) 'Du capitalisme rhénan au capitalisme américain, la mutation de l'économie s'accélère', *Le Monde*, 29 July.

MEDEF/AFEP (2002) *Pour un meilleur gouvernement des entreprises cotées* (Bouton Report).

Morin, F. (2000) 'A transformation in the French model of shareholding and management', *Economy and Society*, 29(1) (February): 31–53.

Nayak, A., M. Maclean, C. Harvey and R. Chia (2007) 'Entrepreneurship, corporate governance and Indian business elites', *International Journal of Indian Culture and Business Management*, 1(1): 9–27.

Palmeri, C. and S. Lacy (2004) 'CalPERS: getting back to business', *Business Week*, 13 December.

Pasqua, C. (1999) 'La mondialisation n'est pas inéluctable', *Le Monde*, 8 December.

Péan, P. and P. Cohen (2003) *La Face cachée du monde: du contre-pouvoir aux abus de pouvoir*, Paris: Mille et Une Nuits.

Rhodes, M. and B. van Apeldoorn (1998) 'Capital unbound? The transformation of European corporate governance', *Journal of European Public Policy*, 5(3) (September): 406–27.

Rocard, M. (2000) 'Le développement, oui, mais comment ?', *La Vie*, 10 February.

Roe, M.J. (1994) 'Some differences in corporate governance in Germany, Japan and America', in T. Baums et al. (eds), *Institutional Investors and Corporate Governance*, Berlin: De Gruyter.

Romano, R. (2004) 'The Sarbanes-Oxley Act and the making of quack corporate governance', ECGI Working Paper Series in Finance, 52, 1–216.

Schmidt, V. (2003) 'French capitalism transformed, yet still a third variety of capitalism', *Economy and Society*, 32(4): 526–54.

Servan-Schreiber, J.-J. (1967) *Le Défi américain*, Paris: Denoël.

Stoléru, L. (1969) *L'Impératif industriel*, Paris: Seuil.

Trouille, J.-M. (2001) 'The Franco-German industrial partnership', in M. Maclean and J.-M. Trouille (eds), *France, Germany and Britain: Partners in a Changing World*, Basingstoke: Palgrave Macmillan, pp. 70–84.

Trouille, J.-M. and H. Uterwedde (2001) 'Franco-German relations, Europe and globalisation', *Modern and Contemporary France*, 9(3) (August): 339–53.

UN (United Nations) (1999, 2000, 2001, 2002, 2003, 2004, 2005), *World Investment Report*, New York and Geneva: UN.

UNCTAD (United Nations Conference on Trade and Development) (2006) *World Investment Report 2006*, http://www.unctad.org/en/docs/wir2006_en.pdf, consulted 14 June 2007.

Vernholes, A. (2001) 'La France n'accepte pas de payer le prix de ses ambitions', *Modern and Contemporary France*, 9(3) (August): 289–300.

Weber, H. (1986) *Le Parti des patrons: le CNPF (1946–1986)*, Paris: Seuil.

Whitley, R. (1999) *Divergent Capitalisms: the Social Structuring of Change and Business Systems*, Oxford: Oxford University Press.

Yeo, H.-J. et al. (2003) 'CEO reciprocal interlocks in French corporations', *Journal of Management and Governance*, 7(1): 87–108.

10
From Industrial Policy to Competitiveness Policy? The New French Strategy

Jean-Marc Trouille and Henrik Uterwedde

> France can only find its place within the new international division of labour if it takes the initiative in the remobilisation of its industrial capacities and its research potential.
>
> (Jean-Louis Beffa)

Introduction

France has traditionally advocated proactive, interventionist supply-side policies as a means of asserting its position as a strong industrial nation on the world stage. During the *Trente Glorieuses*, the 'Thirty Glorious Years' of uninterrupted post-war economic expansion, modernisation strategies relied upon major industrial projects (nuclear energy, transport infrastructures, defence and space technologies, high-speed trains and so on) initiated by the state in the framework of a large public sector (Maclean, 2002: 78–88). From the mid-1980s onwards, the concept of 'industrial policy' became gradually obsolete, and the expression itself went out of fashion. Whilst French firms were rapidly adjusting to the imperatives of economic globalisation, economic planning, national grants and sectoral policies were gradually losing momentum in the run-up towards the Single European Market. As a result, industrial policy was eclipsed for many years. However, after 2002, the economic crisis and the need to take up the industrial challenge brought the principle of having a policy to support industry back to centre stage.

This sudden renaissance is to be understood in the context of (largely unfounded) fears that economic globalisation would lead to massive relocations, and that de-industrialisation in France would exacerbate social problems. The changes which had occurred since the 1980s (liberalisation and the opening of the French economy) produced problems which had still to be overcome. Increasingly, there was a strong awareness that France, like Germany, had preserved a large manufacturing base; that a national economy based primarily on services might have little weight in tomorrow's world; and that preserving French industry was therefore vital for the whole economy. Reinstating microeconomic policies was perceived as the best way to safeguard the national economic model and the primacy of industrial logic against financial logic (Colletis, 2006). Since 2003, numerous public claims have been made, both at national and at EU level, in favour of launching a new, vigorous industrial policy (Trouille, 2007). Major initiatives were subsequently taken by the state to initiate the revival of industrial policy. These new measures now need to be examined.

The term 'industrial policy' has frequently been associated across many EU member states with the kind of interventionist supply-side policies consistently conducted in France until the mid-1980s; synonymous with *dirigisme* or state intervention, state aid to protect declining sectors, and distorted competition. However, defining industrial policy is not as straightforward as defining other policy areas. The lack of a single definition of what it entails explains its relative absence from economic theory (Cohen and Lorenzi, 2000). Two conceptions, nonetheless, tend to prevail: the 'horizontal' laissez-faire, market-oriented approach, which focuses on creating a favourable economic and legal environment for business investment by allowing markets to operate as fully as possible, with a view to generating sustainable economic development, and the 'vertical', proactive and interventionist approach, which expects the nation state to preserve long-established corporate structures by means of selective sectoral interventions in order to protect domains perceived as strategic, save jobs and create national industrial champions. Arguably, this classification is over-simplistic and does not reflect the fact that an increased number of countries have adopted a mix of indirect (horizontal) and direct (vertical) policy measures to boost their industries (Levet, 2005). In this context, it is pertinent to examine whether France has merely 'recycled' its own old recipes from the 1960s and 1970s, or whether new initiatives and recently launched policy instruments offer innovative solutions adapted to current challenges. Is boosting national champions the most efficient way to promote 'economic patriotism', or is it preferable to create a favourable business environment to attract foreign direct investment? Is there a special role for the Franco-German partnership to play in a renewed supranational industrial cooperation? And finally, does the 'revamped' French industrial policy contribute to consolidating the economic position of France on the world stage?

French industry and global competition

More than in other countries, economic globalisation is considered in France as a threat to national interests. According to this view, uncontrolled globalisation boosts economic liberalism and undermines the French social model, based on state intervention and a large public sector; the domination of international capital markets tends to impose a 'shareholder value' strategy on the management of companies which threatens industrial development with its short-term views and narrow financial perspective; national production is damaged by industrial *délocalisations* to low-wage countries; and transnational takeovers have a tendency to transform leading French groups into agencies steered by foreign decision centres. This interpretation is reinforced by a recurrent debate on a supposed 'French decline', asserting that the French economy is losing its substance in global competition (Baverez, 2003).

These arguments, which strongly influence public debate (mainly, but not only on the political left), seem to be confirmed by a relatively poor macroeconomic performance in recent years, coupled with a persistently high unemployment rate and the social consequences this entails. The importance of anti-liberal discourses and networks became particularly visible in the 2004–05 campaign for the referendum on the European Constitutional Treaty – marked by an aggressive battle against 'liberal Europe' (that is, an EU dominated by economic liberalism), by campaigns to stop industrial relocations and, more recently, in calls for 'economic patriotism' when fighting to preserve 'French' companies from unfriendly takeovers (see Chapters 6 and 7).

However, this political agitation is not justified by the analyses and public reports evaluating the strengths and weaknesses of French industry (for example, Debonneuil and Fontagné, 2003; Jacquet and Darmon, 2005). Far from being in decline, French industry, which has largely opened up to global competition in the last 30 years (in 2004 foreign trade accounted for 26 per cent exports and 25.7 per cent imports of GDP), maintained its global market share in the long run (1970–99), whereas Germany, the US and the UK all lost market share in the same period. However, France has suffered a deterioration in the course of the past decade, its market share in global exports falling from 6.3 per cent (1992) to 5.1 per cent (2003). The apparent reasons for this deterioration are that French export specialisation is insufficiently attuned to the dynamic markets (Asia and Eastern Europe), and that France has suffered a decline in technological competitiveness. The problems are, therefore, not so much caused by globalisation, but rather by weaknesses inherent in France's industrial structure.

French capital exports have risen substantially since 1985. Globally, French groups have been very active in acquiring foreign companies. Today there are 22,000 foreign subsidiaries with nearly 5 million employees worldwide. France has no fewer than 15 companies in the world's top 100 list (see Chapter 9 by Mairi Maclean). Leading French companies realise more than half of their business volume outside France. This high degree of externalisation produces positive economic consequences for France in terms of employment, revenues and trade balance. As for the relocation debate, all studies converge to show that the impact of relocation (that is, closing down French production sites in favour of new ones in low-cost countries, with re-export to France) is marginal in macroeconomic terms, except in particular industries such as clothing, textiles or household equipment (Fontagné and Lorenzi, 2005).

Foreign investment in France has risen, too, in a significant way. The national statistics office, the Institut national de la statistique et des études économiques (INSEE), shows that in 2003, 1.9 million French employees worked in firms held by foreign owners, compared to 1.1 million in 1994 (Angel and Régnier, 2006: 1). In industry, foreign-owned companies account for 28 per cent of total revenue. Foreigners hold 44.2 per cent of capital in the leading 40 groups listed in the Cotation Assistée en Continu (CAC-40) index. Openness to foreign capital is more significant than in any other leading economy. Previous fears that foreign influence on French firms could be harmful to the French economy have given way to a positive view, which is confirmed by studies underlining the overall positive impact of foreign investment on France. Notwithstanding this, some cross-national takeovers involving leading French companies have prompted anxious public debates about alleged threats to the French economy. For instance, the takeover of Péchiney, world leader in aluminium production, and regarded as a jewel of French industry, by the Canadian company Alcan in 2003, made a huge impact in France, where the nationality of companies remains a sensitive issue.

When faced with cross-national takeovers, French governments tend to exert massive political influence. In 2005, the government urged the (Franco-German) chemical group Aventis to accept a takeover bid from the French company Sanofi-Synthélabo instead of the Swiss Novartis. In 2005, it opposed the takeover of the steel group Arcelor by Mittal, and in the same year it tried to counter a bid by the Italian group Enel for Suez by proposing a merger of Suez (private) with Gaz de France (public). Also in 2005, when rumours suggested that PepsiCo was trying to take over the French food group Danone, Prime Minister Dominique de Villepin pledged to tighten government controls on cross-national mergers and acquisitions involving French firms, with pompous announcements about 'economic patriotism'.

The measures taken do not really substantiate allegations about everlasting French 'Colbertism' or a 'Maginot Line for corporate France' (*Financial Times*, 3 March 2006). Nevertheless, they reflect the concerns of the French state, fearful of losing influence. The transposition of an EU directive on takeovers into French law lists eleven 'strategic' sectors in which French firms may be protected against foreign takeover bids: it covers sectors including casinos, security activities, biotechnology, cryptology, and defence industries. Furthermore, 'poison pills' will allow management to increase the company's capital in order to counter a takeover bid, and clauses of reciprocity will assure that French firms can defend themselves under conditions equal to those in the country of the assailant group. More important are measures to improve the capital structure of French groups, which is too small and dispersed, making them vulnerable to takeovers, being sometimes referred to as 'capitalism without capital' (Izraelewicz, 1999). If most of these dispositions can be found in other countries, a special law voted in summer 2005 obliges any company wanting to absorb a French group to buy all its foreign assets, which would considerably increase the price of any takeover.

While there seems to be a consensus about the legitimacy of protective measures for French firms against unfriendly takeovers, the notion of 'economic patriotism' is largely criticised by French experts. Elie Cohen (2007) points to the inconsistency of the French 'obsession' about the 'nationality' of its large companies, and the hypocrisy of saluting every foreign takeover pulled off by French firms while opposing foreign takeovers in France. He asserts that the French problems are home-made: it was indeed the French state that privatised the public companies without giving them a sufficiently strong capital structure, exposing them to the international capital markets and to foreign institutional investors.

At the same time, there has been a shift in political perspective. The global strategy of large companies has disconnected the conditions of the national economy from those of its former 'national' companies: what is good for Danone, AXA and so on is no longer automatically good for France. In fact, there seems to be a large gap between the economic success of these few French global players and the rest of the French economy, which has more problems meeting the challenges of global competition and benefiting from the dynamics of globalisation. In this context 'made in France' becomes more important for the government than 'made by Danone'. However, French policy should be more concerned about the competitiveness of the French production site as a whole rather than protecting 'French' (in fact, largely globalised) firms. This new approach is expressed in the paradigm of territorial attractiveness (the capacity to attract investment capital). In this perspective, various studies have been commissioned by the government, and in 2002 Prime Minister Jean-Pierre Raffarin declared French attractiveness a crucial political concern (Hanotaux and Wendling, 2001; Lavenir et al., 2001; Badre and Ferrand, 2001).

Industrial policy: the new paradigm

The notion of 'industrial policy' has a special meaning in French public debate. It is closely linked to the post-war modernisation of the French economy, which transformed a backward and mainly rural economy into one of the world's leading industrial nations. The special role of state interventionism in this modernisation process shaped a specific state-led capitalism. In this context, industrial policy meant sectoral development plans initiated, financed and controlled by the state, public control of the banking and finance sector, a huge public sector, mainly in infrastructure, and the shaping of 'national champions' by state-influenced mergers in private business, as well as comprehensive industrial development projects in emerging and high-tech sectors such as aeronautics, high-speed trains or information and communication technologies, all of this being encapsulated in the phrase 'high-tech Colbertism' (Cohen, 1992).

However, in the light of a changing international economic context, which highlighted the many contradictions and limitations of French state capitalism, public interventionism in general and industrial policy in particular became discredited. The U-turn in French economic policy in 1982–83 initiated a gradual but important shift towards a more liberal policy which materialised during the 1980s and 1990s. Privatisation, liberalisation and deregulation, as well as the opening of the French economy to international capital, changed the role of state intervention. The European framework, especially the Single European Market project and European Monetary Union, accentuated the shift towards an economic policy concentrating mainly on the general economic framework, macroeconomic stability, and regulation.

Notwithstanding the actual positive effects of this new approach, it soon became clear that French industry continued to suffer from structural weaknesses which required specific public action. The persistent employment crisis, the effects of globalisation and fears of de-industrialisation, reinforced the call for a revival of industrial policy in recent years. As Jean-Louis Beffa, head of Saint-Gobain and author of a report commissioned by President Chirac noted: 'France can only find its place within the new international division of labour if it takes the initiative in the remobilisation of its industrial capacities and its research potential' (Beffa, 2005: 2).

Whereas the traditional understanding of industrial policy as interventionist and potentially protectionist is still present in the political debate, concepts developed since the 1990s are now at the core of the new policy. These concepts, articulated in numerous public reports (Commissariat général du Plan (CGP), 1992; Blanc, 2004; Délégation à l'aménagement du territoire et à l'action régionale (DATAR), 2004), indicate that the main bottlenecks for France's industrial competitiveness lie in qualitative fields, such as the weakness of medium-sized firms, of business networks and of local or regional clusters, the insufficient efforts in innovation or the characteristics of France's industrial specialisation, which has not been sufficiently focused on high technologies. Given the changed framework for international competitiveness and the emerging key role of a knowledge-based economy, the reports propose a renewed approach to industrial policy (CGP/Deutsch-Französisches Institut, 2001):

- A policy that gives the key role of industrial development and competitiveness to firms.
- A comprehensive strategy of 'overall competitiveness', that is, a competitiveness that goes far beyond the microeconomic, reaching to a macro-societal level (*compétitivité globale*) and covering a great variety of policy fields, in particular education and professional training, innovation, research and development, and technology transfer.
- A multi-actor approach including public, mixed and private actors such as the state, regional and local public actors, private business, research and training institutions, and so on, transforming the role of the state with regard to regulation, setting framework conditions, guaranteeing vital public infrastructures and coordinating governance processes.
- A new emphasis on decentralisation, which in turn should liberate the potential of endogenous local or regional development, which, up to now, seems under-exploited in centralised France.
- A new emphasis on the innovation cycle (education, university, research, public and private R&D, creation of innovative firms, patents and the like).

As a whole, the new approach turns its back on the former state-led, centralist 'top-down' model of industrial policy and development.

The new industrial policy initiated by the French government in 2005 follows these guidelines. State intervention in mobilising public funds for new research and development projects is now combined with new partnerships between central state, business, research and training institutions, and regional public actors. Research and innovation are at the core of the new policy, which features three main pillars:

(1) A revival of public research, with supplementary public funds (€20 bn for the period 2005–10), the setting up in February 2005 of a National Research Agency, and new guidelines concerning research management, evaluation, the transfer to business of the outcome of publicly-funded research, the emergence of centres of excellence and so on.
(2) The renaissance of large-scale programmes in high-tech industries, led by a new state agency, the *Agence de l'Innovation Industrielle* (AII), the Industrial Innovation Agency, initiating business-research partnerships in key technologies.
(3) The promotion of regional cluster-based development initiatives (*pôles de compétitivité*).

The Mobilising Programmes for Industrial Innovation (*Programmes mobilisateurs pour l'innovation industrielle*) launched in 2005 were first proposed by Jean-Louis Beffa (2005) in his report *Renewing Industrial Policy*. Based on the idea that the main problem of the French economy lies in the weakness of its research, industrial development and innovation effort, and that France should revive the *grands projets* policy of the 1960s, that is, the development of new product lines in high-tech industries such as nuclear power, aerospace, electronics and so on, the Beffa report proposed the creation of the AII, which effectively was set up by a law in July 2005, with Beffa as its president. With a budget of €2 bn, the mission of the agency is to initiate and support large-scale high-tech industrial projects conceived by a multi-actor partnership of large and small businesses, and private and public research and development organisations, under the leadership of a large company. The first programmes were selected in spring 2006 (see Table 10.1); some thirty other proposals were to be considered by December 2006. The key characteristics of these programmes are an ambition to achieve global technological leadership in the respective domain, a mixed public-private sharing of finance and risks and a new governance of private and public actors.

The French government was particularly keen to invite European partners to join R&D programmes under the aegis of the AII, emphasising its

Table 10.1   The Mobilising Programmes for Industrial Innovation (February 2007)

Programme	Description of programme	Industrial leader	Sums invested (€ millions)	Subsidies (€ millions)	Term (years)
The five initial programmes					
BioHub	Valorisation of agricultural resources for biotechnology (Agreed by EU Commission in December 2006)	Roquette	98	43	6
HOMES	Energy-efficient buildings	Schneider Electronics	88	39	5
NeoVal	Modular automatic transport systems (Agreed by EU Commission in February 2007)	Siemens France	61	26	6
Quaero	Developing multimedia and multilingual search engines	Thomson	250	90	5
TVMSL	Unlimited mobile TV	Alcatel	98	38	4
Programmes recently selected by the AII Supervisory Board					
VHD	Hybrid diesel-electric cars	Peugeot	271	110	–
MaXSIMM	Multimedia services on mobile phones	Gemalto	122	35	2½
MINimage	Micro-camera applications	STMicroelectronics /Saint-Gobain	141	69.9	4
OSIRIS	Biotechnology applied to agricultural resources	Soufflet	77	31.2	8
Iseult/Inumac	Imaging of neuro-disease using high field MR and contrastophores	Guerbet/Siemens	–	55	–
ADNA	Molecular diagnosis, gene therapy, immuno-monitoring	Mérieux Alliance	231	103.5	10
NanoSmart	Innovative substrata for opto- and microelectronics	Soitec	162	80	–

Source: AII (http://www.aii.fr/srt/aii/home).

Franco-German and European dimension. For President Chirac, 'the Agency is one of the cornerstones for placing European industrial policy on a new footing, an objective France and Germany are unremittingly pursuing' (speech, 25 April 2006). Two (out of four initially planned) fully-fledged Franco-German projects, Iseult/Inumac, jointly led by Siemens and Guerbet, and NeoVal, which brings together Systems Transportation Systems and Lohr Industrie, have so far been launched as the fruit of renewed bilateral industrial cooperation with Germany. In addition, a number of German, Dutch and Italian companies as well as several foreign laboratories are involved in several of the projects listed in Table 10.1.

The recent promotion of *pôles de compétitivité*, combining industrial policy and regional development, is the outcome of more than a decade's debate about competitive regions. The academic discussion about regional competitiveness in the contest to attract investors, inspired by the theory of industrial districts promoted by Alfred Marshall (1946) and the examples of prosperous Italian regions, had stressed the endogenous factors of competitiveness and the capacity of regional actors to 'produce' competitive advantages (Benko and Lipietz, 1992; Pecqueur, 1989). This gradually led to a shift in the French spatial development policy from centralist top-down approaches towards decentralised programmes giving more freedom of action to regional actors. Thus, in 1997, the government called for the establishment of local innovative production networks (*systèmes productifs locaux*), selecting and financing about 100 networks.

The success of this formula led to another approach calling for regional *pôles de compétitivité* focusing more on innovative activities. These are defined as:

> the combination, in a given geographic area, of firms, job training centres and private or public research institutions engaged in a synergy by defining common innovative projects. This partnership is focused on a specific market and on a corresponding technological and technical domain and is searching for critical mass in order to achieve international competitiveness and visibility.
>
> (Jacquet and Darmon, 2005: 64)

A public call for projects launched in November 2005 received an overwhelming response. Out of 105 proposals, 67 local *pôles de compétitivité* were selected; 15 of these classified as having a 'global dimension'. Over the next three years, they will be granted subsidies and tax relief for

R&D measures to the sum of €1.5bn, financed by the state and specific public institutions. Small and medium-sized companies will receive a substantial part of these subsidies (40 per cent). Officials and experts stress that the main responsibility for defining and launching innovative networks lies with private business, public actors being confined to an 'enabling' role.

While it is too early to evaluate the new approaches, it seems clear that the emphasis laid on innovation processes, the mobilisation of local and regional actors and the promotion of productive networks including a multitude of partners in business, research and formation contribute to a shift in the fundamental paradigm of industrial policy, which, arguably, should be renamed competitiveness policy (see Table 10.2). Having said

Table 10.2 From industrial policy to competitiveness policy? Old and new paradigms

	Old paradigm	New paradigm
	Industrial policy	**Competitiveness policy**
Objectives	Industrial modernisation, Coherence of national industry	Competitiveness of national territory
Actor system	Single actor; hierarchical governance	Multi-actor; horizontal governance
Actors	Central state Nationalised companies	Central and local public actors, private companies, educational and research centres, regulation agencies, etc.
Public intervention	Direct, vertical (sectoral) subsidies, national champions	Indirect, horizontal economic framework, incentives, regulation
State-market dimension	Interventionist state: numerous public interventions, market restrictions and controls	Enabling state: accompanying markets, private-public partnerships
Territorial dimension	Central state domination	Decentralisation; endogenous regional development
International dimension	Colbertism: national industries, Industrial cooperation in public industries (aerospace, arms, etc.)	Open economy Defence of French companies Territorial attractiveness European framework setting Call for European policies and industrial partnerships

this, it has to be remembered that the new approaches, if they are to constitute the prestigious 'spearhead' of the new French policy, cannot be separated from other elements that constitute the business environment, namely the general economic framework (market regulations, tax policy, labour market policy, entrepreneurial climate and so on). The perspective of a knowledge-based economy calls for more flexibility and change, and for new forms of decentralised and public-private governance. One possible bottleneck in the new policy may be the capacity of the central state to rethink its role and to concede local and regional autonomy. As Christian Blanc (2004: 1) puts it in his report: 'Our actors are fossilised in national hierarchical and vertical systems, with the result that the interactions between research, education and enterprise lose all vitality out of which innovation and competitiveness are born.' It will take a cultural revolution in the French high administration and the political class to introduce change. In this respect, another critical point is the propensity – observable in the Beffa report – to rely on high technology as a panacea to French competitiveness problems. Does this express a 'quasi cultural adhesion of certain elites to the "fairytale technology" whose magic would eliminate all problems' (Colletis, 2006: 33)? This remark refers to innovation as a societal process far beyond technology, calling for rules and frameworks enabling productive networks and economic change.

The partnership with Germany: a changing approach to industrial cooperation

Throughout the post-war era, Paris has regarded cooperation with Germany as an important constituent of French economic and industrial development strategy. As early as 1950, the Schuman Plan for the European Coal and Steel Community, initiated from behind the political scenes by Jean Monnet and approved by Konrad Adenauer, marked the beginning of European construction on the basis of a supra-national industrial policy project. Other instances of industrial cooperation soon materialised in the aeronautics industry, then in the late 1960s in missiles, satellites and space technology. The 1970s and 1980s saw increased bilateral projects in these fields, whilst the 1990s witnessed new cooperation projects in nuclear energy, including Framatome ANP (Advanced Nuclear Power); life science (Aventis); and the setting up of the European Aeronautics, Defence and Space Company (EADS). These bilateral alliances were politically initiated (or at least encouraged by the political establishment when they occurred in the private sector), and often backed up financially. Industrial cooperation projects were hailed in political discourse as the 'natural' outcome of the undeniably unique relationship that has bound the two countries for more than 55 years. However, Franco-German industrial relations have remained a very sensitive domain, with state-led cooperation frequently hampered by rivalries and power struggles.

As far as economic cooperation is concerned, France and Germany have been each other's main supplier and purchaser of goods and services year after year. In terms of direct investment, Germany is the fourth highest investor in France, whilst French firms are the third highest investors in Germany. Investment volumes have been growing steadily in recent years, reflecting a high level of industrial interdependence between the two sides of the Rhine. Approximately 2400 German companies have settled in France, accounting directly for 200,000 jobs and a total turnover of €60 bn. At the same time, 1043 French companies do business in Germany, accounting for 170,000 jobs and a total turnover of €46 bn (*Cahiers Industries*, 2004). Recent research on interfirm linkages established between French and German companies from 1990 to 2005 (Trouille, 2006) provided a realistic assessment of bilateral industrial cooperation, its real impact and limitations. The study focused on mergers, acquisitions, joint ventures and capital participations between French and German firms. It revealed a high level of interpenetration in virtually all sectors of activity. The list of Franco-German mergers appeared to be extremely limited, whereas takeovers were by far the preferred market entry option. In the majority (60 per cent) of takeover cases, the dominant bidding company was French, a discrepancy caused by a larger opening of local and regional public utilities in Germany than in France, and by a more aggressive expansion strategy of French firms in certain sectors such as banking and credit. The number of joint ventures appeared to be quite substantial, though three times less frequent than acquisitions. Interestingly, the study revealed that Franco-German partnerships were more likely to be successful when these were not state controlled. Indeed, a long series of failures called into question the very principle of state-initiated interfirm linkages established on the basis of a political agenda, rather than according to business logic. The forced partnership between France Télécom and Deutsche Telekom, Sanofi-Synthélabo's bid for Aventis fully endorsed by Paris, or French manoeuvring to prevent Siemens from buying key activities of the troubled French engineering conglomerate Alstom, are only a few examples of a long list of points of contention between Paris and Berlin. Even the sole apparently successful Franco-German merger of equals, EADS, with its flagship subsidiary, Airbus, has not remained unscathed by political divergences, with attempts to replace the conglomerate's bicephalous leadership by French-shaped corporate governance. Such cases were not isolated. They showed that beyond the official rhetoric on the alleged benefits of developing bilateral cooperation, and behind discourses on the promotion of European 'champions', the two countries remain largely divided by issues of industrial nationalism.

However, rather than a deliberate attempt on the part of France to regress to past interventionist supply-side policies, the Sanofi/Aventis and Alstom/Siemens affairs were symptomatic of muddled, uncoordinated activism among French political elites in favour of French-led alliances and reacting with anxiety in the face of economic globalisation. These fears were triggered in 2003 when Péchiney was taken over by Alcan, raising the sensitive issue of the nationality of companies and highlighting the fact that many 'home' companies were an easy prey for takeover bids. The following year, fears that Sanofi-Synthélabo was too easy a target for major American life-science groups, which would deprive France of its 'national champion' in this domain, overrode French scruples towards the German partners in Aventis.

Apparent lack of consideration for German interests in Aventis, EADS and a possible Alstom/Siemens linkage raised suspicions in Berlin about French willingness to cooperate on an equal basis with Germany. Further attempts to promote Franco-German industrial groupings and create what Jacques Chirac referred to in his 2005 New Year's speech as 'the Airbuses of tomorrow' have failed so far. Building a Franco-German 'Airbus of the rails' or a 'maritime Airbus' (Becker and Marx, 2005) or restructuring the defence industry under the aegis of EADS systematically comes up against the need to ensure the fairest possible mix of power between the political and industrial actors involved. In view of the difficulties and limitations encountered in running Franco-German champions jointly, let alone generating new ones, the focus has gradually shifted towards relaunching bilateral industrial cooperation in a more pertinent way, with a clear emphasis on R&D projects in future technologies.

In January 2003, shortly after the 40-year celebrations of the Elysée Treaty, French and German industry ministers signed a joint declaration on future cooperation, setting the new scene. The report called for the development of a European industrial policy no longer linked to sectoral plans, structural protection and high-tech Colbertism (Cohen, 1992), but with the emphasis on innovation and on investment in large supranational technological projects, such as Galileo or the International Thermonuclear Experimental Reactor (ITER). One year later, in January 2004, the first Franco-German symposium for industrial competitiveness was held, jointly organised by the two countries' respective ministries of industry and employers' organisations, providing a forum to debate the attractiveness of their sites for industrial investment, the need for structural reforms, the Lisbon strategy for growth and competitiveness, and potential projects to boost European industry. A platform of common objectives was defined to promote action at bilateral and EU level:

- To encourage the creation of European university groupings, and to increase joint integrated study courses between French and German institutions of higher education under the aegis of the Franco-German University.
- To enhance interregional cooperation between French *régions* and German *Länder* to encourage joint research and innovation projects, using grants from the German Federal Ministry for Education and Research, the *Technologiezentrum*, the *Verein deutscher Ingenieure* (VDI), the Union of German Engineers, and the French DATAR.
- To establish new networks by linking together existing clusters (French *pôles de compétitivité* with German *Technologiezentren*) and thereby to capitalise on technological expertise (Uterwedde, 2005).
- To encourage industrial investment and R&D projects financed by public-private partnerships.
- To make concrete proposals to shape European industrial policy, to develop a range of measures at EU level to increase attractiveness and innovation, and to achieve a better balance between competitiveness and the environment.

In October of the same year, Jean-Louis Beffa and Gerhard Cromme (ThyssenKrupp) launched the Franco-German Working Group on Economic Cooperation, a task-force consisting of five French and five German industrial leaders, to study the potential for increased cooperation between French and German companies (Cromme, 2005). In fact, the main mission entrusted to the working group was to overcome the political crisis provoked by the Aventis and Alstom affairs. Fora such as this, or the symposium for industrial competitiveness, offer the advantage of providing a framework for key players from both countries where they can exchange views and compare their visions and strategies. Furthermore, Beffa launched the AII with the clear intention of opening the agency's resources to other EU companies, in particular to German business, and adopting a cooperative approach in selecting research projects. Two 'Mobilising Programmes for Industrial Innovation', Iseult/Inumal and NeoVal (see Table 10.1), are joint Franco-German R&D initiatives, and several other French-led programmes also involve German medium-sized companies and research laboratories. However, the Quaero project, initially supposed to be a bilateral venture, will remain a French venture due to a lack of entente between Bertelsmann and Thompson. The projects, initially announced at the Fifth Franco-German Council of Ministers in April 2005, were nonetheless carefully selected by Beffa and Heinrich von Pierer (President of Siemens' Supervisory Council) in the framework of the Working Group on Economic Cooperation. They bring together research laboratories across the Rhine and are co-financed equally by public procurement (AII on the French side) and industrial partners.

These joint initiatives demonstrate that, despite numerous points of contention in their industrial cooperation, both countries were able to reach a consensus as regards the kind of measures to adopt and the type of industrial policies that require implementing. Achieving such consensus with Germany was largely facilitated by the de facto convergence of the new paradigm adopted in French industrial policy with the German approach to supply-side policies. The renewed bilateral industrial cooperation with Germany can therefore be regarded as an outcome of this new French paradigm. One of its aims is also to adopt a common approach towards European decisions and promote EU-wide supply-side policies. On many occasions, European Commission directives have been criticised by Paris and Berlin for being 'too bureaucratic, too biased in favour of environmental and consumer interests', and both capital cities frequently criticise an overly strict interpretation of EU competition rules. In 2003 and 2004, joint letters by Chirac, Schröder and Blair were addressed to the EU presidency (Uterwedde, 2004). The first requested from Brussels an inquiry into the process of de-industrialisation, and proposals on how to improve the international competitiveness of European businesses. The second requested less bureaucracy, more leeway for member states to sustain innovative small and medium-sized enterprises (SMEs) and more flexibility in applying competition rules, in order to pay more attention to specific needs for industrial development, and to devote more attention to the compatibility of EU policy initiatives with the competitiveness of European companies. These intergovernmental initiatives clearly highlight a shared desire to influence decision-making and promote a more proactive approach to industrial policy at EU level.

Conclusion

The recent launch of a new industrial policy is an attempt to address the stunning pace of economic change on the world stage at a time when

French industry has reached a turning point. France's industrial base is still strong, but ageing. Its industrial specialisation is no longer sufficient for it to remain competitive in a number of high-tech sectors. Increased awareness that international competitors have a clear strategy of global expansion (the USA and Japan) or a highly effective 'catching up' strategy, not just in manufacturing industries and services but also in high-tech industries (China and India), have raised concerns regarding France's future position in the international division of labour. In a rapidly changing external market place, where technology is used ever more efficiently, boosting innovation and R&D and providing the necessary investment have become urgent necessities, particularly in research geared towards industrial innovation. The renewed French industrial policy aims at responding to this challenge.

However, the recent revival of a microeconomic policy in a country where supply-side measures have traditionally been 'vertical', that is, strongly interventionist, has led to a number of criticisms. For instance, the rhetoric on 'economic patriotism', attempts to shelter 'strategic' sectors, and a preference for national champions denote a nationalist approach viewed by European partners with suspicion. Such issues tend to dominate headlines and strengthen widespread views on French protectionism, whilst concealing other more worthwhile and forward-looking initiatives. The Beffa report, too, has been criticised for being too 'national' and too overtly inspired by de Gaulle's vision of *grands projets*. Furthermore, electoral considerations may have played a role in granting the label *'pôle de compétitivité'* to no less than 67 regional clusters, resulting in funding being spread too thinly. Whilst these criticisms are to a large extent justified, any assessment of the new French policies has to differentiate between a government-led, interventionist political rhetoric, eager to match public expectations, and real policies open to modern approaches. Today's France has, in reality, become more liberal than is generally recognised by its neighbours, many of whom still tend to regard it as interventionist. France's new approach to industrial policy no longer corresponds to the former state-led, rigid, centralist 'top-down' model of industrial development, where businesses, funding and orders were all under state control (Trouille and Uterwedde, 2001). The nature of state intervention has changed. Private businesses are now responsible for industrial development and competitiveness. They hold the main responsibility for defining and launching innovative networks, whilst public actors are confined to an 'enabling' role. At the core of the new policy are new concepts that differ enormously from the old-style 'vertical' policies pursued by France in the 1960s and 1970s. The new emphasis is laid on innovation processes, R&D, private-public partnerships, the mobilisation of local and regional actors, and the promotion of productive networks involving numerous partners.

The renewed French industrial policy undeniably consists of innovative, forward-looking strategies which, at the same time, do indeed rely partly on old recipes. In the new paradigm, in which industrial policy de facto has become a policy of competitiveness, the state is no longer the sole project manager, but still fulfils an important, proactive role as a catalyst whose support will help firms develop long-term projects. Yet is the state the best judge in deciding which projects to fund? Should the aim of the AII be to retain 'French' companies whose long-term interests may be to move to buoyant emergent markets, or would it be more appropriate to attract new investment, whatever its origin? Whilst it is too early to evaluate the efficiency of the renewed approach to industrial policy, such crucial questions will remain at the heart of the debate. At this juncture, however, the focus of the new industrial policy on innovation, on co-financing and on new partnerships within and beyond national boundaries nonetheless seems to be proceeding in the right direction.

Acknowledgement

The authors wish to thank Joanna Ardizzone for a much appreciated critical reading and useful comments.

References

Angel, J.-W. and V. Régnier (2006) 'Les groupes étrangers en France: en dix ans, 1,8 fois plus de salariés', *INSEE Première*, 1069 (March): 1–4.

Badre, D. and A. Ferrand (2001) 'Mondialisation: réagir ou subir? La France face à l'expatriation des compétences, des capitaux et des entreprises', Paris: Sénat, rapport d'information no. 386.

Baverez, N. (2003) *La France qui tombe*, Paris: Perrin.

Becker, P. and S. Marx (2005) 'Europäische Champions – Aufgabe europäischer Industriepolitik? Fallbeispiel maritime Industrie', Berlin: Deutsches Institut für Internationale Politik und Sicherheit, Research Group on EU Integration, Science and Politics Foundation, Working Paper, 1 February.

Beffa, J.-L. (2005) *Renewing Industrial Policy*, Paris: La documentation française.

Benko, G. and A. Lipietz (eds) (1992) *Les Régions qui gagnent: districts et réseaux: les nouveaux paradigmes de la géographie industrielle*, Paris: PUF.

Blanc, C. (ed.) (2004) *Pour un écosystème de la croissance*, Paris: La documentation française.

Cahiers Industries (2004) 'Coopération industrielle franco-allemande', *Cahiers Industries*, 92 (January): 9–21.

CGP (1992) *France, le choix de la performance globale*, Paris: La documentation française.

CGP/Deutsch-Französisches Institut (2001) *Compétitivité globale: une perspective franco-allemande*, Paris: La documentation française.

Cohen, E. (1992) *Le Colbertisme 'high tech': économie des télécom et du grand projet*, Paris: Hachette.

Cohen, E. (2007) 'Industrial policies in France: the old and the new', *Journal of Industry, Competition and Trade*, 17(3) (December): 213–27.

Cohen, E. and J.-H. Lorenzi (eds) (2000) *Politiques industrielles pour l'Europe*, Paris: La documentation française.

Colletis, G. (2006) 'Enjeux des mutations industrielles en France', in G. Colletis and Y. Lung (eds), *La France industrielle en question*, Paris: La documentation française, pp. 11–36.

Cromme, G. (2005) 'Politique industrielle: l'action commune est possible', *Revue des deux mondes*, 10–11 (October–November): 177–86.

DATAR (2004) *La France, puissance industrielle*, Paris: DATAR.

Debonneuil, M. and L. Fontagné (eds) (2003) *Compétitivité: rapport du Conseil d'analyse économique*, Paris: La documentation française.

Fontagné, L. and J.-H. Lorenzi (eds) (2005), *Désindustrialisation, délocations: rapport du Conseil d'analyse économique, No. 55*, Paris: La Documentation française.

Hanotaux, P. and C. Wendling (2001) 'Rapport au Premier Ministre sur l'attractivité du territoire français', Paris: Assemblée nationale.

Izraelewicz, E. (1999) *Le Capitalisme zinzin*, Paris: Grasset.

Jacquet, N. and D. Darmon (2005) *Les Pôles de compétitivité: le modèle français*, Paris: La documentation française.

Lavenir, F., A. Joubert-Bompart and C. Wendling (2001) *L'Entreprise et l'hexagone: rapport au Ministre de l'Economie*, Paris: Les Éditions de Bercy.

Levet, J.-L. (2005) 'Les politiques industrielle dans le monde: illustrations, enseignements et perspectives', in L. Fontagné and J.-H. Lorenzi (eds), *Désindustrialisation, délocalisations*, Paris: La documentation française, pp. 315–56.

Maclean, M. (2002) *Economic Management and French Business from de Gaulle to Chirac*, Basingstoke: Palgrave Macmillan.

Marshall, A. (1946) *Principles of Economics*, London: Macmillan.

Pecqueur, B. (1989) *Le Développement local: mode ou modèle?*, Paris: Syros/Alternatives.

Trouille, J.-M. (2006) 'Die Kooperation deutscher und französischer Unternehmen: Zwischen Konkurrenz und Partnerschaften', *Dokumente*, 62(1): 31–42.

Trouille, J.-M. (2007) 'Re-inventing industrial policy in the EU: a Franco-German approach', *West European Politics*, 3 (May): 502–23.

Trouille, J.-M. and H. Uterwedde (2001) 'Franco-German relations, Europe and globalisation', *Modern and Contemporary France*, 9(3): 339–53.

Uterwedde, H. (2004) 'Deutsch-französische Industriepolitik: mehr als Illusionen?' *Dokumente*, 60(5): 21–7.

Uterwedde, H. (2005) 'Y a-t-il une politique industrielle commune pour la France et l'Allemagne?', *Visions franco-allemandes*, 4, Paris: Institut français des relations internationales.

11
Facing Global Climate Risk: International Negotiations, European Policy Measures and French Policy Style

Joseph Szarka

Introduction

The photograph of Earth from space taken by the Apollo 17 mission has become the icon of global environmental consciousness. Jasanoff (2001: 310) observed that it was 'a deeply political image, subordinating as it does the notional boundaries of sovereign power in favour of swirling clouds that do not respect the lines configured by human conquest or legislation'. The icon's resonances of planetary interconnectedness – of common origins and single destiny – are mixed with the forebodings of vulnerability. During its now canonical prescription for sustainable development, the Brundlandt report evoked 'a small and fragile ball, dominated not by human activity and edifice but by a pattern of clouds, oceans, greenery and soils' (WCED, 1987: 308). Ironically, it is this 'pattern of clouds' – the global atmosphere – which is threatened by unsustainable human activities. Ongoing climate change caused mainly (but not solely) by greenhouse gas (GHG) release from fossil fuels poses *worldwide* risks, yet solutions lie in the hands of *national* policy-makers, firms and local communities. Thus whereas climate risk is global, climate policy is marked by a logic of disaggregation and re-appropriation in which territorially constituted actors – notably sovereign states – assert their interests and preferences within an international order, whilst shaping and being shaped by new global regimes.

Addink et al. (2003: 78–9) argued that climate issues link with globalisation in three major ways: (1) environmental interests now structure particular processes of globalisation, (2) reciprocally, environmental problems and their solutions are themselves structured by relationships within international society, and (3) environmental resources are increasingly exploited in world politics and the global economy, not only in the 'traditional' contexts of natural resources and raw materials, but also in terms of technology transfers and financial flows related to GHG emissions control. In consequence, national governments are faced with complex opportunity sets within which the drive to innovate is constrained by the institutional and economic dimensions of path dependence. Thus climate change strategies are emblematic of the dilemmas posed by globalisation for the nation state, which is at once sovereign and dependent, entrepreneurial and reactive, acting and acted upon.

The French case aptly illustrates these tensions since the Gaullist ideology of national *independence* – as applied to foreign policy, defence and energy sourcing – has in recent decades been tempered by the consequences of *interdependence* arising from economic and political globalisation. Further, France has proposed a distinctive model for the design of climate policy based on emissions per capita. Yet whilst this model may yet prevail in the long term, in recent years a sectoral logic of emissions control has assumed dominance which marginalised the French position and set particular challenges. Accordingly this chapter will first review the ways in which the French authorities have engaged with the process of international regime-building for climate protection. The second section will review the rationale of burden-sharing and the main policy measures developed by the EU, including their impact on France. The third section looks more closely at France's distinctive national strategy. The overall aim of the analysis is to explain why French policy style in relation to climate protection is approaching its limits, identifying the factors which encourage its renewal as well as pointing to the forces of path dependence which encourage its persistence.

International negotiations

As noted by Addink et al. (2003: 78–9), the international climate policy regime has structured particular processes of globalisation and a substantial literature now exists on its development.[1] Hence the present discussion will concentrate on French responses during the landmark stages of its evolution.

Negotiated during the World Summit in Rio in 1992, the United Nations Framework Convention on Climate Change (UNFCCC) set out in article three the principle that 'the Parties should protect the climate system for the benefit of present and future generations of humankind, on the basis of equity and in accordance with their common but differentiated responsibilities and respective capabilities'. This principle has since been embedded in agreements undertaken during successive Conferences of the Parties (COP). The most salient of these is COP-3 in December 1997 when the Kyoto Protocol was signed, putting in place GHG targets for industrialised countries and identifying 'flexible mechanisms' to contribute to their attainment (the Clean Development Mechanism, Joint Implementation and emissions trading). Subsequent conferences developed the institutional architecture, for example the 2001 Marrakech Accord arising from COP-7 established compliance procedures and in November 2006, COP-12 was held in Nairobi. The principle of 'common but differentiated responsibilities' has been consistently maintained, with the industrialised nations agreeing to take the lead in achieving emissions targets in the first commitment period of 2008–12, with other nations aiming for greater participation at dates yet to be agreed.

A problem from the outset has been to define the basis of 'differentiated responsibilities' in a manner that translates into quantified national targets. An implied question has been whether the attribution of burdens is conducted on an arbitrary basis or modelled on an inner logic. As one of the first signatories of the UNFCCC, France put forward a distinctive strategy for GHG reduction by stressing emissions per capita. This was coherent with national circumstances in that France has relatively low emissions compared to other industrialised countries. In EU-25, France has the third lowest emissions per capita and the second lowest GHG emissions per unit of GDP (EEA, 2004: 9–10).

The major reason for this arises from the structure of the electricity-generating industry. In the 1960s and 1970s, the French electricity sector was reconfigured by the expansion of first hydro and then nuclear power.[2] Together they accounted for around 90 per cent of French electricity sourcing by the 1990s. Since nuclear and hydro power are virtually carbon free at the point of generation, they made substantial cuts in CO_2 emissions from the power sector. Energy related emissions fell by 23 per cent between 1980 and 1990, with electricity generation accounting for 11 per cent of French CO_2 emissions – as compared to an Organisation for Economic Co-operation and Development (OECD) average of 34 per cent – due to the switch away from oil and coal which had accounted for 60 per cent of total electricity generation in 1973 (IEA, 1996: 73–6). The development of a world-leading nuclear power sector led to a significant instance of path dependence. The French economy became dependent on the nuclear industry because of sunk costs and the need to amortise heavy R&D investment by international sales of the technology. Further, the establishment of a climate regime placing caps on GHG emissions left France with no way back to a fossil fuel-sourced electricity sector. This contrasts markedly with the UK where the 'dash to gas' of the 1990s reconfigured a predominantly coal-based electricity sector and considerably *reduced* CO_2 emissions. In France, however, a switch to gas would *increase* emissions. This, combined with high prices, means that gas will remain a marginal source for French electricity generation.

These developments led to a particular construction of French national interest in relation to energy and climate. Achieving major CO_2 cuts ahead of its neighbours had left France curiously vulnerable. According to the French government 'the costs of new and additional measures are expected to be higher than in many other OECD countries' (quoted in IEA, 1996: 74). Ironically, becoming an 'inadvertent pioneer' (Szarka, 2006) entailed a reduction in the scope for low-cost GHG cuts in France, once an international climate regime was created. In contrast, competitor nations retained greater potential for 'picking the low-hanging fruit' of cheap emissions reductions. This explains why France chose to emphasise emissions per capita as its preferred guideline for burden differentiation.

In its 1993 programme for combating climate change, the government set out a policy perspective which still informs the French approach. France argued that the indicator for assessing emissions reduction liability should be emissions per capita. In this early stage, France set as its target the stabilisation of emissions at below two metric tonnes of carbon per capita per year by 2000, a level some 10 per cent higher than the 1990 outcome (IEA, 1996: 74). A negotiating strategy based on capping per capita emission levels put pressure on the biggest emitters (globally the USA, in Europe, Germany) to make large reductions. The French approach bears a similarity to the 'contraction and convergence' model promoted by Meyer (2000), which favours a transition to common levels of GHG emissions by promoting deep cuts on the part of industrialised nations. This model views the atmosphere as a 'global commons' and seeks to distribute national burdens on the basis of international and intergenerational equity. It holds big emitters responsible for increased atmospheric concentration of GHGs and argues that they can reduce emissions at lower cost, whilst upholding the position of developing countries whose capacity for cuts is generally limited. However, France's espousal of the emissions per capita approach was also more narrowly advantageous in terms of national interest.

Conversely, this approach was clearly disadvantageous for the European neighbours. Thus France proved unable to convince key EU partners to adopt it. Indeed, in the run-up to COP-3, disagreements between member states on the differentiation of responsibilities *within* the EU threatened the achievement of a joint position. A lack of consensus would encourage member states to 'go it alone', bargaining in international negotiations to achieve the national GHG targets that suited them and potentially undermining the *acquis* of European economic integration. It would also render the EU incapable of achieving global leadership in climate protection, a goal considered as beneficial to Europe's long-term future since – as argued by Addink et al. (2003: 78–9) – climate protection opens new dimensions for exploitation of environmental resources involving technology transfers and financial flows related to GHG emissions control. Achieving a burden-sharing agreement within the EU was therefore treated as an essential goal. In the early 1990s, an initial attempt by the European Commission to solve the burden-sharing problem identified three groups of member states with distinct obligations. Countries emitting above the EU average (Germany, Denmark and the Netherlands) would be asked to reduce emissions by 5 per cent, those emitting around the average (France, Luxembourg, UK, Italy) would stabilise emissions, whilst the 'cohesion countries' would be allowed an increase of 15 per cent (Ringius, 1999: 139). However, France, Italy and the UK resisted this idea as unrealistic.

To settle the disputes, the Dutch presidency of the European Council adopted the 'triptych' approach in early 1997. Developed by energy specialists at Utrecht University, this approach combined data on energy supply systems and industrial energy efficiency to allocate fair shares of CO_2 reductions (Andersen, 2005: 139). It divided national economies into three broad components: the electricity-generating sector, the energy-intensive, export-oriented sector and the domestic sector (Phylipsen et al., 1998). This division captured effects of scale (related to quantity of emissions) and issues of competitiveness. Singling out the power sector allowed incorporation of the differential impacts of fuel mix, so distinguishing between the high emissions caused by German and Danish coal-fired generation and the low emissions characterising the French and Swedish 'nuclear plus hydro' electricity sectors. Henceforth national industrial structure was to determine the emissions burden. This allowed a more objective and instrumental allocation of targets by the identification of *sectoral pathways* towards emissions control, rather than fixating on national-level aggregates, emissions per capita or problematic flat-rate reductions.

The 'triptych' approach enabled a joint European position – but with less ambitious aims than originally mooted. Early calls for an EU-wide reduction of 15 per cent were diluted to around 10 per cent in the run-up to Kyoto. The final burden-sharing agreement of 1998 – the so-called 'EU bubble' – programmed an aggregate 8 per cent reduction for the 2008–12 commitment period. Germany, Denmark and the UK pledged big cuts, whilst Spain and Portugal were allowed large increases. France was required to stabilise emissions at the 1990 level, due in large part to low per capita emissions. As a consequence of this complex equation, cuts within Germany and the UK alone were equivalent to the EU's projected reduction of 310 $MtCO_2$ for 2010 from a total of 3286 $MtCO_2$ in 1990. Ringius (1999: 136–7) argued that asymmetrical distribution had the advantages of encouraging participation, enhancing cost-effectiveness and allowing lead countries to increase pressure for rigorous targets, whereas equal distribution tends to lowest common denominator outcomes. Thus the EU could take up a leadership role during negotiation of the Kyoto Protocol, pressuring other industrialised nations to commit to meaningful cuts and facilitating eventual ratification. Moreover, the protocol's implementation was strengthened by subjecting the GHG commitments of member states to the enforcement powers of the EU (Oberthür, 2006: 68).

The COP-6 talks in the Hague in 2000 aimed to finalise arrangements made in Kyoto. From the outset talks were mired in disagreements over precise measures, with national positions hardening during negotiations. Once again, the French found it impossible to persuade EU partners to take their preferences on board. France wished to include nuclear power within the Clean Development Mechanism but only Finland was in favour, with the remaining 13 of EU-15 states opposing (Lajoinie, 2001: 102–3). An important bone of contention for all parties related to the accountancy of carbon 'sinks' and the extent to which forestry reserves could be used to 'offset' CO_2 emissions, with the USA pushing for large allowances in the face of EU scepticism. Pressing for domestic GHG cuts, the French presidency of the EU (led by Environment Minister Dominique Voynet) resisted use of 'carbon sinks' (MATE, 2000). When a compromise deal with the USA – brokered by British Deputy Prime Minister John Prescott – was not defended by the French presidency, recriminations broke out among EU members (Grubb and Yamin, 2001: 263). The talks collapsed in confusion over who was responsible, with each side blaming the other and NGOs blaming them all (Fisher, 2004: 38). Subsequently, the new Bush administration withdrew from negotiations in March 2001 and the prospect of the protocol being 'dead' was raised. However, the remaining parties patched up implementation issues in following rounds of COP talks. Once Russia was persuaded to participate (on the basis of substantial concessions), the route to making the Kyoto Protocol operational was re-opened and it came into force on 16 February 2005. These developments bear out the contention of Addink et al. (2003: 78–9) that global environmental problems and paths to their solution are structured by relationships within international society.

However, the Kyoto Protocol remains flawed on a number of counts. The USA as the largest emitter of GHGs has not signed, other major emitters such as China and India have pledged no reductions, whilst such commitments as have been made fall on a few states and are too small to make a practical difference. Countries making binding commitments account for only 19 per cent of global emissions (Barrett, 2003: 382). Uncertainties hang over the protocol's future – the first commitment period ends in 2012 yet no second period has been negotiated, nor is it known which of the major emitters will participate actively and to what extent. Nevertheless, in February 2007 the EU reasserted its will to leadership and unilaterally pledged a 20 per cent emissions cut by 2020.

European policy measures

Meeting the EU's current commitment to reduce emissions has proved challenging. Fuel substitution in the power sector has realised major emissions savings but emissions have increased in other sectors, such as transport. Failure to hit targets is not an option, since the 2001 Marrakech Accord set up a compliance mechanism for signatory countries to the Kyoto Protocol. A target overshoot during 2008–12 incurs a penalty for the subsequent period, whereby assigned reductions will be increased by 0.3 (Jagt, 2003). For the EU, a penalty would be spread across member states.

To support its aspirations to leadership in climate protection, the EU has sought to innovate in terms of policy measures. In the 1990s, repeated attempts were made to set up carbon taxation (Zito, 2000). Initially, France was supportive of a carbon tax provided that it was based entirely on the carbon content of fuel (and not on energy content, since the latter would also have taxed nuclear power) and that it was implemented in all EU states, with precautions taken to maintain competitiveness if other OECD states did not implement it (IEA, 1996: 75; Godard, 1997: 37–8). But shortly before the 1992 Rio Summit, with several member states (including France after an about-turn) declaring reservations, the EU made establishment of the carbon tax conditional on similar measures in other OECD countries (Barrett, 2003: 368), a development that the United States and Japan would not countenance.

The inability to pioneer an international carbon abatement policy left the EU searching for measures operable within Europe's frontiers. Only in the 2000s was an alternative implemented, with the establishment of the Emissions Trading Scheme (ETS) as the centrepiece of European climate policy.

During negotiations at the Hague the EU had resisted US proposals for emissions trading, yet it has moved first to implementation.[3] The EU ETS was set up under directive 2003/87/CE. It operates in two phases: a trial phase that ran between 2005–07 and an operational phase between 2008–12 (to coincide with the Kyoto Protocol's first commitment period). In phase-one, 'national allocation plans' (NAPs) had to be approved by the European Commission during 2004 so that trading could start on 1 January 2005. The scheme established a European framework for carbon trading, targeting the highest industrial emitters of CO_2, namely the electricity, energy, steel, cement, chalk, glass, ceramics, paper and cardboard sectors. It covers some 12,000 factories producing 45 per cent of industrial CO_2, equivalent to 35 per cent of total GHG emissions in the EU (Andersen, 2005: 143). In theory, the caps set on emissions are progressively lowered, triggering serial reductions on a least-cost basis. Allocations to firms are made by governments on the 'grandfathering' principle: in other words permits are assigned in proportion to historical emissions and distributed free.[4] Companies are incentivised to cut emissions below quota by the prospect of selling the balance of permits to underperformers – who are obliged either to buy up quotas or pay a fine (€40 per tonne during phase one, rising to €100 in phase-two). A peculiarity of the scheme is that caps are unspecified at the European level, leaving their setting to domestic negotiations – and business lobbying. This peculiarity arises from the principle of differentiated national targets and from variations in the scope for CO_2 reductions in particular industrial and technological contexts, but has led to opacity regarding the setting of caps and the distribution of burdens across industries. The danger of inappropriate quota allocation leading to market distortions was recognised from the outset (Delalande and Martinez, 2004: 108–9). Furthermore, the persistence of national jurisdiction highlights the inability of the EU to implement a single European scheme.

Because the EU ETS focuses on a limited number of industries, the total number of quotas allocated is dependent on the economic structure of each of the member states. This sectoral approach reflects and continues the 'triptych' approach to the distribution of emission reduction burdens. Whilst emissions from the power sector form the lion's share of total emissions in Germany, Denmark and the UK, they are very low in France for the reasons discussed above. In consequence, France is a small player within EU ETS – Germany accounted for 23 per cent of quotas under phase-one, Italy, Poland and the UK for 11 per cent each, Spain for 8 per cent and France for 7 per cent. Further, the structure of allocation is distinctive with 50 per cent of quotas at EU level going to the electricity sector, but only 25 per cent in the French case (Arnaud, 2005: 94). In consequence, a large number of small establishments have been roped into the French allocation plan; yet only 26 per cent of total CO_2 emissions are covered (Arnaud, 2005: 95). The impact of the scheme in France was further reduced by the modest phase-one reduction target of 2.43 per cent overall, which itself was moderated by factors such as allowance for economic growth and 'headroom' for new entrants (MEDD, 2004b).

When phase-one NAPs went before the European Commission during 2004, criticisms of over-allocation were made in several cases. The French NAP received only qualified approval, with conditions placed to reduce so-called 'economic growth reserves' and to include categories of establishment present in other NAPs (EurActiv, 2004). This necessitated an increase in the number of plants targeted to some 1400, with France having a more diverse spread of establishments than in other countries. The final approved version allocated quotas for some 156 $MtCO_2$.

In most European countries initial fears of a huge extra burden on industry due to carbon pricing proved unfounded due to over-allocation of quotas by national governments desirous to protect domestic firms. Although total emissions trades were valued at €9–10 bn for 2006, actual emissions were below the cap with the exception of Austria, Spain and the UK (Brough, 2006). The analysis by Entec (2006) showed an aggregate level of over-allocation across the EU of some 4.4 per cent – but with significant differences among member states with Germany at 4 per cent, France at 15 per cent and Poland at 25 per cent, whilst the UK was *minus* 13 per cent – with the most likely cause being over-generosity in the allocation process. However, because of low levels of market intelligence and because smaller players were disincentivised from selling credits, many market participants were unaware of the extent of over-allocation. Once information on national over-allocations was released in April 2006, carbon prices collapsed from a peak of circa €30 to €9. This has led to calls from concerned parties that phase-two allocations should be much tighter if the carbon market is to work correctly in reducing industrial CO_2 emissions.[5]

The early version of the phase-two French NAP, as presented to the European Commission in September 2006, proposed a ceiling on emissions of 151 MtCO$_2$ equivalent per year as compared to an actual outcome of 131 MtCO$_2$ in 2005 (Actu-Environnement, 2006). Although the remit of the phase-two NAP was extended, the extra establishments included were too few in number to justify the height of the ceiling. The plan was roundly criticised by French NGOs who requested that the Commission reject it on grounds of 'laxity', namely over-allocation of quotas and a likely short-fall to France's Kyoto target.[6] With the Commission sending strong signals that it would not tolerate a repeat of the phase-one fiasco, the French government withdrew its original proposal. In December 2006, it put forward a considerably revised plan. It programmed quotas of 128.86 MtCO$_2$-equivalent per year under 'grandfathered' emissions, plus a further 3.94 MtCO$_2$ reserved for new entrants, making a total of 132.8 MtCO$_2$ (MEDD, 2006a: 7). In effect, the new French NAP required a small, supplementary effort on the part of established players, whilst allowing for growth by new entrants. The net result is likely to be a stabilisation of industrial emissions at recent levels, albeit after a period of substantial reductions.[7] This revised NAP was approved in March 2007, subject to minor technical clarifications (Actu-Environnement, 2007).

French policy style and measures

Given that the sectoral methodology which characterised the 'triptych' approach has informed the design of the EU ETS, how well have French policy style and measures fitted with the continuity in climate strategy? Although emissions trading was viewed with suspicion in France during the 1990s (Godard, 2001), its implementation has afforded a comfortable fit with national policy traditions. This is because French policy style in the environmental domain has also been based on a sectoral methodology. This style has been characterised in terms of 'environmental meso-corporatism',[8] by which is meant the ring-fencing of a policy sector within which organised producer interests are entrusted with stewardship whilst being subject to the supervision of public institutions.[9] Despite the prominence of state actors and appearances of 'command and control' regulation, in reality environmental policy has been subtended by bilateral meso-corporatist bargains. As argued by Szarka (2006), this policy style has proved amenable to the organisation of emissions trading, engendering institutional arrangements comparable to those found in pre-existing environmental policy arenas. The French authorities once again ring-fenced a meso-corporatist domain within which negotiation is undertaken between industry representatives and public officials. The French NAP was drawn up by the ADEME (the Environment and Energy Efficiency Agency) and the register of emissions is kept by the Caisse des Dépots et des Consignations (a state-owned organisation).The accuracy of carbon accounts is checked by the Inspection des installations classées (Licensed Sites Inspectorate), supervised by the Environment Ministry. Although producer interests have an influence on the quantity and distribution of ETS quotas, the authority of the central state is asserted by its right to set caps and apply sanctions as last resort.

This closed policy community has recently seen its prerogatives subjected to greater scrutiny. Directive 2003/87/CE which established the EU ETS requires a consultation procedure, whose aim is to encourage public participation and improve transparency in the setting of quotas. Public consultation did not occur with the phase-one French NAP, but did occur in phase-two. However, Réseau Action Climat-France (2006) complained that civil society had little opportunity to participate, whilst industrialists continued to exercise predominant influence. But because the French government withdrew and then resubmitted its phase-two NAP, it was forced to engage in a further round of consultation. This generated a larger number of critical submissions by the public (albeit under NGO prompting). Thus the requirements for greater transparency imposed by the EU and eagerly demanded by NGOs have put pressure on the meso-corporatist policy frame.

In other areas of climate and energy policy, signs of emerging meso-corporatist bargains can also be detected. The production of energy crops has been identified as a promising development for both enhancing energy security and reducing emissions. The French agricultural sector is highly corporatist, with the farmers' lobby exercising considerable influence. A context of reform of the Common Agricultural Policy and greater international competition has sparked a crisis for French farmers. The production of energy crops offers significant opportunities for agricultural diversification (Bal, 2005). It may even renew the Gaullist tradition of subsidising intensive agriculture whilst contributing to 'national independence' in energy supply. European directive 2003/30/CE set the objective of substituting 5.75 per cent of vehicle fuels by biofuels in 2010. France brought this deadline forward to 2008, and set targets of 7 per cent for 2010 and 10 per cent for 2015 (MEDD, 2006b: 8). Acceleration has, however, proved faltering with output of biodiesel falling by 2.5 per cent between 2003 and 2004 to 348,000 tonnes, whereas it increased by 44 per cent in Germany to reach 1,035,000 tonnes (*Systèmes solaires*, 2005: 42). New tax measures introduced in 2005 are expected to incentivise an expansion in production and use. By way of comparison, in the biomass sector tax credits to households buying high-efficiency wood-burning stoves have stimulated expansion (Delannoy, 2007: 138–9), contributing to the success of the 2000–06 *Plan bois-énergie* (national 'Wood Energy Plan'). France has become the biggest producer of energy from wood in the EU. In summary, domestic production of biomass and biofuels offers scope to respond to energy and climate challenges via a renewed form of the 'economic patriotism' that has long characterised French economic management. Thus the potential for new meso-corporatist bargains is far from exhausted.

On the other hand, France has already missed opportunities to develop electricity generation from wind energy and extend the national engineering base.[10] At the start of 2007, Germany, Spain and Denmark – the wind power market leaders – had 20,622 MW, 11,615 MW and 3136 MW of capacity respectively, compared with 1958 MW in the UK and 1469 MW in France (*Windpower Monthly*, 2007: 90). Unlike the market leaders, France has not proved successful in building up a wind power engineering sector. The French wind turbine industry is limited to two, fairly small players, Vergnet and Jeumont. To stake out a presence, Areva – the French nuclear giant – has built up its holdings in the German firm REpower, which held a 29 per cent share of the French domestic market in 2005. But given the relatively slow rate of expansion, France will have difficulties in meeting its 2010 target of 21 per cent of electricity consumption from renewable energy sources (RES), as programmed by European directive 2001/77/EC. In France, electricity generation from renewables stood at 12.5 per cent of output in 2004; wind energy accounted for one terawatt hour (TWh) compared to 65 TWh from hydro, 448 TWh from nuclear and 53 TWh from fossil fuels (IEA, 2005: I.36–7). But given that 90 per cent of French generation is virtually carbon free, emissions reductions can only be achieved from the residual 10 per cent which – though still considerable in volume terms – is problematic to substitute by new categories of RES given that coal-fired generation is used to smooth demand peaks, a usage for which wind power in particular is unsuited given its intermittency and limited predictability.

In terms of overall energy usage, renewables account for 6 per cent of French energy consumption, which is also the EU average (Comité 21, 2007: 120). However, the EU target for energy sourcing from renewables is 12 per cent by 2010, with a new target of 20 per cent for 2020 agreed in early 2007. During negotiations France showed reluctance to accept the increase despite being rich in RES, including wind, biomass and geothermal energy. Limited political will has meant that France has not to date been able to fashion support for renewable energies into opportunities for industrial policy to the extent that Germany has done. But clear opportunities exist to seize the initiative. Meanwhile, energy policy continues to favour one of the main neo-corporatist bargains existing in France, namely in the nuclear sector. The 2005 Energy Bill reinstated the French preference for the nuclear option by the decision to build a demonstrator European Pressurised Reactor plant in France by 2012, with a view to renewing the fleet of nuclear reactors post-2015.

Because of the limited scope for achieving emission reductions in the power sector, national policy has needed to identify opportunities for cuts in a diverse range of domains. The danger of escalating emissions was identified in the 2004 Climate Plan, with increases for transport and buildings of 44 per cent and 30 per cent respectively projected by 2010 (MEDD, 2004a: 14). Thus whilst aggregate emissions in 2004 were 558 $MtCO_2$ equivalent as compared to the 1990 level of 563.9 $MtCO_2$ (MEDD, 2006b: 3), France could not afford to be complacent. Without supplementary measures, emissions would overshoot the target by an estimated 10 per cent (MEDD, 2006b: 3). Thus the 2004 Climate Plan put forward around 60 measures to reduce emissions, of which the five main ones were incentives for buying low-emission vehicles, support for biofuels, increased tax credits for energy efficient appliances, use of energy labelling on a wider range of goods, regular servicing of air-conditioning equipment and energy efficiency certificates for housing. Further, a new standard has been developed to improve the environmental and energy performance of buildings. In total, supplementary domestic measures were projected to 'save' 72 $MtCO_2$ equivalent and bring aggregate emissions to slightly below the 1990 level for the first Kyoto commitment period (MEDD, 2004a: 77). The 2006 update of the climate strategy reinforced the 2004 measures with the aim of 'saving' a further 6–8 $MtCO_2$ equivalent in 2008–12 (MEDD, 2006b: 3). If the official scenarios are proved correct, France will do no worse than meet its GHG emissions stabilisation target and possibly do slightly better, with a fall of around 2–3 per cent.

Conclusions

A conundrum for the international climate regime has been how to apportion 'common but differentiated responsibilities' on an equitable and pragmatic basis. The policy architecture put in place by COP agreements sets parameters for GHG accounting, specifies emissions targets for climate change mitigation and identifies 'flexible mechanisms' for their achievement, but leaves choice of means to sovereign states. However, the reasons explaining the specification of national targets in the Kyoto Protocol remain fuzzy, being the outcome of bargaining rather than the result of an explicit methodology. France's distinctive solution stressed GHG emissions per capita, but it has not been adopted internationally nor even in the EU. In contrast, a sectoral logic has prevailed towards burden differentiation in the EU with (a) the development of the 'triptych' methodology to establish a rationale for burden-sharing, (b) the design of ETS (the EU's main climate policy instrument) and (c) the stress on renewable energy conversion technologies. For France, with low GHG emissions per capita and per unit of GDP, and with exceptionally low CO_2 emissions from the electricity generation sector, all these choices represent second-best solutions since they fail to reward an early (if somewhat relative) decarbonisation of the economy. These factors explain why France is not striving for rapid emission cuts, but is aiming merely to stabilise emissions at 1990 levels for the first commitment period.

Although these features point to national distinctiveness, they do not add up to a new form of French exceptionalism. The climate challenges faced by France are comparable to those in other industrialised nations, but for structural reasons their scale and timing varies. In relation to emissions control in the industrial and power sectors, France currently has less 'low hanging fruit' to pick than neighbouring countries. But these differentials are set to decrease quite rapidly. Further, the sectoral approach favoured by EU climate policy sits relatively easily with the conventions of French 'environmental meso-corporatism'. This has already been demonstrated as regards the EU ETS. In addition, the underdevelopment of the meso-corporatist framework in relation to emergent RES technologies (especially biofuels) offers *domestic* opportunities to renew and re-legitimise the 'economic patriotism' long associated with French economic management. Meanwhile the French nuclear lobby is seeking to reposition itself as an *international* supplier of 'turnkey' climate change solutions. Thus as regards technology transfers and accompanying financial flows, traditional 'national recipes' retain their purchase in the new arena of global climate strategy.

Yet their capacity to deliver against the very ambitious emissions targets now mooted is open to question. To respond to the seriousness of global climate risk, a 'factor four' reduction target – namely a 75 per cent reduction in GHG emissions by 2050 – was first announced by President Chirac and then pledged by Prime Minister Raffarin in 2003 at the 20th plenary session of the International Panel on Climate Change in Paris (Boissieu et al., 2006: 13). The goal was subsequently incorporated into the 2005 Energy Bill. However, a scenario in which French emissions fell from 564 to 550 $MtCO_2$ equivalent between 1990 and 2010 yields a reduction per decade of only 1.5 per cent. Compare this with the 'factor four' target which requires a reduction of 18 per cent per decade. As French climate policy has worked relatively hard to stand still, a clear step change is required for the long term.

Notes

1. Useful historical surveys of the international climate change regime can be found in Mintzer and Leonard (1994); Luterbacher and Sprinz (2001); Dunn (2002); Barrett (2003); Yamin and Depledge (2004) and Dessler and Parson (2006). Proposals to reconfigure the regime's architecture can be found in Baumert et al. (2002); Bodansky et al. (2004); Barrett (2003) and Helm (2005). For presentations of the physical science bases, see IPCC (2001) and IPCC (2007).
2. For discussion, see Maclean (2002: 110–12).
3. See Christiansen and Wettestad (2002) for discussion of the EU's change of mind.
4. Auctioning of 10 per cent of allocations is allowed, but has not so far been tried out.
5. See for example Carbon Trust (2006).
6. See Réseau Action Climat-France (2006).
7. GHG emissions from industry fell by 22 per cent between 1990 and 2004 (MEDD, 2006b: 10).
8. In 'meso-corporatism', interests are aggregated at the sectoral level (namely industrial branches such as chemicals, cement and so on), with interest group representatives and state officials engaging in *bipartite* policy discussions.
9. The analytical framework of 'environmental meso-corporatism' is developed by Szarka (2002: 132–9 and 146–65).
10. For detailed discussion of the wind power sector, see Szarka (2007).

References

Actu-Environnement (2006) 'Neuf états de l'Union Européenne se voient contraints de modifier leur plan national d'allocation de quotas', http://www.actu-environnement.com/ae/news/2114.php4, consulted 13 April 2007.

Actu-Environnement (2007) 'La Commission européenne approuve le PNAQ II français', http://www.actu-environnement.com/ae/news/pnaq_commission_climat_co2_france_2362.php4 consulted 13 April 2007.

Addink, H., B. Arts and A. Mol (2003) 'Climate change policy in changing contexts: globalisation, political modernisation and legal innovation', in E.C. van Ierland, J. Gupta and M.T.J. Kok (eds), *Issues in International Climate Policy:*

Theory and Policy, Cheltenham, UK and Northampton, MA, USA: Edward Elgar, pp. 75–94.

Andersen, M.S. (2005) 'Regulation or coordination: European climate policy between Scylla and Charybdis', in B. Hansjürgens (ed.), *Emissions Trading for Climate Policy: US and European Perspectives*, Cambridge: Cambridge University Press, pp. 135–49.

Arnaud, E. (2005) 'Plan national d'allocations des quotas et territoires', *Revue de l'énergie*, 564 (March–April): 92–9.

Bal, J.-L. (2005) 'Les multiple enjeux du développement des biocarburants en France', *Revue de l'énergie*, 565 (May–June): 173–8.

Barrett, S. (2003) *Environment and Statecraft. The Strategy of Environmental Treaty-Making*, Oxford: Oxford University Press.

Baumert, K. et al. (2002) *Building on the Kyoto Protocol – Options for Protecting the Climate*, Washington, DC: World Resources Institute.

Bodansky, D. et al. (2004) *International Climate Change Efforts Beyond 2012: a Survey of Approaches*, Washington DC: Pew Centre on Global Climate Change.

Boissieu. C. de et al. (2006) *Division par quatre des émissions de gaz à effet de serre de la France à l'horizon 2050*, Paris: La Documentation française.

Brough, M. (2006) 'European emissions trading: is it working?' http://www.oxera. com/cmsDocuments/Agenda_September%2006/European%20emissions%20 trading.pdf, consulted 28 September 2006.

Carbon Trust (2006) 'EU ETS hits crunch time', http://www.carbontrust.co.uk/ about/presscentre/071106_euets.htm, consulted 27 November 2006.

Christiansen, A.C. and J. Wettestad (2002) 'The EU as a frontrunner on greenhouse gas emissions trading: how did it happen and will the EU succeed?', *Climate Policy*, 3: 3–18.

Comité 21 (2007) *L'Avenir en vert*, Paris: Seuil.

Delalande, D. and E. Martinez (2004) 'Le plan national des allocations de quotas dans le système d'échange européen de CO_2 et la compétitivité', in D. Bureau et al., *Politiques environnementales et compétitivité*, Paris: La Documentation française, pp. 97–112.

Delannoy, I. (2007) *Environnement: les candidats au banc d'essai*, Paris: Editions de la Martinière.

Dessler, A.E. and E.A. Parson (2006) *The Science and Politics of Climate Change: a Guide to the Debate*, Cambridge: Cambridge University Press.

Dunn, S. (2002) 'Reading the Weathervane. Climate Policy from Rio to Johannesburg', Washington DC, World Watch Paper 160.

EEA (European Environment Agency) (2004) 'Greenhouse gas emission trends and projections in Europe 2004', Copenhagen, EEA report no. 5.

Entec (2006) 'Analysis of EU ETS news flow for an investor audience: final report', http:// www.carbontrust.co.uk/Publications/publicationdetail.htm? productid=CTC619&metaNoCache=1, consulted 27 November 2006.

EurActiv (2004) 'French carbon allocation plan fails Commission test', http://www.euractiv.com/Article?tcmuri=tcm:29-131260-16&type, consulted 12 March 2005.

Fisher, D.R. (2004) *National Governance and the Global Climate Change Regime*, Lanham MD: Rowman and Littlefield.

Godard, O. (1997) 'Les enjeux des négotiations sur le climat', *Futuribles*, 224 (October): 33–66.

Godard, O. (2001) 'Les permis négociables, une option crédible en France?', in M. Boyer et al. (eds), *L'Environnment, question sociale. Dix ans de recherches pour le Ministere de l'environnement*, Paris: Odile Jacob, pp. 263–72.

Grubb, M. and F. Yamin (2001) 'Climatic collapse at the Hague: what happened, why and where do we go from here?' *International Affairs*, 77(2): 261–76.

Helm, D. (ed.) (2005) *Climate-change Policy*, Oxford: Oxford University Press.

IEA (International Energy Agency) (1996) *Climate Change Policy Initiatives*, Paris: OECD/IEA.

IEA (2005) *Electricity Information*, Paris: OECD/IEA.

IPCC (Intergovernmental Panel on Climate Change) (2001) *Climate Change 2001: Synthesis Report*, Cambridge: Cambridge University Press.

IPCC (2007) 'Climate change 2007: the physical basis. Summary for policy makers', http://www.ipcc.ch/SPM2feb07.pdf, consulted 23 February 2007.

Jagt, J. van der (2003) 'Elaborating an international compliance regime under the Kyoto Protocol', in E.C. van Ierland, J. Gupta and M.T.J. Kok (eds), *Issues in International Climate Policy: Theory and Policy*, Cheltenham, UK and Northampton, MA, USA: Edward Elgar, pp. 223–41.

Jasanoff, S. (2001) 'Image and imagination: the formation of global environmental consciousness', in C.A. Miller and P.E. Edwards (eds), *Changing the Atmosphere: Expert Knowledge and Environmental Governance*, Cambridge, Mass.: MIT Press, pp. 309–37.

Lajoinie, A. (2001) *L'Energie: repères pour demain*, Paris: Assemblée nationale, report no. 2907.

Luterbacher, U. and D.F. Sprinz (eds) (2001) *International Relations and Global Climate Change*, Cambridge, Mass.: MIT Press.

Maclean, M. (2002) *Economic Management and French Business: From de Gaulle to Chirac*, Basingstoke: Palgrave Macmillan.

MATE (Ministère de l'Aménagement du territoire et de l'environnement) (2000) 'La Haye: obtenir un bon accord, pas un accord à tout prix', *Dépêches*, 4 (24 November).

MEDD (Ministère de l'écologie et du développement durable) (2004a) 'Plan Climat 2004–2012', http://www.ecologie.gouv.fr, consulted 1 December 2004.

MEDD (2004b) 'Plan national d'affectation des quotas – période de référence 2005–2007', http://www.ecologie.gouv.fr/article.php3?id_article=2207, consulted 28 February 2005.

MEDD (2006a) 'Projet de plan national d'affectation des quotas d'émissions de gaz à effet de serre (PNAQ II). Période: 2008 à 2010', http://www.consultation publiquepnaq.com/download/PNAQII_v19ter.pdf, consulted 8 March 2007.

MEDD (2006b) 'Actualisation 2006 du Plan Climat 2004–2012', http://www.ecologie.gouv.fr/IMG/pdf/1er_doc_INTRO_PLAN_CLIMAT_final.pdf, consulted 16 November 2006.

Meyer, A. (2000) *Contraction and Convergence. The Global Solution to Climate Change*, Totnes: Green Books.

Mintzer, I.M. and J.A. Leonard (eds) (1994) *Negotiating Climate Change: the Inside Story of the Rio Convention*, Cambridge: Cambridge University Press.

Oberthür, S. (2006) 'The climate change regime: interactions with ICAO, IMO and the EU', in S. Oberthür and T. Gehring (eds), *Institutional Interaction in Global Environmental Governance: Synergy and Conflict among International and EU Policies*, Cambridge, Mass.: MIT Press, pp. 53–77.

Phylipsen, G.J.M. et al. (1998) 'A triptych sectoral approach to burden-differentiation: GHG emissions in the European bubble', *Energy Policy*, 26(12): 929–43.

Réseau Action Climat-France (2006) 'Commentaires du RAC-France et de ses associations membres sur le projet de deuxième Plan National d'Affectation des Quotas de la France (PNAQ2)', http://www.rac-f.org/IMG/pdf/commentaires_des_ONG_sur_PNAQ_2_de_la_France.3_octobre_06.pdf, consulted 8 March 2007.

Ringius, L. (1999) 'Differentiation, leaders and fairness: negotiating climate commitments in the European Community', *International Negotiation*, 4: 133–66.

Systèmes solaires (2005) 'Le baromètre des biocarburants', *Systèmes solaires*, 167 (May–June): 39–56.

Szarka, J. (2002) *The Shaping of Environmental Policy in France*, Oxford: Berghahn.

Szarka, J. (2006) 'From inadvertent to reluctant pioneer? Climate strategies and policy style in France', *Climate Policy*, 5: 625–36.

Szarka, J. (2007) *Wind Power in Europe: Politics, Business and Society*, Basingstoke: Palgrave Macmillan.

WCED (World Commission on Environment and Development) (1987) *Our Common Future*, Oxford: Oxford University Press.

Windpower Monthly (2007) 'Operating wind power capacity', *Windpower Monthly*, 23(4) (April): 90.

Yamin, F. and J. Depledge (2004) *The International Climate Change Regime: a Guide to Rules, Institutions and Procedures*, Cambridge: Cambridge University Press.

Zito, A.R. (2000) *Creating Environmental Policy in the European Union*, Basingstoke: Macmillan.

12
Pushing Back and Reaching Out: French Television in the Global Age

Raymond Kuhn

In common with all other national broadcasters in Europe, French television is increasingly affected by developments in what has become an ever more interdependent global media system. Technological innovation, new patterns of ownership in media industries and cross-border trade in programme content and formats are just some facets of the contemporary era of media globalisation. This chapter focuses on selected key aspects of the changing nature of French television in the digital age of global media, notably the response of stakeholders in the national policy community to the growing transnationalisation of the medium in recent years. In particular, the chapter analyses and evaluates the effectiveness of some of the 'pushing back' and 'reaching out' measures taken by policy stakeholders – notably, political elites, broadcasting regulators and media professionals – in response to the challenges they face in what is now the third age of French television's historical evolution. In this context 'pushing back' refers to regulatory measures designed to protect the national status of French television from perceived external threats, while 'reaching out' embraces the active promotion of French cultural and economic interests in non-domestic broadcasting markets.

The French television landscape

From national ...

Let us start with a brief historical freeze-frame, which could easily be expanded into a more detailed analysis of the evolution of the French television landscape since regular transmissions began after the end of the Second World War (Kuhn, 1995: 109–228). We start by going back just over 25 years – the time span of only a generation – to the immediate aftermath of the first presidential election victory of François Mitterrand in 1981. It was relatively easy at that time to talk about French television as an overwhelmingly *national* medium that was protected by a combination of technological constraints due to the limited transmission range of terrestrial networks and public policy decisions in support of the legal framework of the state monopoly. The results were a territorially-bounded television landscape overwhelmingly dominated by national actors and a policy field in which national concerns and issues were paramount. In this context one would, of course, have to define the concept of 'national' and establish criteria to allow for an assessment of the system's credentials with reference to this conceptual label, as for example Susan Hayward has done in her study of French national cinema (Hayward, 2005: 1–16). With regard to the closely related but significantly different medium of television, a wide-ranging list of variables could be considered relevant to this task. These include the configuration of ownership and control, the main bases of production and origin of programme content, the nature of dominant programming formats and genres, the source and content of regulatory provisions, and patterns of audience reception.

The first age of French television (Kuhn, 2005), which lasted roughly from the 1950s up to the Socialist government's 1982 reform (with the *loi Fillioud*), was characterised by the following key features:

- limited supply consisting of a maximum of three channels with restricted daytime schedules;
- public ownership enshrined in a legal framework of state monopoly which allowed for no private, commercial competition;
- highly regulated output with all three channels subject to French-style public service obligations;
- terrestrial transmission, which meant that the overwhelming majority of the French audience was restricted to the output of the three national channels;
- no minority, niche or thematic channels, and so programme schedules were for the most part designed for mass audience consumption;
- a small and relatively tightly integrated policy community, made up predominantly, if not exclusively, of *national* political and media actors;
- much television content produced in France and catering for French interests and tastes, ranging from news and sport to drama, current affairs and entertainment.

In short, up until 1982 France possessed a strong *national* television culture (Steemers, 2004: 1–19). This is hardly surprising, since in the years when the medium went through the formative period of this first age – the 1960s – television was consciously and explicitly used by politicians and state officials, most notably President de Gaulle, as a cultural, educational and informational tool to help construct a popular national consensus around the new political institutions of the Fifth Republic (Chalaby, 2002).

...to transnational?

If we fast-forward to the present day, the French television landscape has changed – in many respects radically. Indeed, to a new generation of French audiences, socialised to believe in the virtues of consumer sovereignty and market choice in many areas of their daily lives, the highly restricted state monopoly provision of a quarter of a century ago must seem like a relic from the Jurassic age of broadcasting. As one scans through the development of the medium from our freeze-frame of the dying days of the first age through a turbulent period of marketisation, liberalisation and limited deregulation in the 1980s and early 1990s (the second age) up to the contemporary digital era of multimedia convergence (the third age), then the more one needs to take account of the impact of three important features: commercialisation, digitisation and transnationalisation.

Commercialisation has seen the entry into the French television landscape of new private actors at all levels of the value chain of production, programming and distribution. While much of this process of commercialisation has been incremental, it has also been punctuated by radical public policy initiatives, such as the Chirac government's 1986 law on Freedom of Communication (*la loi Léotard*) and the subsequent privatisation of the main free-to-air public television channel, TF1. Since the abolition of the state monopoly by the Socialists in 1982, the power of commercial television interests has grown, with a significant share of ownership in the hands of industrial conglomerates such as the construction company Bouygues which is by far the main shareholder in TF1.

Digitisation is the most important technological change in television since the medium was invented. The relatively recently introduced process of compressed distribution of signals via a variety of digital platforms – cable, satellite, terrestrial and ADSL (for example, broadband) – not only allows more content to be made available to audiences in a significant increase in programme supply, but also encourages greater segmentation in the form of thematic and minority channels, as well as access to near video-on-demand services and a host of interactive possibilities. The impact of digitisation, therefore, cannot simply be evaluated in terms of an increase in the quantity of content transmitted to viewers: more television output in a traditional flow model of distribution, whereby programmes are selected and packaged for audiences within the framework of a constructed schedule. Instead, the advent of the digital age opens up a different type of television compared to its analogue predecessor, with content capable of being accessed via the internet and mobile phone as well as the traditional television monitor, and with greater empowerment for the service user (no longer just a 'viewer') to construct their own patterns of content access and medium usage. In the eyes of some, digitisation radically alters the power balance between producer and consumer, as a previously highly restricted, producer-dominated market is replaced by a more competitive set of arrangements in which consumers can now exercise greater freedom of choice.

The third feature of the digital era – the phenomenon of transnationalisation – has various facets. These include transnational distribution technologies, notably satellite broadcasting and the internet, which allow audiences to access audio and video content distributed from outside the national territory; transnational media ownership, with companies owning media assets across different national systems and global regions; an increase in cross-border trade in programme content and formats, from game shows such as *Who Wants To Be A Millionaire?* to 'reality' programming such as *Big Brother* and its original French variant, *Loft Story*; cooperation between national broadcasters in transnational ventures, such as the Franco-German cultural channel, Arte; the regulatory intervention of supranational and global actors, such as the European Union (EU) and the World Trade Organisation (WTO), with the former particularly important in imposing common standards across member states in areas such as media competition as well as in pushing through regulatory initiatives such as the Television Without Frontiers Directive (Harcourt, 2005); and, finally, the cross-border transfer of ideas and practices between national governments and regulatory authorities in the area of media and communications policy.

Transnationalisation is, of course, a complex process and one should be wary of oversimplification in emphasising the scale, scope and pace of the transition from national to transnational. Even in the first age of French television, where the media landscape was dominated by national features, there existed some transnational elements: the cross-border import and export of programmes, the attempt – largely a failure – to export the French transmission standard (known as SECAM), and instances of international cooperation through bodies such as the European Broadcasting Union. Conversely, even in the contemporary third age of French television, *national* actors, rules, patterns of ownership, content and audience tastes continue to exist and, in many important respects, retain a strong hold within the broadcasting system. Even what seem to be transnational features of the contemporary French television landscape are usually filtered through national prisms, leading to complex patterns of mutual interaction which are characterised by processes of cross-fertilisation, mutual adjustment among policy actors, hybridity, fusion, recuperation and the tweaking of global content for local consumption by transnational broadcasters in the practice labelled 'glocalisation'. In short, transnationalisation is not simply an innovation of the contemporary era, nor are the boundaries between the national and transnational as clear cut as might initially be assumed.

How do stakeholders in the French media policy community – politicians, regulators, owners, chief executives and lobby groups – seek both to influence and adapt to this increasing complexity in the nature of the television landscape? One potential response is to see change as largely unwelcome and even threatening. Such a reaction would be in accord with a significant swathe of French public opinion, itself aided and abetted by much media and political elite discourse (from Bové on the *altermondialiste* left to Le Pen on the extreme right) regarding the phenomenon of globalisation. From this perspective globalisation is regarded, first, as an external force imposed on France and the French in a more or less conspiratorial manner by the hegemonic forces of Anglo-Saxon neo-liberalism and, second, as exerting an overwhelmingly negative impact on the French economy, cultural values, social model and national identity.

A contrasting approach is to try to take advantage of the opportunities offered by transnationalisation, notably the opening up of foreign media markets to French interests. Outside of the media sector, several French companies have successfully exploited the liberalisation of markets at supranational and global levels to become European or even world leaders in their fields (Gordon and Meunier, 2001: 13–40). There is a clear and demonstrable willingness on the part of many economic and corporate elites in France to adapt positively to forces of change in areas ranging from pharmaceuticals to telecommunications. In the media policy community there is evidence of both sets of responses to the transnationalisation of the television landscape – protectionism and entrepreneurship – as stakeholders engage in practices of 'pushing back' and 'reaching out' to defend and promote cultural values, economic interests and political objectives.

Pushing back

Since the advent of television as a mass medium of information, education and entertainment, French policy-makers have been highly interventionist in its regulation (Dagnaud, 2000). For example, regulation has been used to control market entry, traditionally justified on the grounds of spectrum scarcity, with state officials and regulatory authorities acting as gatekeepers in decisions about who should be authorised (and who not) to broadcast within the confines of the sovereign territory. Even when new entrants were allowed into the market as part of the economic liberalisation of broadcasting in the 1980s, the process was managed in a top-down fashion and controlled by a state-appointed regulatory agency, first the High Authority for Audiovisual Communication (1982–86) and then the National Commission for Communication and Freedoms (1986–89) (Chauveau, 1997). This controlled liberalisation contrasted with the so-called 'savage deregulation' of the television systems in Greece, Portugal and Italy at the same time (Hallin and Mancini, 2004: 124–7). Media-specific regulation, as opposed to legislation such as competition law which applies to the functioning of the media as part of its general regulatory ambit, currently operates in two main spheres in France: ownership and content.

Media regulation sets limits on ownership within an individual television network, across the television sector as a whole and across the totality of different media markets (press, radio and television). Upper thresholds on maximum ownership shares are specified in national media legislation in an attempt to promote editorial pluralism and content diversity. For instance, no single individual or company is allowed to own more than 49 per cent of a single national terrestrial commercial television network; a company may not hold more than one licence for the provision of a national terrestrial commercial television service; and there are complex rules regarding cross-media ownership involving television, radio and the press (Open Society Institute, 2005: 48–50). A particular facet of French media ownership regulation within the context of 'pushing back' is the restriction placed on foreign (that is, non-EU) ownership of a national terrestrial commercial television network. This is fixed at a maximum of below 20 per cent, in stark contrast to recent communications legislation in the UK which places no limits on the share that foreign interests, including US companies, may own in such networks. French governments of all ideological complexions have been keen to ensure that significant sections of the national media remain wherever possible under French control, on the basis that in this way it is easier for government to exert influence over their operations.

Regulation of content has traditionally embraced both positive and negative rules. The mandatory inclusion of both different types and prescribed amounts of programming in television schedules has been included in the operating agreements (*cahiers des charges*) of television companies, while other types of content have been excluded by regulation from the output of at least some content distributors. The specific obligations of content regulation vary across service providers, with the toughest obligations being imposed on the channels of France Télévisions and other public service broadcasters. Quotas on French-produced programming, for instance, have long been an integral part of the television regulatory context and are undoubtedly the product of the lobbying power of different stakeholders in media and audiovisual policy communities.

Quotas have been defended in national and international policy fora on the grounds of cultural protection in the face of unfair international competition dominated by the US entertainment and film industries. Such quotas can be regarded as the policy outcome of either a half-digested interpretation of media imperialism theories or a perfectly understandable desire to protect French artefacts in an interdependent global cultural market. They can also be seen as a form of economic protectionism, providing support to internationally uncompetitive domestic sources of production, or as a defensible concern with maintaining a national production base in an important area of the global media economy.

Reaching out

Alongside the 'pushing back' of cultural and economic protectionist measures, stakeholders in the media policy community have also been involved in promoting French interests in non-domestic broadcasting markets. These 'reaching out' activities can be divided into different analytic categories, such as the export of programme content and formats, the holding of ownership stakes in foreign media companies, the establishment of French companies in external broadcasting markets and the launch of transnational channels. Thus, France is an important exporter of television product, particularly to French-speaking markets. French companies have acquired shares in foreign media groups, such as Vivendi's stake in the British satellite broadcaster, BSkyB, in the 1990s. They have entered foreign markets directly as broadcasters, most notably Canal+ with its pay-TV operations in Spain, Italy and Poland among others. French interests have also been involved in transnational television ventures, including the European news channel, Euronews, and the global Francophone channel, TV5 Monde. From the many examples that could be cited, this section concentrates on two case studies of the French practice of 'reaching out' on to the world stage in recent years: the multimedia conglomerate, Vivendi Universal, and the global rolling news channel, France 24.

Vivendi Universal

The merger of Vivendi with the American film giant Universal in 2000 represented an audacious attempt by a French company to become a global multi-media player (also see Chapter 9 by Mairi Maclean). There are fewer than ten major transnational media conglomerates, which between them dominate global entertainment and communications markets. These include TimeWarner, Viacom, Disney, Bertelsmann and News Corporation, all of which are either in US ownership or have a major base in the United States (Tunstall and Machin, 1999; Herman and McChesney, 1997). These companies do not just have a worldwide media presence across different global regions; they also tend to be vertically integrated, with a stake in each stage of the production/programming/distribution chain. Rupert Murdoch's News Corporation, for example, has media interests in Australia, Asia, the UK, continental Europe and the USA. The company owns satellite distribution systems; it runs several television channels including the rolling news network, Fox News, and various sports, film and general entertainment channels; it controls the Twentieth Century Fox film business which gives it a stake in programme production; it owns the social networking website MySpace; it has been a leading player in the acquisition of sports rights for television coverage; and is involved in the businesses of encryption technology and subscriber management systems, two key areas of activity in digital television. Murdoch's interests have always been media-focused.

In contrast, Vivendi was originally a water utility company (called the *Compagnie générale des eaux*) which became involved in the distribution of cable services in the 1980s and, after its takeover of the advertising company Havas in 1997, entered the French media market as a major player by gaining control of the pay-TV company Canal+. This move guaranteed Vivendi a role not just in the media sector in France but also in the media markets of those other countries where Canal+ was involved in the supply of pay-TV. Under the leadership of its dynamic chief executive, Jean-Marie Messier (Briançon, 2002), Vivendi expanded its media portfolio in an attempt to take advantage of technological convergence in media industries across telephony, television and the internet, becoming involved in mobile phone services and setting up its own internet portal, Vizzavi. Control of sports and film rights are generally considered to be major economic drivers in the pay-TV industry. Consequently, a deal with a major US movie company such as Universal was an attractive proposition to Vivendi management, as it seemed to offer Vivendi the opportunity to move their corporate game to a higher level and to compete with the major players of the global media economy. At its height, Vivendi Universal was one of the leading media companies on the world stage.

Messier's convergence strategy may have appeared sound in theory. The growth of digital broadcasting and the expansion in internet services appeared to underline the importance to media companies of combining ownership of programme rights with control of the means of distribution to audiences: the holy grail of a combined stake in both content and conduits. The US mega-merger in 1999 between the media giant Time Warner and the internet company America OnLine (AOL) seemed to demonstrate the compatibility between traditional media organisations and new internet companies. Yet even this particular conjunction of US interests failed to live up to stock market expectations following the end of the speculative dot.com boom only a few months after the merger. Messier's convergence strategy also quickly encountered major problems. His investment decisions proved to be overly ambitious, with either the technology failing to deliver or customers unwilling to sign up to the promised new services. Vivendi Universal quickly ran into financial difficulties and the stock markets lost confidence in Messier's capacity to steer the company through troubled waters. As the share price plummeted, Messier continued to defend his decisions, making statements increasingly at odds with the reality of the company's market position. In 2002 Pierre Lescure, head of Canal+, was sacked in a diversionary attempt to shift responsibility for Vivendi's economic woes. A few weeks later Messier himself resigned, leaving behind a media conglomerate which was a pale shadow of the company of only a few years previously. Vivendi Universal had been severely damaged by a mix of Messier's personal hubris, corporate overreach and poor investment decisions (Orange and

Johnson, 2003). It was little consolation that around the same time other European media companies, such as Kirch in Germany and ITVDigital in the UK, made similar costly errors in their attempts to benefit from television's digital expansion.

The failure of Vivendi Universal under Messier deprived France – at least temporarily – of a media company with truly global ambitions. The complicated ownership structure of Vivendi Universal also revealed the complexities of successfully reaching out in the highly competitive, interdependent global media economy of the early twenty-first century. The Vivendi saga can certainly be viewed as an example of failed French outreach into world markets. At the same time, it can also be regarded as the Americanisation of a previously wholly French company – a view taken by many in the French cinema industry (Hayward, 2005: 70), which, if accurate, demonstrates the complex nature of ownership and control in the era of global media.

France 24

France 24 represents a belated attempt by stakeholders in the French media policy community to enter the competitive world of global television news providers. Global news channels originated with the launch of CNN in the 1980s, with the service establishing its reputation through its coverage of the first Gulf War in 1990–91. Since then other global news channels have been launched, with the most notable examples including BBC World (UK), Deutsche Welle (Germany) and Al Jazeera (Quatar). Al Jazeera has been particularly successful in providing an Arab perspective on events in the Middle East, including the war in Iraq, and at the end of 2006 the company launched an English language version of its service, Al Jazeera English. During this period of growing international competition, France was notable by its absence from this market, which is surprising given the country's long-standing commitment to the dissemination of French cultural artefacts and values around the world.

The immediate stimulus to the decision to go ahead with the France 24 project appears to have been official concern that the French government's position in the run-up to the Iraq war was not given sufficient space on the main English language news channels, especially those based in the USA. French political elites across the party spectrum argued that France's voice in international matters was at best being marginalised and at worst being vilified in the news reporting of channels such as CNN and Fox News. More generally, in the new international climate of post-9/11, there was a strong sense that the battle 'for hearts and minds' required an international rolling news channel which would provide a French perspective on world events. The impetus for the creation of France 24 was, therefore, overtly political, with President Chirac one of the early supporters of the project after his re-election in 2002.

Despite official backing, however, French news broadcasters had to overcome a series of difficulties in the run-up to the launch of the new service. The first was that France has no organisational equivalent of the BBC, whose size and output of English-language content make it a natural player in global news markets. In contrast, not only is the largest single French television network, TF1, in private hands, but the public service provider, France Télévisions, benefits from neither the status nor legitimacy in the French media landscape that the BBC routinely enjoys in the UK. Nor does France Télévisions enjoy a reputation among international audiences on a par with the BBC. In part this is because the experience of governmental intervention in news production in the early years of French television prevented public broadcasting as a whole from developing a tradition of political independence which would allow the organisation to foster a positive relationship with civil society and embed itself in popular consciousness as a national icon. There has never been a French equivalent of 'the Beeb'. In addition, the break-up of the unitary broadcasting organisation of the Office de radiodiffusion-télévision française (ORTF) in 1975 split public radio and television, with the result that for over 30 years there has been no single public broadcasting organisation which could maximise its influence internationally. Finally, while the BBC has for long regarded news and information provision as a central component of its mission – indeed arguably *the* principal defining feature – this has been much less true of either TF1 or France Télévisions. Thus, while the contemporary BBC regards itself not just as a *broadcaster* but as a major public *communications* actor, embracing radio, television and on-line services, TF1 and France Télévisions are still in many ways old-fashioned suppliers of television programming with some web content as an add-on service. The project was held up by discussions among stakeholders about which national broadcaster would take the lead role. The government wanted TF1 to be involved, while France Télévisions wanted to be in total charge. In the end, ownership of France 24 is equally shared between these two private and public companies.

Second, a prolonged debate took place – and, given the sensitivities involved, probably needed to take place – regarding the language(s) in which France 24 would broadcast. In particular, the question of whether the news channel should broadcast in French was an important aspect of the pre-launch debate. In the end it was decided that the channel would broadcast in three languages – French, English and Arabic – so as to maximise audiences and extend its potential for influence among elite opinion formers who were regarded as the channel's main target audience. Broadcasting in the French language was not considered to be a point of principle.

Third, TF1 did not want France 24 to be available within France for fear that this would provide unwanted competition for its own domestic rolling news service, LCI. Finally, the project was held up by disagreements about the amount of financing required and where the money would come from. Its initial operating budget of €80 million, most of it from the public purse, is comparatively small by the standards of international rolling news channels.

Launched in December 2006, the channel was praised by *Le Monde* for its coverage of the conflict in Iraq, the amount of space devoted to cultural issues and its reporting of events in Africa (Larrochelle, 2007). Only time will tell whether the objective of reaching out to key international opinion-formers has been a success. The channel's capacity to reach out to economic, business and political elites rather than simply to a mass audience will therefore be the key criterion of evaluation by all those involved in the journalistic enterprise.

Conclusion

How successful have stakeholders in the national media policy community been in ensuring France's place in global television markets in the early years of the twenty-first century? The answer is at best mixed.

In terms of 'pushing back', there has been a strong and concerted attempt to maintain a distinct French identity to French television content through the use of prescriptive and proscriptive regulation. Has this ensured the distinctiveness of French television when compared to that of other European nations of similar size? Not particularly. In terms of the amount of imported programming, French television is not especially exceptional or distinct when compared to the UK or Germany. However, in fairness to the French authorities it could be argued that without regulatory constraints on content the amount of domestic product shown on French television would probably be significantly lower, as French companies took advantage of the financial savings to be made through a policy based on cheap imports. If so, then regulation does allow for a certain amount of cultural and economic protectionism.

In terms of 'reaching out', France has certainly not been as successful as it would have wished. As regards producing a Gaullist style 'national champion' in global media markets, the results are poor. Vivendi Universal represented a 'heroic failure', while Canal+ has pulled back from foreign incursions – for example its forced withdrawal from the Italian pay-TV market, in which it was forced to sell its holdings to Murdoch's News Corporation. Meanwhile TF1 has been largely content to dominate the domestic television market. The company remains a major player within France, but not a big global player in terms of its portfolio of assets/activities in foreign markets. It is certainly not a rival to the BBC in terms of external commercial activities such as programme sales. Nor is France Télévisions. Moreover, French production companies are often weak and under-capitalised by international standards. In addition, programme exports have been hindered by language constraints, by the cultural specificity of much of the content and by idiosyncratic national particularities regarding length of programmes – 90 minutes is quite common in French production, while the international standard is 52 minutes (one hour including time for commercial breaks).

Another aspect of the failure of France's 'reaching out' strategy has been political confusion. Turf wars between the ministries of foreign affairs on the one hand and culture on the other have not helped forge a 'joined-up' policy. The result has been a fragmentation of effort across different broadcasting actors, including Radio-France internationale, TV5 Monde and France 24 among others (Brochand, 2006: 435–68). Yet it is also the case that fragmentation is to some extent inevitable: the mission of TV5 Monde is to supply French language content to those with a knowledge of French, while that of France 24 is to put across a French perspective on global events. These are two quite separate objectives, catering for different audiences and requiring different skills on the part of the content providers.

What of the future? As national borders become more porous in the face of global technological change, corporate transnational ownership strategies and liberal WTO and European regulations, a defensive national strategy of 'pushing back' will become more difficult to deliver. This will be true whether 'pushing back' is evaluated in cultural or economic terms. In an age of multi-channel television, content segmentation and audience fragmentation, there will be increasing pressures on the financial bottom-line. French product will have to compete to secure its privileged position on domestic television. At the same time, the regulatory tradition in French television is well entrenched and so the significance of defensive strategies in the face of external competition should not be underestimated. It is also important to remember that

French-produced television content is much appreciated by the national audience.

As far as 'reaching out' is concerned, more emphasis needs to be placed on this activity. French television is important in certain global regions (notably French-speaking markets in Europe, Africa and North America), but tangential in other global regions (English- and Spanish-speaking markets, India and China). At present there are insufficient incentives for many policy stakeholders as well as significant corporate resistance. In particular, the lack of a powerful global media company represents a major constraint to French efforts to play a major role on the world stage.

References

Briançon, P. (2002) *Messier Story*, Paris: Grasset.

Brochand, C. (2006) *Histoire générale de la radio et de la télévision en France, Tome III 1974–2000*, Paris: La Documentation française.

Chalaby, J.K. (2002) *The de Gaulle Presidency and the Media*, Basingstoke: Palgrave Macmillan.

Chauveau, A. (1997) *L'Audiovisuel en liberté*, Paris: Presses de Sciences Po.

Dagnaud, M. (2000) *L'État et les médias*, Paris: Éditions Odile Jacob.

Gordon, P.H. and S. Meunier (2001) *The French Challenge? Adapting to Globalisation*, Washington, DC: Brookings Institution.

Hallin, D.C. and P. Mancini (2004) *Comparing Media Systems*, Cambridge: Cambridge University Press.

Harcourt, A. (2005) *The European Union and the Regulation of Media Markets*, Manchester: Manchester University Press.

Hayward, S. (2005) *French National Cinema*, 2nd edn, London: Routledge.

Herman, E.S. and R.W. McChesney (1997) *The Global Media*, London: Cassell.

Kuhn, R. (1995) *The Media in France*, London: Routledge.

Kuhn, R. (2005) 'The myth of exceptionalism? French television in a West European context', in E. Godin and T. Chafer (eds), *The French Exception*, Oxford: Berghahn.

Larrochelle, J.-J. (2007) '24 heures sur France 24', *Le Monde*, 4–5 February.

Open Society Institute (2005) *Television across Europe: Regulation, Policy and Independence – France*, http://www.soros.org/initiatives/media/articles_publications/publications/eurotv_20051011, consulted 18 April 2007.

Orange, M. and J. Johnson (2003) *Une Faillite française*, Paris: Albin Michel.

Steemers, J. (2004) *Selling Television*, London: British Film Institute.

Tunstall, J. and D. Machin (1999) *The Anglo-American Media Connection*, Oxford: Oxford University Press.

13
Globalisation and the Specificity of the French Republic: the End of the French Counter-Model?

Gino Raymond

Introduction

When the deprived suburbs of Paris and other French conurbations erupted in the autumn of 2005, in the worst display of civil unrest in France for four decades, there was no shortage of commentators willing to recall the attempt to overturn the authority of the state that was led by the students at the Sorbonne in 1968. In his memoirs, the president at the time, Charles de Gaulle, had himself admitted that one of the specificities of French democracy was that nothing seemed to change in France unless the people took to the streets, and the period generated numerous academic studies that underlined France's failings as a society incapable of overcoming a sense of stifling immobilism (Crozier, 1970). Certainly, the scale of the unrest was evocative of a major urban challenge to the peace and security of civil society, lasting for a full three weeks, and resulting in over 8000 vehicles being torched. Moreover, the special measures taken by the government to bring the situation under control, notably the resort to emergency curfew powers, seemed like an atavistic response from the worst days of the Fifth Republic under de Gaulle. Some have argued that France had been in revolt for a decade already, starting with the mass mobilisation against the plans drawn up by the government of Prime Minister Alain Juppé in 1995 to reform the country's generous social security system; that the challenge to the authority of the state peaked again in 2003 in response to government proposals to reform the pensions system; and that the challenge posed by the youth of urban France in 2005 was the most dramatic expression of the frustration felt by a significant portion of society at the impoverishment and social neglect caused by the neo-liberal agenda imposed by governments of Left and Right in France since the early 1980s (Wolfreys, 2006).

A closer analysis of the social realities, however, leads to a more nuanced view of what the riots of 2005 signified, and especially what the youth involved represented. Statistical analyses after the event showed that half the young people arrested were under 18 years of age, operating in groups of 30–200 individuals according to the *banlieue* in which they lived. On no occasion could it be said that a representative cross-section of the population of the suburbs concerned took to the streets in an act of defiance against the state. They were, in fact, the principal victims of the disorder due to the damage done by the rioters to their property and the amenities they used. Attempts to interpret the riots as the reaction of a generation fighting the discrimination suffered by the Muslim community in France overlook the fact that the many thousands of often highly politicised students of Muslim origin or persuasion in French universities did not join the unrest. Apart from the occasional piece of abusive graffiti regarding the then French Interior Minister, Nicolas Sarkozy, later elected President of France in May 2007, the rioters had no political agenda as such. There were no demands, no spokespersons, there was no network of support and no organisation.

In contrast to this, the students of 1968 were highly politicised and could be seen as invoking their rights as citizens, according to that first, heady declaration of the rights of man and the citizen in 1789, to wrest sovereignty back from an authoritarian government, while the rioting adolescents of 2005 seemed to be turning their backs on the blueprint for citizenship that the French revolution bequeathed to the modern world. For them, the rights of citizenship and the concomitant obligation to participate in the life of the polity and shape its future were at best hollow, and at worst a deliberate deception aimed at masking the fact that there was no upward socio-economic mobility for them in contemporary France. In short, for these young rebels, and in contrast to their predecessors in 1968, the grand narrative of modernity flowing from the Revolution of 1789 that allied the progress of a democratic state with the empowerment of the individual citizen with universal rights, had broken down. What this chapter will do, therefore, will be to survey first of all some of the essentially conservative arguments suggesting that the revolutionary impetus, and the political culture that it engendered and that underpinned the specificity of the French polity, has come to an end. It will then examine the view that rather than marking a dangerous form of *anomie*, the decline of the old Republican paradigm has, in fact, released new forces and provided a platform for a new politics. And in the final section, a synthesis will be offered which suggests that the French Republican model for assuming citizenship through action in the public space remains pertinent, albeit in a more modest manner where its specificity has accommodated the prospect of convergence with other post-modern liberal democratic societies.

The decline of the French Republican paradigm

Observations and anxiety about the failure of a growing number of citizens to take an active part in political life through the processes of representative democracy are not new, and certainly not unique to France. Empirical surveys, notably in the USA in the 1950s and 1960s, illustrated the considerable gulf that existed between the active citizen envisaged by the fathers of the American Revolution or the *citoyen actif* conceptualised by the authors of the French Revolution and his modern twentieth-century counterpart (Berelson et al., 1966). What emerged was the image of a citizen who was poorly informed politically, undynamic and lacking in self-motivation with regard to participation in the life of the body politic. Subsequent surveys in Britain and France during the two following decades suggested that democracies that had enjoyed generations or even centuries of stability had developed a complacent coexistence with the apathy of many of their citizens. The sociological interpretation of this that emerged, especially from the research of individuals such as Pierre Bourdieu in France, shed a particular light on the classic notion of the active citizen by asking whether it was only ever an illusion. The nineteenth-century barriers to participation posed by property qualification had gone, but, according to Bourdieu, the right to influence decision-making remains illusory due to the cultural capital that is shared by modern political elites in a market from which the ordinary citizen is excluded. And Bourdieu's ideas were fed back into the debates occurring in English-speaking countries about the cultural underpinning of political representation (Bourdieu, 1991).

But one could argue that, notwithstanding the parallels with other modern liberal democracies, the specificity of France's political culture made the sense of anxiety engendered by the crisis of representation more acute there than elsewhere. As Jürgen Habermas has observed, the eighteenth century marked a watershed in the context framing the relationship between the governing and the governed in Europe by offering the individual the principle of public deliberation as a means of legitimate control over political authority (Habermas, 1993). The relationship between those exercising power and the people was expressed by the emergence of a public space or dimension that conditioned new forms of sociability, defining the individual through his or her commitment to action in that space. The ambition to create a *res publica* or public entity that emerged from the Revolution of 1789 can be seen as setting a new template and temporal framework for modernity, and the depth of that conviction was evoked by George Steiner (1988: 151) when he argued that 'the cycle of lived history, was deemed to have begun a second time'.

Such hyperbole provides an implicit link to the metaphysical understanding of citizenship that characterises the specificity of the French approach in contrast to the empiricism of the Anglo-American one, and points to the inevitable sense of anxiety that must surface when the Republican ideal collides with reality. Almost from the beginning of that new dawn in history, as Steiner would have it, there has been a tension between the prerogatives afforded to the citizen according to the Republican ideal, and the way this was translated in terms of political practice. Entry and action in the public space did not conform to the idealised image of the active citizen. It is noteworthy that, when, on 29 October 1789, the National Assembly passed the decree introducing the category of 'active citizens' (male and tax-paying), this was challenged by figures like Camille Desmoulins who asked: 'But what is this much repeated word "active citizen" supposed to mean? The active citizens are the ones who took the Bastille' (Wickham Legg, 1905: 173–4).

Those who in previous generations had theorised the way the role offered to the citizen by the Revolution had not been realised in terms of political practice would have recognised the 'democracy minus the people' identified by Maurice Duverger (1967) in the early life of the Fifth Republic, when the operation of the public space was incomparably more transparent and the processes of representation more established. As Duverger argued, the fundamental mediating role that should be played by political parties in translating the preferences of civil society into the choices of the state, is weaker in France than in other comparable democracies such as Britain or Germany. Whereas the mass party memberships in those democracies provided a form of leverage that allowed considerable direct pressure to be brought on the leaderships in question, the weak membership bases of mainstream French political parties (with the historical exception of the French Communist Party), and the reliance on tendencies and factions as the conduit for changes in party policy, has resulted in what has been perceived as the rise of a class of party notables who have come to dominate public life. Furthermore, by operating through a form of *centrisme* that perpetuates itself precisely by occluding the fundamental oppositions that should separate the adversaries, the parties deprive the voters of a genuine choice and preside over a system that could be termed *la démocratie sans le peuple* or democracy minus the people.

The frustration identified underlined the enduring challenge of reuniting the citizen with the vocation defined by the Revolution, and whether it was Duverger or other figures exercising a seminal intellectual influence, the guiding assumption was that the citizen cannot fulfil himself or herself without engaging actively in the life of the Republic. But as the end of the twentieth century approached, the focus of anxiety moved from the obstacles in the way of participation to the fundamental relationship between the individual citizen and politics in the Republic. The interaction between the citizen and those mediating institutions identified by Duverger and others was conceived, originally, in a way that buttressed the specificity of the French Republic. The ethical voluntarism that characterised the Revolution posited the notion of a citizen emancipated from the claims of heredity, and whose judgement was founded on the exercise of reason alone. In terms of political fidelity, the claims of genealogy had to give way to the choices constructed within a broad set of values defined by the collectivity, the nation. The inevitable corollary of Jacobin ideology was that the children of the revolution were 'constitutionally innocent' (Borie, 1981: 215), because any kind of social determinism passed from one generation to the next would militate against the democratic structuring of political choices that individuals would make as free and equal citizens.

Political theorists from other democratic cultures could be tempted to establish a causal link between the political convictions of parents and the partisan preferences of their children, even to the point of extrapolating from this a fundamental factor responsible for the stability of a mature democracy like that of the United States. However, Anglo-American political scientists have tended to cast France as an idealised counter-model where, it has been argued, the weakness of family-based factors in the formation and transmission of political loyalties is a determining factor in the turbulence that sometimes characterises political life, and especially the susceptibility to the sudden emergence of new movements (Converse and Dupeux, 1962: 23). The typical reaction in France itself to the notion that a correlation could be drawn between the state of the polity and the state of the family was to query the criterion chosen as the basis for such a model. The indicator of continuity in terms of political commitment could lie within a broad ideological tradition that in a country like France was perpetuated by classic divisions such as those between Left and Right, and constituted non-family factors of political socialisation that were just as influential and self-perpetuating as family factors were perceived to be elsewhere (Percheron and Jennings, 1993).

A difficulty arises when defending the specificity of political sociali-sation in France, if those non-family factors that had characterised the strength of the Republic are perceived to have faded. It can justifiably be argued that the very notions of Left and Right, and the ideological antitheses they imply, were universalised from the French revolution-ary tradition. The ensuing narrative of social transformation perpetuated allegiances and galvanised constituencies as it was defined through strug-gles such as anti-clericalism in the inextricably linked pursuit of freedom and secularism, and the attempt to give concrete social form to the ideal of equality in the face of the inequalities generated by the amoral forces of money and markets. But as some commentators observed, as the French Republic reached the threshold of the new millennium the concept of liberty as a project building on the visions of the kind of new society described by figures like Rousseau and Saint-Just was in retreat, faced with the rise of a 'parasitic' notion of liberty, that is liberty as a niche or individual space to be hollowed out of the body politic; a process accel-erated by what was regarded by an increasing number of French citizens as the redundancy of the political cleavages and causes emanating from 1789 (Tenzer, 1990: 216). This desertion of *l'espace public*, the public space that is supposed to be the privileged platform for the actions of the citizen as a political animal, was the consequence of what had been identified elsewhere as the distancing of the individual from both nor-mative systems of belief, such as ideology, and a sense of their social origins, resulting in an imperative of fulfilment that had become power-fully and personally differentiated in a kind of vacuum (Lipovetsky, 1983: 14).

Empirical studies, as opposed to theoretical speculations, suggested that although it was premature to conclude that old cleavages like Left and Right no longer conditioned political commitment, it could cer-tainly be asserted that they were far from sufficient in operating as coherent global indicators of the way political identities were formed in individuals. The analysis of attitudes among the electorate suggested rather that their fidelities and choices were subject to a process of *déstruc-turation* or dismantling, with the fading of former patterns of allegiance (Schweisguth, 1994). In an implicit admission of the declining specificity of the French counter-model, due to the growing failure of mediating institutions to condition the participation of the individual citizen in the life of the polity, surveys carried out in France as the 1990s drew to a close appeared to acknowledge that the existence of a pre-existing parental template of political preferences could play a significant part in anchoring the individual citizen in his or her role as a political actor, as in the USA or Britain. In an analysis of the post-electoral Cevipof survey of 1995, it was argued that the transmission of political convictions from one generation to the next in a family context could operate as a conditioning factor, and moreover a positive one, since those citizens without it could find themselves less able to make clear choices as voters and therefore be relegated to the sidelines as *hors jeu politiques*. In the wider context of the functioning of the political system itself, the rise in the number of individual citizens without a parental legacy of political commitment might lead to a worst-case scenario where they would comprise the constituency most vulnerable to expressions of political extremism (Jaffré and Muxel, 1997: 85).

Such an implication, however qualified by the usual caveats that accompany empirical research, would suggest an undermining of the vocation of the French Republic on two related fronts. On the first front is the *déstructuration* diminishing the range of binary oppositions that once defined the variety of options to which the individual could commit as an active citizen. On the second front, the 'metaphysical' conception of the citizen that had given the Republic its specificity might in fact be inadequate faced with the new realities of French society, and the yardstick of stability used by Anglo-American commentators might not be entirely inappropriate for France after all. In short, the *déstructuration* of political choice at home and the convergence with other liberal democracies abroad might represent a fatal blow to the singular and very specific ideal of the French Republic.

At the most pessimistic end of the scale, one kind of reaction to the decline of the ideal of the Republic has been to declare its veritable demise as a mobilising concept for the active citizen. The notion of *filiation politique* or inherited political conviction, whether attributable to familial factors or the broader context of ideological ones, could not withstand the kind of *idolâtrie démocratique* that has pushed the individuality of choice to an extreme that is neither sustainable nor desirable. It is the fruit of an unhealthy adulation of the individual that has severed him or her from the ties that provide a framework of orientation (Finkielkraut, 1999). This is an evolution that, in some eyes, constitutes a reversal of the modernising thrust of the Revolution. With the unravelling of the nexus provided by a political culture that once bound the citizen to the Republic, comes a situation where the boundaries determined by its institutions are occluded by 'grey zones' no longer susceptible to the authority of those institutions, thereby undoing the integrating impetus of 1789 and, in so doing, drawing France into a kind of new 'middle ages' (Minc, 1993).

Conversely, there is a much more sanguine reading of the *déstructuration* of the range of political options to which the active citizen can commit. Rather than the retreat of the Republic being seen as the abandonment of *l'espace public* to its inevitable transformation into a wilderness, it has also been interpreted as a new horizon of possibility in which the notion of commitment and the sphere of politics can be fundamentally rethought.

Politics outside the paradigm

As has already been implied, the perception of the Republic and its vocation is inextricably woven into the great narrative of modernisation. The inculcation of the Republic's values was crucial to the political socialisation of its citizens, and its institutions were the key to their integration. But the viability of that narrative, and therefore the credibility of the Republic's mission, rested on the claim to universality that translated practically into a monopoly of the forms of engagement in the public space by which the citizen could define him or herself. The desire to step outside the *offre politique* or choices provided by its mediating institutions would inevitably be perceived as a crisis for the concept of 'the community of citizens' (Schnapper, 1994) whose fulfilment is meant to be defined and underwritten by the universalism of the Republic's values. As has been cogently argued elsewhere, the claim to embody the values that would elevate and gratify the fundamental aspirations of all citizens, was sustained by the corresponding resort to a process of 'othering' (Silverman, 1999: 133). The ambitions of the Republic were historically underpinned by the systematically negative construction placed on what was portrayed as the embodiment of antithetical values, whether it was the caricatural contrasting of ethno-cultural concepts of citizenship with France's universalist one (Brubaker, 1992: 2), or the depiction of those (such as in the colonies) who could not be elevated to the metaphysical citizenship offered by the Republic, and were therefore categorised as subjects to be administered, as opposed to citizens empowered to act by rights.

This projection of particularism, corporality and difference on others outside the Republic could sustain the contract with the active citizen operating in the public space as long as the Republican state could maintain the credibility of its modernising mission of securing economic progress, cultural unification and the formulation of political responses

to social demands. But the increasing difficulty of responding successfully to those challenges is what can be characterised as the crisis of
modernity for Western countries (Dubet and Wieviorka, 1995), and,
one could argue, especially for France, where it constituted the essential trade-off between the concrete particularisms defining the individual
and the disembodied universalist rights empowering him or her as a citizen. Implicit in the complaint, 'nobody knows today what it is to be
a citizen' (Castoriadis, 1996: 92), is the fear that if the Republic loses
the monopoly of defining the nature of citizenship then the cohesion
of the collectivity it embodies is seriously threatened. Conversely, the
argument can be turned on its head with the proposition that it is the
opening up of the public space to the clash of particularisms that now
drives the definition of citizenship (Naïr, 1992) and that by extension
should redefine the role of the Republic, bringing it into line with the
evolution of post-modern democracy globally.

Empirical evidence suggests that the Republic's monopolistic definition of action in the public space is being increasingly challenged by
bottom-up pressures in French society. On the one hand, the political life
of the Republic over the last three decades has been characterised by the
ever-rising tidemark of abstention among its citizens from the rationalist
and universalist activity that evokes Ernest Renan's nineteenth-century
description of the nation as a 'daily plebiscite'. In the definition offered
to a representative cross-section of the electorate of what constituted a
good citizen, the characteristic of being a 'regular voter' had, in 1976,
been cited by 51 per cent of the respondents, in 1983 this figure had
dropped to 43 per cent, and by 1989 it was down to 38 per cent (Jaffré,
1990). In the referendum that marked the opening of the new millennium, the disinclination to engage was starkly illustrated by the 69.2
per cent of citizens who abstained from voting on the reform of the
presidential mandate (Ponceyri, 2000: 14). On the other hand, recent
surveys of French society reveal a remarkable willingness on the part of
its citizens to commit themselves to a multiplicity of projects that challenge and impact on the life of the collectivity (Crettiez and Sommier,
2002). Although individuals are unquestionably less willing than in
previous generations to subscribe and effectively fold their individuality into organisations with programmes that operate in the public
space, many from varied backgrounds and generations are now prepared to invest in a project that is limited in time and space while
preserving the distance that safeguards their individuality, an *engagement
distancié* or arms' length commitment (Ion, 1997: 88). The investment
in parochial concerns and punctual objectives has seen a remarkable

flourishing of *la France associative*. Up to 1970 the number of new associations created annually was less than 20,000, but by the 1990s the figure was nudging up to 70,000. While in an obvious respect comprised of individuals committed to collective interaction, the typical *association* is nonetheless task-driven rather than ideologically-driven, whether responding to changing social needs, humanitarian or cultural imperatives, eschewing the assumptions that would characterise an enveloping political project. Such has been the rise in the popularity of these vehicles for action that, by some estimates, France entered the new millennium with up to 800,000 officially registered *associations* (Waters, 2003: 22).

More pertinently for the mission of the Republic is the way mobilisations have occurred in recent years, challenging the institutions that mediate its role in formulating responses to social needs. A salient example is the emergence in the 1990s of varied and widespread expressions of militancy by a social group that up to then had been envisaged in the kind of passive terms that reflected their economic inactivity. The marches of the unemployed launched by AC! (Agir ensemble contre le chômage) in 1994 encouraged a growing determination that a once virtually invisible section of society should deploy its demands in the public space, and do so on its own terms. The wave of protest that culminated in the winter of 1997–98 was vigorously independent of any kind of *récupération politique* or instrumentalisation by established parties or organisations like trade unions.

As for the Republic's vocation of cultural integration, the mobilisation against racism that took shape in France during the 1990s provides a rich example of how the traditional expectations regarding the political mediation of social change are challenged by the multiplicity of ways that social change is ramified culturally. In many ways, SOS Racisme (SOSR), formed in 1984, became an archetype of the 'mediatised' social movement, with all the short-term advantages and medium-term disadvantages that entails. In the short term, the accomplished performances in the media of their charismatic first leader, Harlem Désir, set a benchmark with regard to the ability to communicate a message to a mass audience, since televised appearances provided the profile for an orchestrated campaign using the tools of regular press conferences and the co-opting of various celebrities to support the cause, which in turn provided more fodder for television exposure. That the movement succeeded in alerting the nation to the dangers posed by the rise of racism in 1980s France, especially the rise of the Front National (FN), is generally uncontested. The most optimistic interpretations of the significance of the movement credited it with being no less than the only force to have understood and subsequently mobilised the 'moral generation' (Joffrin, 1987: 13).

In retrospect, the anti-racism movements might not have obtained a measurable institutional impact commensurate with the initial enthusiasm they generated, but the impact on the consciousness of individuals and the processes of self-understanding, though less quantifiable, was nonetheless very significant. Many individuals who, by their ethnic and/ or cultural origin, had lived with the implicit pressure to conform to an abstract Republican identity that denied them the positive display of those defining characteristics as citizens, began to assume those particularist attributes, but in a way that circumvented the traditional political practices of the public space.

What these movements appeared to challenge in practice was what others had articulated in theory, namely that a universalist concept of citizenship predicated on the value of equality can in fact veil hegemonic processes that can be experienced as controlling, oppressive and in effect inegalitarian. The greater the tension this creates in society, the more the need emerges for an understanding of citizenship that gives individuals the opportunity to participate in a democracy that is radical and plural (Mouffe, 1992). This would translate into an opening up of the public space to citizens as social actors where the interaction of plural identities would, by definition, work through antagonistic processes that are nonetheless positive rather than the unsustainable assumption of an abstract consensus. This concern with concrete rights and the prerogatives that citizens ought to possess in order to constitute the public space from below, as opposed to its being something imposed from above, has led some to argue for a fracturing of the traditional integration between the concepts of citizen and state in the Republic. If the evolution of society has transformed France into what is in reality a 'multiple and moving border', undermining national specificity (Balibar, 1998: 6), then the understanding of citizenship should reflect that evolution and be framed in transnational terms. For its most enthusiastic advocates, recasting French citizenship into a European mould may be the only way to preserve the relationship between the individual citizen and his or her role as a political actor, by preventing the triumph of those global liberal economic forces that provoke a kind of fatalism that disempowers and depoliticises the individual citizen (Bourdieu, 1998: 74).

However attractive these transnational reconceptualisations may be with regard to breaking the homology between the citizen and the nation as represented by the Republic, they are evocations of a society that may or may not – depending on the evolution of the European

Union (EU) – be in the process of being fulfilled (see Chapters 6 and 7). However great the potential may be for a European notion of citizenship to transcend the limitations of a national one, the absence of factors like the shared cultural symbols that are constitutive of a common identity mean that, so far, the EU has been more inclined to define the membership of individuals and states through the elaboration of regulations. The reality for the Republic of today is that the established conceptualisation of the public space is still operational and may possess a greater potential for adaptation than its critics are prepared to admit.

Revitalising the vocation of the French Republic

The presidential elections of 2002, and more precisely the shock result of the first round when the Socialist, Lionel Jospin, was beaten to the second place spot by the FN's Jean-Marie Le Pen, focused a profound and wide-ranging debate about the relationship between the citizen and the Republic and the consequences for its mediating institutions. One of the paradoxes observed was, at one end of the spectrum, the unchanging nature of the *offre politique* or the options in terms of the prospective leaders entering the race. Unlike other systems where a losing candidate normally gives up the leadership of his or her party and retires to the political sidelines, the system in France repeatedly throws up the same faces. Lionel Jospin and Robert Hue were entering the contest for the second time, Jacques Chirac and Jean-Marie Le Pen for the fourth time, and Arlette Laguiller for a remarkable fifth time. This over-familiarity, it has been argued, bore a causal relationship to the explosion of options at the other end of the spectrum among those candidates with little established profile. With a total of sixteen candidates entering the first round, on the surface there appeared to be a balanced political choice, with eight candidates coming from the Left or extreme Left, and eight coming from the centre Right, the Right and the extreme Right. But in reality the results of the first round testified to the *émiettement* or break-up of the vote that had little to do with Left-Right allegiances: fifteen of the sixteen candidates each gathered more than 1 per cent of the votes cast, and none of them crossed the threshold of 20 per cent. Moreover, for the first time in the life of the Fifth Republic, there were four women candidates standing for the supreme office and a youth (in political terms) of twenty-seven, Olivier Besancenot, standing as the candidate of the Ligue Communiste Révolutionnaire (LCR), who, according to the Louis Harris poll of 21 April 2002, attracted 14 per cent of the votes cast by 18–24-year-olds (Gattolin and Miquet-Marty, 2003: 28). There was, therefore, on the one hand, a striking number of voters who were prepared to step outside of the mainstream in their choice of candidates, and on the other hand, with a first-round rate of abstentions and spoilt ballots touching 30.05 per cent, no shortage of commentators to remark on the reluctance of citizens to exercise their rights actively in the public space.

Well before the events of 21 April 2002, however, there had been interpretations of the abstentionist phenomenon that did not see it as an inevitable and cataclysmic indicator of disengagement. A rising level of abstention may be read as signalling political engagement by another means. Studies have shown that there are very few permanent abstentionists in France, and that they are difficult to categorise in fixed terms demographically and socio-economically. The refusal to vote among erstwhile supporters of mainstream parties, can express a desire not to 'betray' the party with which they are most closely aligned, but which they also reproach for not fulfilling their expectations. On a broader and related level, abstention can be a deliberate choice in response to what is perceived as the absence of genuine alternatives. The voter may therefore opt to abstain, but this is not a blanket response, being instead one that is modulated according to a possible host of variables, resulting in multiple modes of behaviour, and constituting an eloquent reflection on what is on offer politically (Subileau and Toinet, 1993: 193). It may be that the voter may temper his or her incursion in the public space in a way that balances his or her sensibilities as an individual subject and as a citizen. Thus, the *sujet-citoyen* intervenes when there is a *correspondance* or alignment of personal and collective convictions, and withdraws when they can safely diverge, leaving the public space to be filled by a second-order partisan discourse.

Less interest in party politics does not mean that there is less interest in democracy, as the massive mobilisation behind Jacques Chirac in the second round of the presidential election illustrated, allowing him to be elected on 5 May 2002 with 81.75 per cent of the vote, and crushing his far-right rival Le Pen. This result, followed by the solid presidential majority acquired as a result of the legislative elections of the following month, can be translated as a return to the sources of the Fifth Republic (Cole, 2005: 43). It may also be viewed as a clear contradiction of the argument advanced by some commentators that France was on a path of convergence with other parliamentary regimes in Europe where the head of state is an arbiter but where the key consideration is who heads the government and therefore exercises real executive power

(Avril, 2003), given, notably, the way *cohabitation* had clipped the wings of the presidency. However, resurgent abstention in the first round of the legislative elections of June, at 35.20 per cent, allows for a more nuanced interpretation, certainly of the behaviour of the *sujet-citoyen*. The mobilisation behind Chirac in May 2002 could be read as evidence of a new *engagement légitimiste*, or legitimism that asserted a conviction, beyond partisan politics, in the enduring value of French democratic ideals and institutions and the need to defend them. By the same token, it is not the kind of engagement that is drawn by the ritualised conflict of party politics. Instead, it is an engagement that mobilises around themes, such as the right to work, education or residency when that coincides with the defence of fundamental democratic rights, or the demand that those rights should be actualised. It is a kind of engagement that requires a rethinking of *l'espace public*, possibly along the lines of an *espace commun* or common space, opening up and grounding the understanding of citizenship to accommodate the needs of 'subjectivation', and freeing the ends of action from the pressure for uniformity expressing itself as consensus, thereby removing the obstacles to active participation in the shaping of the Republic by the *sujet-citoyen* previously held back by the conflicting and identifying particularisms of his or her subjectivity. Interestingly, participation in the 2007 presidential elections was significantly higher than in 2002, with 85 per cent and 84 per cent of the French electorate voting in the first and second rounds respectively.

If, as the notion of *l'engagement légitimiste* suggests, the appetite exists for a re-affirmation of the legitimacy of the French Republic's democratic ideals, then the onus is thrown back on its mediating institutions to frame the political options in a way that is capable of drawing that engagement. France is characterised by democratic structures that are deeply rooted, and in a sense the Republic has always been running to catch up with its citizens. Those movements whose relation to the polity falls outside the established modes of action in the public space may represent, today, what the battle for the third estate was two centuries ago, but focusing instead on new divisions, such as that between those with homes and the homeless (Guilhaumou, 1998: 32), and engaging above all with everyday social realities instead of abstract projects.

Conclusion

The suggestion by some commentators that the Revolution is not only over, but that the specificity it gave to the Republic has been defeated by the excesses of individualism, is exaggerated and overlooks the fact that if there is one thing that embodies the leap forward it represents it is way the rights of the individual came to constitute the beating heart of the French Republican project. Conversely, the suggestion that as in the USA and elsewhere 'citizens doing it for themselves' by wresting universal rights out of the abstract and giving them individual and embodied particularities is the best way of revitalising the Republic overlooks the prospect that, even with a much broader concept of the public space which accepts as normal the perpetual collision of actors in pursuit of individual and communal difference, the need for a *modus vivendi* to be defined remains, and that the best embodiment of that consensus is the Republic.

As was argued at the beginning of this chapter, the actions of the youth who rioted in autumn 2005 in urban France were apolitical and did not mark the demise of the specific French model of polity. The rioters attacked the police, the emergency services and sometimes journalists in the same way that they might attack gangs from other neighbourhoods. As for the demand for economic opportunities, too often these young people had excluded themselves from the processes of socialisation afforded by the world of work by their contempt for the kind of employment their parents, notably their fathers, had settled for, instead living on a combination of welfare payments and petty crime. It could be argued that the events of autumn 2005 illustrated the extent to which the reality of the French Republic was marked by a pattern of social convergence with other post-industrial liberal democracies. In spite of their identification by others as young people of Arab and Muslim origin, the rioters constitute a social sub-class whose model is not Cairo or Mecca, but the alienated young blacks of urban America (Roy, 2005).

It is also impossible to ignore, however, the weight of France's modern history and the political culture that gives the Republic its specificity. France remains susceptible to what has been called 'spontaneous aggregation' and social crisis, because a significant proportion of its citizens find themselves in a double-bind (Pernot, 2004: 134). On the one hand, there is the feeling that they are deprived of effective political representation; and, on the other, there is the enduring expectation that the organisational and institutional infrastructure of democracy in France will allow the Republic to assume its social vocation. Looking to the future, the French Republican state will be less inclined to resort to the 'othering' that was a historic aspect of nation-building after 1879; and the evolution of political practices such as the gathering of information about its citizens according to race, illustrates the convergence with Anglo-American style liberal democracies. But, at the same time, the conditioned expectations of the governing elites and the constituencies at the grassroots of society will continue to make action in the public space the privileged arena for defining the options for a society in search of reconciliation with itself.

References

Avril, P. (2003) 'Les conséquences des élections sur la nature du régime. L'improbable phénix', in P. Perrineau and C. Ysmal (eds), *Le Vote de tous les refus*, Paris: Presses de Sciences Po.

Balibar, E. (1998) *Droit de cité: culture et politique en démocratie*, Paris: Editions de l'Aube.

Berelson, B., P. Lazarsfeld and W. MacPhee (1966) *Voting*, Chicago: Chicago University Press.

Borie, J. (1981) *Mythologies de l'hérédité au XIXe siècle*, Paris: Galilée.

Bourdieu, P. (1991) *Language and Symbolic Power*, trans. G. Raymond and M. Adamson, Cambridge: Polity Press.

Bourdieu, P. (1998) *Contre-feux: propos pour servir à la résistance contre l'invasion néo-libérale*, Paris: Liber-Raisons d'Agir.

Brubaker, R. (1992) *Citizenship and Nationhood in France and Germany*, Cambridge, MA: Harvard University Press.

Castoriadis, C. (1996) *La Montée de l'insignifiance: les carrefours du labyrinthe IV*, Paris: Seuil.

Cole, A. (2005) *French Politics and Society*, London: Pearson Longman.

Converse, P.E. and G. Dupeux (1962) 'Politicisation of the electorate in France and the United States', *Public Opinion Quarterly*, XXVI: 23.

Crettiez, X. and I. Sommier (2002) *La France rebelle, tous les foyers, mouvements et acteurs de la contestation*, Paris: Michalon.

Crozier, M. (1970) *La Société bloquée*, Paris: Seuil.

Dubet, F. and M. Wieviorka (eds) (1995) *Penser le sujet: autour d'Alain Touraine*, Paris: Fayard.

Duverger, M. (1967) *La Démocratie sans le peuple*, Paris: Seuil.

Finkielkraut, A. (1999) *Ingratitude*, Paris: Gallimard.

Gattolin, A. and F. Miquet-Marty (2003) *La France blessée*, Paris: Denoël.

Guilhaumou, J. (1998) *La Parole des sans: les mouvements actuels à l'épreuve de la Révolution française*, Paris: ENS Edition.

Habermas, J. (1993) *L'Espace public*, Paris: Payot.

Ion, J. (1997) *La Fin des militants?* Paris: Editions de l'Atelier.

Jaffré, J. (1990) 'Après les municipales et les européennes: le nouveau décor électoral', *Pouvoirs*, 55: 147–62.

Jaffré, J. and A. Muxel (1997) 'Les repères politiques', in D. Boy and N. Mayer (eds), *L'Electeur a ses raisons*, Paris: Presses de Sciences Po, pp. 67–100.

Joffrin, L. (1987) *Un coup de jeune: portrait d'une génération morale*, Paris: Arléa.

Lipovetsky, G. (1983) *L'Ere du vide: essais sur l'individualisme contemporain*, Paris: Gallimard.

Minc, A. (1993) *Le nouveau moyen âge*, Paris: Gallimard.

Mouffe, C. (ed.) (1992) *Dimensions of Radical Democracy: Pluralism, Citizenship, Community*, London: Verso.

Naïr, S. (1992) *Le Regard des vainqueurs: les enjeux français de l'immigration*, Paris: Grasset.

Percheron, A. and M.K. Jennings (1993) 'Le mythe de l'exceptionalité française', in N. Mayer and A. Muxel (eds), *La Socialisation politique*, Paris: Armand Colin, pp. 119–29.

Pernot, J.-M. (2004) 'Pleins et déliés de la contestation: du repli de la grève au mouvement sur les retraites', in S. Béroud and R. Mouriaux (eds), *L'Année sociale 2003–4*, Paris: Editions Syllepse, p. 134.

Ponceyri, R. (2000) 'La fin de la République gaullienne', *Revue Politique et Parlementaire* (September–October): 9–34.

Roy, O. (2005) 'Intifada des banlieues ou émeutes de jeunes déclassés?', *Esprit*: 12.

Schnapper, D. (1994) *La Communauté des citoyens: sur l'idée moderne de la nation*, Paris: Gallimard.

Schweisguth, E. (1994) 'L'affaiblissement du clivage gauche-droite', in P. Perrineau, (ed.), *L'Engagement politique: déclin ou mutation*, Paris: Presses de Sciences Po, pp. 215–37.

Silverman, M. (1999) *Contemporary French Thought on Culture and Society*, London: Routledge.

Steiner, G. (1988) 'Aspects of counter-revolution', in G. Best (ed.), *The Permanent Revolution*, London: Fontana Press, pp. 129–53.

Subileau, F. and M.-F. Toinet (1993) *Les Chemins de l'abstention*, Paris: La Découverte.

Tenzer, N. (1990) *La Société dépolitisée*, Paris: Presses universitaires de France.

Waters, S. (2003) *Social Movements in France: Towards a New Citizenship*, Basingstoke: Palgrave Macmillan.

Wickham Legg, L.G. (1905) *Select Documents Illustrative of the History of the French Revolution: the Constituent Assembly*, 2 vols, Oxford: Clarendon Press.

Wolfreys, J. (2006) 'France in revolt: 1995–2005', *International Socialism*, 109: 3–20.

Index

Bold type indicates main entries.